The Origins of the
National Recovery Administration

The Origins of the National Recovery Administration

Business, Government, and the Trade Association Issue,
1921–1933

ROBERT F. HIMMELBERG

New York
FORDHAM UNIVERSITY PRESS
1976

Printed in the United States of America

Contents

Selected Abbreviations

API	American Petroleum Institute
ATAE	American Trade Association Executives
CTI	Cotton Textile Institute
FOCB	Federal Oil Conservation Board
NAM	National Association of Manufacturers
NCF	National Civic Federation
NEMA	National Electric Manufacturers' Association
NICB	National Industrial Conference Board
NRC	National Resources Committee
PRA	President's Reemployment Agreement
RFC	Reconstruction Finance Corporation
TNEC	Temporary National Economic Committee

Acknowledgments

I owe thanks to a number of individuals and to certain institutions for assistance during the years in which this book has developed. At Pennsylvania State University, where it was initiated, Neil McNall's advice and criticism were especially important, but Robert K. Murray, Philip S. Klein, and Ari Hoogenboom, among others, helped clarify ideas and gave encouragement. Fordham University, where I have taught for a number of years, has assisted me several times with research travel grants and twice with semester fellowships.

Over the past decade a number of new manuscript collections of major importance for this study have been opened, most notably the Herbert Hoover Papers in the Presidential Library at West Branch, Iowa, and the Raymond Moley Papers in the Hoover Institution at Stanford University. These sources, together with other newly available collections, as well as those discovered through further combing of the National Archives, have made possible—indeed necessitated—the amplification and reconstruction of the original version of this study which was completed in 1963. The competence and helpfulness of the staffs of these institutions (and of others where I worked, including the Franklin D. Roosevelt Library, the Baker Library, the Manuscripts Division of the Library of Congress, the New York Public Library, Columbia University's Butler Library, and the Ohio Historical Society) were greatly appreciated.

The greatest aid came from my wife, Jo Ann Boone Himmelberg, whose efforts have made it possible for me to combine scholarship and family raising, inevitably antipathetical undertakings. Though not an historian, she has played a direct role in the writing of this book, first by reacting to ideas, second by helping with the chores of typing and editing.

Introduction

THIS BOOK is the history of the business community's efforts during the 1920s and early 'thirties to emasculate the federal policy, stemming from the Sherman Act and subsequent antitrust legislation, of maintaining a competitive enterprise system. The period begins with the Harding Administration and ends with the coming of the New Deal. The central issue, pressed quite continuously by trade association spokesmen and other business leaders, was the redefinition of the legal limits upon industrial cooperation. Businessmen, of course, wished to expand their right to cooperate, to shrink the potential of the traditional antitrust policy for interfering with business agreements to fix prices, regulate the rate of production, or otherwise limit competition. The specific goals of this business campaign for antitrust revision varied substantially during the period. They could be limited or extravagant, for formal legal change or administrative relaxation, depending upon the political climate and other circumstances.

Thus, not only are the demands of the businessmen and the political pressures they exerted recounted here, but also the changing pattern of government attitudes and policies toward competition and cooperation—a pattern much more complex than has hitherto been supposed. The view embedded in much of the literature on the period—that government economic policy during the Republican era reflected, directly and emphatically, what businessmen wanted—is no doubt recognized nowadays as too simple, but there are few studies precisely tracing the economic policies of the succeeding Presidents and gauging the influences which shaped them. The policies toward cooperation and competition which Harding, Coolidge, and Hoover fashioned were, for much of the period, far from meeting the wishes of the business community. The values of the Presidents and their lieutenants, the political climate and economic circumstances, had as much as or more to do with policy formation than business pressure.

Just as the history of the revision movement offers an opportunity for a fresh look at the way the antitrust laws were interpreted and enforced during the Republican era, so it furnishes a new angle of approach for investigating certain fundamental questions about the structure and ideology of the business community during the 'twenties. Sharp differences between different segments of the business community over goals and tactics emerged at an early stage of the protracted effort to secure antitrust liberalization. A fault line ran through the business community, dividing those who actively supported thoroughgoing revision from those who were satisfied with the status quo or were willing to back liberalization efforts only if they were entirely risk-free. This was not a division between "big" and "little" businessmen. The basis of division was a factor quite other than size but nonetheless quite as tangible; and it continued to have its effect even during the last stages, during the depths of the Depression, of what had by then become a crusade for antitrust relaxation.

Behind the business concepts of what constituted the ideal economic order—and for much of the business community this clearly was not the traditional American ideal of a market-directed enterprise capitalism—lay ideas about the ideal structure of political and social power. Especially when they became most intensive during the Depression years of the early 'thirties, the business efforts to substitute the fostering of cartelism for the maintenance of competition rather clearly implied a concept of society as hierarchical, and evidenced a determination on the part of businessmen to shore up the advantageous position they enjoyed in this framework and to maintain their pre-eminent role in the formation of national economic and social policy.

A central purpose of this investigation has been to illuminate what is recognized as a pivotal event in the history of business–government relations, which occurred as the Republican era ended and the Democratic era of the New Deal began: the creation of the National Recovery Administration. The NRA has found several historians, most recently and extensively in Louis Galambos in *Competition or Cooperation*, a study of the Cotton Textile Institute which throws much light on many aspects of business–government relations in the antitrust field, and in Ellis Hawley with his *New Deal and the Problem of Monopoly*, which has confirmed the fact of domination of the agency by the business program of cartelism. In May and June 1933, Congress and the President established the NRA as one of the two key measures of the early New Deal. The preamble of the Act which created the agency, and Roosevelt's description of its purpose in introducing it to the people, stressed the aim of recovery through improved wages and wider employment. Through the summer and fall of 1933 business leaders from the major and the minor industries trooped into Washington to draft and secure NRA approval for the codes the Act had provided for. Under the energetic, even frenetic, direction of Hugh Johnson, a former aide to Bernard Baruch, the people were led to expect recovery to issue from the excitement in the capital; to believe that a great cooperative effort between business and government, carried off in a spirit of patriotism reminiscent of the Great War, was underway to save the nation from the cruel misfortune of the Great Depression.

The novelty of this spectacle and the plausibility of its pretensions began rather soon to wear thin, primarily because the promise of substantial industrial recovery went largely unredeemed, but also because the NRA codes began to be perceived as suppressing competition and encouraging price-fixing and monopoly. The codes which Johnson and his associates in the mushrooming NRA bureaucracy approved contained, at the behest of the trade associations or other industry representatives which had negotiated them, a wide array of terms which influenced the dynamic of competition, always in the direction of enfeeblement. Soon Congressional critics were denouncing the codes on the grounds that they almost always led to price-fixing and in many instances injured small competitors and aided the natural advantage of the more powerful firms of codified industries. Airing of these charges in Congressional committees and in the press was followed by the celebrated investigation of the NRA headed by Clarence Darrow early in 1934 which ended by confirming the strictures against the agency already current and widely accepted. Riven now by internal controversy over fundamental policy, the NRA perished in May 1935, shortly before its enabling legislation would have expired in any case, unless renewed by Congress, at the hands of the Supreme Court which found the National Industrial Recovery Act unconstitutional.

Despite the elimination of the legal basis of the NRA codes, many of them seem to have retained much of their force. It was not until 1937 that the Administration seriously revived the antitrust policy and began to prosecute cartelistic arrangements, with Robert Jackson and then Thurman Arnold in direction of a major effort to encourage price flexibility, increase production, and break up the "bottlenecks of business."

In a general sense the business efforts of the 1920s and early 'thirties to escape competition are relevant for a better understanding of government policies and business attitudes during this New Deal era. But they are especially relevant for an understanding of how the NRA came to be created and why it took the form it did. How it happened that Franklin Roosevelt, at the outset of the New Deal, conceded so much to the anticompetitive philosophy has remained somewhat obscure. Most historians who have attempted to re-create the immediate origins of the NRA have taken an eclectic position, tracing the birth of the experiment to the convergence of the aims of several political groupings and the intertwining of a number of ideological strands. They have focused, too, on the period after the enactment of the N.I.R.A. and the establishment of the agency, and have pointed out that the New Dealers conceded to the business viewpoint because this was the only way to secure business cooperation in raising wages and expanding employment. All this is true, but I have here focused attention on the fact that the N.I.R.A. itself gave businessmen an enormous advantage in shaping NRA policy to their purposes and have raised the question why this was so. Through a study in

detail of the forces which actually can be observed in the shaping of the
bill which Congress accepted, I have concluded that the N.I.R.A. represented essentially the culmination of the secular movement for antitrust
revision which extended continuously from the Great War through the
'twenties and early 'thirties.

A word is in order concerning certain usages and considerations in the
following narrative. The familiar terms "antitrust laws" or "antitrust
policy" are usually employed rather than the term "anti-cartel policy"
which has a cumbrous and foreign ring. It should be understood that,
unless otherwise specified, it is this anti-cartel aspect which is intended
when these terms are used. Antitrust policy, of course, has a second
focus: the limitations upon the size and the conduct toward competitors
of individual firms. But in the interwar period, until near its end at least,
the bearing of the law upon such questions as mergers, abuse of power
by large firms, and so on, was regarded as relatively fixed by the great
"Trust" cases of the Progressive era. The question of the legitimate scope
of interfirm cooperation was, however, a major legal and political issue.
Much of the most significant litigation, and many of the Supreme Court
decisions of the period which arose from enforcement of the antitrust
laws, involved this aspect of antitrust policy. Similarly, the terms "businessmen" and "business" are often used although it is principally the men
in the manufacturing, mining, and distribution industries who are affected by the antitrust policy and who therefore have the greatest stake
in its administration. They were the principal campaigners who sought
to change the antitrust policy and, unless otherwise noted, it is men from
these branches of the economy who are signified when the terms are
used.

1

Trade Associations on the Defensive: The First Year of the Harding Administration

IN THE MONTHS immediately following the Armistice of November 1918, businessmen were in an aggressive and confident mood, and their spokesmen, leaders of the major business organizations representative of a wide range of industries, voiced a remarkable demand which apparently had a very broad support. In outspoken terms they called upon political leaders to reform the antitrust policy's restrictions upon industrial cooperation. The president of the National Association of Manufacturers told his members, at their annual meeting in May 1919, that the "march of progress" had made the Sherman Act obsolete. The association should lead a "nationwide movement" to revise this "antiquated enactment" which had proven such an "embarrassment to the Government" when it had taken over direction of the economy during the war that it had been ignored for the duration.[1]

It was precisely the wartime experience which led to the postwar rebellion against the antitrust policy. The ideals and the institutions of industrial cooperation had, of course, been developing for many years before war mobilization, which undoubtedly merely accelerated and reinforced a gathering trend. The state of trade association development—the extent of support among businessmen for legalization of radical cooperative practices—before the war is, however, a virtually unexplored subject. It seems certain that, at least until the first Wilson Administration, there was a tension between larger and smaller firms, both in a concrete sense (in industries in which a dominating firm threatened smaller ones) and in the generalized sense in which big business was universally distrusted and feared as predatory by all smaller businessmen. This tension probably accounts for the reluctance of the political spokesmen for smaller businessmen to support the various proposals for antitrust liberalization which big business representatives made during this period, most notably in 1908. Supreme Court decisions which threatened large firms guilty of abusing their economic power in competitive relations and the creation of the Federal Trade Commission in 1914, which had as a primary purpose the outlawing of unfair competition, would seem, by reducing the tensions between big and small firms, to have laid the groundwork for the acceptance of the associational ideology, which preaches market-sharing among all industry members, regardless of size. In industries in which there was no dominant firm, association ideology and practice, inspired by, or perhaps merely justified by, Jerome Eddy's famous *The New Competition* of 1913, was advancing rapidly.[2]

But mobilization certainly accelerated the formation of trade associations and inspired the radical demands for antitrust revision which businessmen made in the winter of 1918/19. The wartime experience with government regulators (who were mostly businessmen) had proven most palatable. Business emerged from the war confident that if, as the NAM convention of May 1919 resolved, "restraints of trade" were tested "not by the fact of their existence, but by their injurious or beneficial effect upon the public interest," there would be no trouble in securing favorable rulings for them. Chamber of Commerce spokesmen also confidently awaited, in the aftermath of the war, the application of the regulatory principle to competitive industry. "Cordial acceptance by organized business" of regulation was in order, President Harry A. Wheeler advised the Chamber's May 1919 convention, because it would open the door to "broad application of the rule of reason wherein agreements between business men made in the public interest would not be regarded as criminal acts." Wheeler was merely confirming a policy his members already had adopted, for, like the NAM, the Chamber had consistently, from the Armistice onward, demanded from Congress and the Administration a reorientation of antitrust policy. This demand had figured prominently at the so-called Reconstruction Congress which the Chamber had staged in early December 1918. In February 1919, the demand appeared as a referendum proposal when the Chamber's Federal Trade Committee, headed by Rush C. Butler, a Chicago attorney heavily involved in trade association work, commissioned the previous year to compile a report, submitted its recommendations. By April the balloting was complete. The Chamber's members had nearly unanimously endorsed the proposition that Congress should revise the antitrust laws to broaden greatly the scope of permissible cooperative agreements.[3]

Some business advocates of the change chose means more direct than propaganda and exhortation. During November 1918, they pressed Bernard Baruch and his colleagues on the War Industries Board to use the prestige of their wartime success with industrial mobilization to persuade Congress to consider antitrust liberalization. Baruch turned these ideas aside, but certain of his former WIB associates took them up during the following winter. George Peek, until recently Baruch's assistant, and William Ritter, a lumberman with large holdings in that industry and a former WIB official, initiated the steps which led President Wilson to adopt their proposal for an Industrial Board within the Commerce Department. The Industrial Board was supposedly intended merely to ease the transition from war- to peacetime production, but business sponsors and Secretary of Commerce William C. Redfield actually intended it as a device for circumventing and, by precedent, laying the basis for erosion of, the Sherman Act.

By the early summer of 1919, however, the postwar drive for emasculation of the antitrust policy had collapsed. The Industrial Board soon bogged down in a mire of intra-Administration controversy and was abolished in May. After the onset of the unexpected inflationary surge, which began in May 1919, businessmen found the political environment inhospitable to their demands. They were soon thrown on the defensive when, in August, A. Mitchell Palmer, Wilson's new Attorney General, blamed the High Cost of Living, as contemporary usage termed it, upon price-fixing and launched a highly publicized investigation into several industries. The following turbulent months of the fall and winter were those of the great postwar strikes and of the Red Scare, a period of mutual recrimination between capital and labor and of continuing intermittent allegations of business misconduct by the government. The postwar era turned out to be unpropitious for the business plans for blunting the antitrust laws.[4]

This situation took an ugly turn, from the business point of view, early in 1920 when the established practices of many trade associations drew outspoken criticism from several governmental sources and began to become a focus of public concern. Circulation of market information (such as prices, quantities sold, and stocks on hand) had become the primary purpose—at the least, a central activity—of approximately half the trade associations of the manufacturing industries. In a survey in 1921, the FTC located 626 such associations and found that, of these, 276 provided for interchange of statistical market-data among their members. The term "open price association" was sometimes applied to all associations engaged in statistical work, though it was more appropriately reserved for those groups which circulated detailed price-information on current or even prospective transactions, often with the understanding that reported prices would not be changed without prior notice to competitors. Of the 276 statistical associations found in 1921, 107 were genuine open price associations. During the early months of 1920, Attorney General Palmer, prodded by the FTC, which was investigating many trade associations, drew attention to open price associations by attacking them as price-fixing agencies and initiating suits against several, of which the Hardwood Lumber Manufacturers' Association was the most prominent.

The postwar recession which began in February 1920, ending the inflationary wave of the previous year, made public feeling receptive to charges of business price-pegging at a time of decline in wages, employment, and the prices of staple goods. In the nation's two largest cities, state authorities, spurred on by complaints stemming from the postwar housing shortage, soon opened investigations of the construction industries. Heated charges of misconduct, often involving open price trade associations, became consistently newsworthy for the next two years. The New York investigation, which opened in mid-1920, was conducted by a state legislature joint investigating committee chaired by Charles Lockwood. Samuel Untermeyer of Yonkers, made famous by his role as counsel for the Pujo Committee during the Taft Administration, was appointed to the same position for the Lockwood Committee and soon demonstrated his talent for discovering wrongdoing and consistently generating headlines. The Chicago investigation, also the work of the state legislature, began early in 1921. The final report of this Illinois investigation, written late in 1922, illustrated thoroughly the character of the charges which both the New York and Chicago investigations had publicized from 1920 through 1922. The report castigated the " 'Eddy Plan' of 'co-operative competition' " and charged that

> numerous cunningly devised schemes have been used to restrain trade and fix prices. Cost systems are installed so that uniform prices are bound to result. Cost information and selling prices are exchanged between competitors. Information is exchanged as to supplies on hand and in course of manufacture. Production is limited under allotment schemes and the supply thus brought under control. . . . The members of the associations are usually exhorted to remember their homes and their children and the comforts that are due them, and are urged to eliminate by all means "cut throat" competition.[5]

The New York investigation had the greater political impact and probably attracted more attention than the one in Chicago. Beginning in October and early November 1920 with an exposé of labor union corruption and extortion in the building trades, and saddling Mayor Hylan with suspicion of connivance in return for political support, Untermeyer turned later in November and in December to headline-making revelations of price-fixing associations in the building-materials industries which, he alleged, operated on a national level. Summing up the findings of the Lockwood Committee at the end of December 1920, *The New York Times* credited it with showing that "since the war and arising directly out of war conditions the country has been honeycombed with associations of manufacturers and dealers in every conceivable commodity, operating under the Eddy 'open competition' plan of exchanging prices or under some modification of the idea," with unfortunate results for consumers.[6]

Untermeyer's successes and remarkably favorable press gave him the upper hand, too, in a verbal battle with Attorney General Palmer which began late in October 1920. When he accepted the position as counsel for the Lockwood Committee in mid-October, Untermeyer had asked Palmer to assign to him, to help with his investigation, a Justice Department staff member familiar with cases the Department had under consideration or was trying in New York, familiar especially with the case against cement producers which had been initiated the previous spring. When the Department was slow in complying with his request, Untermeyer abruptly, in an interview with the local U. S. District Attorney's assistants on October 31, demanded that he be placed in charge of federal antitrust presentations before the grand jury and of prosecutions in the federal district court, and "berated the United States in general, and the Attorney General in particular, for what he claimed was his lax enforcement of the Anti-Trust Laws." These "open threats of exposure, etc.," the federal attorneys believed, "were made solely for the purpose of coercing the Attorney General into appointing him . . . to the position requested by him." Untermeyer promptly supported his demand by planting, in a willing New York City press, news stories discussing federal inaction respecting antitrust violations and describing the supposed wish of the Lockwood Committee to have its counsel placed in charge of federal prosecutions for the city. Palmer refused Untermeyer's demands but tried to prod Francis Caffey, the local U. S. District Attorney, into moving more rapidly in bringing suit against the trade association conspiracies the Lockwood Committee was turning up in New York. But this scarcely countered Untermeyer's well-publicized and biting criticisms, which characterized Palmer's handling of antitrust violations as "humiliating, blundering and inefficient" and accused the Attorney General of "gross inefficiency and absence of intelligence and political honesty." [7]

Though trade association misconduct had not figured in the campaign of 1920, it was nonetheless a subject capable of blowing up into a major issue as the Harding Administration began in March 1921. By humiliating Palmer, Untermeyer had shown the potential of open price associations as a political issue, and the new Attorney General, Harry Daugherty, might well have pondered how he could avoid the strictures his predecessor had suffered. There were other centers from which outspoken criticism of Republican laxity in antitrust matters could be anticipated. In addition to certain political leaders such as Senator Robert M. La Follette, there was the FTC, still dominated by a Democratic majority and led by Huston Thompson, an able polemicist and an ambitious politician. The Commission had withheld criticism of the Democratic Administration of President Wilson, but had shown considerable zeal in investigating trade associations during the previous year and could be expected to make trouble for the new Republican regime if opportunity arose.

Just as it had to be responsive, with respect to other political questions, to the farm bloc and to other political groups in the turbulent political and depressed economic context in which it began, so the Harding Administration eventually had to respond to pressures for a hostile attitude toward trade association activities. Business spokesmen found to their dismay that the ousting of the Democrats had not changed the uncomfortable situation they had found themselves in during 1920. It was still impossible to advance the cause which had been so bluntly articulated in the postwar months. The question, instead, was whether trade association practices already in common use could be continued. In fact, Harry Daugherty confounded associationists by soon taking up an interpretation of the Sherman Act which threatened, not simply the more extreme kinds of statistical interchange programs which lent themselves readily to price-fixing, but virtually all statistical programs, and set in motion a series of prosecutions designed to enforce this interpretation and secure its acceptance by the federal courts.

There seems little likelihood that Daugherty realized the association question would require major attention at the time the Harding Administration came into power. As for Harding, he probably intended to rely upon his highly respected Secretary of Commerce, Herbert Hoover, to devise Administration economic policy in this area. For Hoover, of course, trade associations were the most important phase of the voluntary associationism which for him was the key to maintaining, under modern conditions, an open, fluid, and yet efficient and stable, political and economic order. As Hoover explained in his brief treatise, *American Individualism*, of 1922 (which contained the sum of the politico-economic philosophy he expounded during the remainder of his public life), a way had to be discovered to reconcile the need of the functional economic groups for stability with the need to prevent the calcification of society, in order to keep open the possibility for individuals of ability to rise within the social order. If stability was stressed, society would be dominated by the few—by bureaucrats, by overweening labor power, by business autocracy, or by all three together in a kind of syndicalism from which only elites would benefit. Voluntary associationism could permit businessmen, farmers, and workers to maintain stability and continuity in their economic condition without destroying the market principle or requiring bureaucratic solutions to problems. In his statement of the early 'twenties, Hoover spelled out in detail how these principles worked in the case of business. Here trade associations were the instruments of voluntary cooperation. The various association practices were the means for promoting economic efficiency and stability, with benefits for both business and consumers. Standardization and simplification of products reduced the waste involved in production, as did the promotion of cost accounting and interfirm cost-comparisons. Interchange of statistics of prices and production could eliminate a more important kind of waste: intermittent slowdown of the entire economy. As he explained to Harding, "a prompt and comprehensive monthly publication of fundamental data . . . would contribute greatly to stabilize commerce and industry as it works strongly to prevent over-expansion and over-speculation, over-stocking of foreign goods, etc." Availability of adequate data, he continued, with an eye on the economic downturn the Republicans had inherited, lent businessmen "courage in times of depression" since it tended to "correct public psychology by giving a properly weighted idea of the very large continuing activities often overlooked in the midst of pessimistic outlook." For Hoover, such practices and purposes were perfectly reconcilable with the principle of market competition which he accepted as the ultimate regulator of the economy.[8] Trade association spokesmen echoed this viewpoint in their writings and speeches of this period, presenting what might be termed an orthodox associationist ideology which labored to reconcile cooperation with the competitive ideal.[9]

Hoover, in early March 1921, apparently had no idea that the legality of trade association practices would be a serious problem for the Administration. Neither Harding nor Hoover, when the latter accepted his appointment, showed any sign that the "general policy" Hoover intended for the Commerce Department—"that we should take up the organization of voluntary action bearing upon foreign and domestic commerce" —might become a center of controversy. While Hoover's most pressing concerns of the earliest months in his new post were to enhance his Department by pulling in functions from other departments which he thought rightly belonged in Commerce; to reorganize, and secure increased appropriations, for the Bureau of Foreign and Domestic Commerce; and to develop an efficient system for collecting and disseminating leading economic statistics, he also proceeded with plans for strengthening trade associations. Hoover gave substantial attention, for example, to a proposal for a major innovation in business–government relations made by an adviser, F. T. Miller, whom he had brought into the Department as a special assistant to advise him on trade association matters. One of Miller's key proposals was for the Department to take advantage of the fact that the FTC had failed to develop procedures for advising business groups of the legality of their proposed cooperative arrangements by providing the service itself, in conjunction with the Justice Department. The Commerce Solicitor, William E. Lamb, also backed procedures of this kind designed to forewarn businessmen of impending conflict with the law and to give them security in arrangements which had been approved. Hoover evidently concurred with his advisers and appears to have discussed the possibility of appropriate implementing legislation with Senator Walter Edge of New Jersey, a sturdy friend of business interests. In an offhand way Hoover even tried to experiment with the practice Miller described for him, twice in early

1921 asking Daugherty to give an opinion upon the legality of a trade group's plan for market cooperation.[10]

Hoover was slow to read properly the signs, in the opening weeks of the Harding Administration, which indicated that open price associations would continue to be subject to hostile criticism and that all trade association work might be included within it. He might have viewed more seriously, for example, an exchange between the President and the FTC in late March and early April 1921. By the latter part of March, Harding felt called upon, by the farm lobby's concern, to seek an explanation of the failure, during the still-worsening economic downswing, of the prices of consumers' goods to keep pace with the decline in the prices of raw materials and of foodstuffs. On March 21, he asked the FTC for illumination. Was the disparity caused by "interference" with normal economic forces? Harding's letter gave the Commission the opening for an authoritative denunciation of the development "among manufacturers" of barriers to the "flow of commodities from producer to consumer." In addition to conspiracies "of the nature condemned by the Sherman law," there had been "widespread development of organization of the kind known as the 'Open Price Association.' " These purported to "lack the element of concerted agreement," but tended, nonetheless, "to bring about uniform prices and maintain them at an artificially high level." The Commission's reply, dated April 7, was published on the 18th in *The New York Times*, and Harding made brief reference to it in his April 12 message to Congress.[11]

While Hoover ignored such indications, Harry Daugherty was taking the first of a series of steps which led him gradually to put the Justice Department into a relation of deadly antagonism not merely to open price programs but even to association statistical work of a moderate type. By the fall of 1921, in fact, Daugherty's Department was engaged in a campaign to narrow the scope of legitimate trade association activities. Though not without flaws in execution and, likely, in motivation, the campaign was intelligently directed, seriously undertaken, and genuinely frightening to the trade association community.

Daugherty's actions apparently were a response to the realization, which his vantage point as Attorney General soon brought home to him, that public hostility toward associationism was too intense safely to ignore. Samuel Untermeyer was an important educating influence. In the latter part of March, Untermeyer met with Daugherty, requesting, as he had demanded of Palmer, support for his New York investigation. Daugherty probably knew something of the popularity of Untermeyer's activities and of the way the New York press had played up his verbal lashings of the previous Attorney General during the preceding months when Palmer had not catered to Untermeyer's demands. But familiar with this record or not, Daugherty seems to have sensed that Untermeyer was relying upon broad public support in making his requests, and he promised appropriate action promptly.

On April 6, Daugherty committed himself to action by appointing an able and experienced attorney as a Special Assistant to investigate association wrongdoing in the building-materials industry. James A. Fowler had been in charge of antitrust prosecutions during the last two years of the Taft Administration and soon proved himself a devoted partisan of stringent Sherman Act enforcement. Fowler was put in charge of a nationwide investigation of the building-materials field. He was to concentrate first on the cement industry's regional open price associations, beginning with the Cement Manufacturers' Protective Association, which represented eastern producers. Daugherty had two specific aims, it appears. The concentration upon conspiracies in building materials, beginning with one centered in New York, was intended to mollify Untermeyer, and for a time it actually did. By the fall of 1921 the other, more fundamental, aim of Fowler's program had become perfectly clear: he was attempting, through his prosecutions, to secure as severe a judicial ruling against price-reporting plans as possible. But certain comments and circumstances of the weeks immediately following Fowler's appointment make it seem likely that these far-reaching purposes had been discussed and agreed upon by Fowler and Daugherty from the very outset. Fowler and his chief assistant, Roger A. Shale, took up the cement investigation with such fervor that it seems almost necessary that some great purpose motivated them. "Those who are now connected with the case," Shale wrote Daugherty on April 16 in a review of the cement investigation then in progress, "have been advised of the objects to be accomplished and an earnest effort has been made to impress upon each man that he has personal responsibility in the matter and that the case cannot be successfully handled unless we receive his loyalty and cooperation. Each man has taken a renewed interest in the case, understands what we are seeking to accomplish, and has his shoulder to the wheel." [12]

Not many weeks had passed after the initiation of this well-conceived investigation, however, before Untermeyer resumed his pressure for more visible action. Untermeyer had little patience with Fowler's deliberate methods, even though they constituted a painstaking attempt to obtain a clear and enforceable construction of the legal status of certain trade association activities. Untermeyer, in fact, was somewhat contemptuous of traditional antitrust policy, considering it useful only as an instrument of harassment. Industry was so permeated with "trade combinations," he had told Daugherty in March, that the most the existing antitrust laws could do was to "make scapegoats of a few of them here and there." He thought associations "should be regulated; that competitors should be allowed to enter into agreements subject to government regulation and control." Because of this, but also, there is good reason to suspect, because he ambitioned to play a personal role in a series of spectacular federal prosecutions, Untermeyer renewed his demands for action upon the evidence of the combinations centered in New York which his investigation allegedly had uncovered.

As a reply to this pressure, Daugherty now appointed a new District Attorney for the Southern District of New York, William D. Hayward, a man fitted by temperament and inclination to produce spectacular results as an antitrust prosecutor. After discussions with Hayward early in June, just after his appointment, Untermeyer again was temporarily mollified, believing that Hayward intended to proceed by criminal rather than equity proceedings, to seek jail sentences for defendants and, most importantly, to share the limelight with Untermeyer. After Hayward had familiarized himself with the New York situation, Untermeyer wrote Daugherty in mid-June, "I expect to collaborate or co-operate with him for presentation to grand juries of all the cases that will justify that action." Two weeks later Untermeyer was again apprehensive, disturbed by the rumor that Fowler, whose investigation of the Cement Manufacturers' Protective Association was now completed, intended to proceed by an equity action, and that this signified a reining in of Hayward's plans for criminal prosecutions in New York. Daugherty, by this time his forces ready to march, met Untermeyer's criticisms with more spunk than before. The government did not intend to limit its antitrust activity to civil proceedings, he shot back and, as for Fowler, Untermeyer would not denigrate him "if you were fully aware of the purposes which he and this Department have in view." Again pacified, Untermeyer sailed for Europe the same day, promising his cooperation upon his return.[13]

Daugherty may have been somewhat disingenuous with Hoover about the far-reaching purposes of the steps he took during the period from April through June. Hoover appears during these months as utterly unaware of the trial trade associationism was about to undergo and seems to have believed he was controlling the Administration's policies in this area. Following Harding's message to Congress which manifestly recognized that open price associations were a matter of public concern, discussion of the problem began within the Administration. On May 23, appearing with Harding and Coolidge at a banquet commemorating the 125th anniversary of the *New York Commercial*, an influential business newspaper, Hoover represented the problem as one susceptible of a ready solution. Statistics of all kinds were to the good, and open price associations were worthy of praise. Situations likely to harm the competitive process and the public interest arose only because some groups circulated their data exclusively to their members. The remedy was publicity. "The free and prompt publicity of such data to the entire public," as Hoover told Harding two weeks later, explaining his solution again, "would go far to cure the viciousness of these operations as it would enlighten the buyer equally with the seller." Businessmen relaxed following Hoover's speech which was taken, according to the *Commercial*, as signifying that the Administration had decided not to take up the hostile attitude toward trade associations which Palmer had at times displayed and which the FTC still held. This feeling of relief persisted for a few more weeks as reassuring news of the Administration's attitude, based on formal interviews with Hoover and, probably, on off-the-record statements by him, were published. Hoover was quoted as saying, two days after a Cabinet meeting of May 31, when the whole issue had been discussed, that the Administration had decided that only "a small minority [of trade associations] have degenerated into ways that make for restraint of trade." These were the associations which handled their statistics secretively. The Attorney General, Hoover said, was in the process of clarifying the law respecting open price associations through litigation. Daugherty, also interviewed and cited, said nothing to conflict with Hoover's soothing interpretation of the Administration's position. For some weeks more, Hoover evidently believed some simple formula, such as the one he had been suggesting, would be adopted to draw the line between legal and illegal statistical work, and the whole isssue would be put to rest.[14]

During July, August, and the fall months of 1921, however, the Justice Department's course of action began to appear as something more than an attempt to clarify the legal status of open price associations. The decision to appoint Hayward as the federal District Attorney in New York returned handsome dividends, within a brief space, in terms of the Justice Department's record for successful trade association prosecutions. On August 31, Hayward secured a grand jury indictment of a combination among New York City tile-setting firms. Indictments against terra cotta producers, glassmakers, and soil-pipe manufacturers followed by the end of the year. In November the first victory was secured when the defendants in the tile case pleaded guilty and received fines. Four of them even received brief jail sentences, a rare event in the history of antitrust enforcement. By mid-December Hayward had secured guilty pleas in the terra cotta case and was still full of his original enthusiasm. His only regret, Hayward told Daugherty, was that Judge Learned Hand, unlike the judge who had heard the tile case, had withheld jail terms.

Hayward's prosecutions were colorful and popular, but Daugherty's decision to turn antitrust administration in New York over to him was at cross purposes with and threatened to disrupt Fowler's quieter but fundamentally more important campaign. On June 30 Fowler had filed a civil suit in New York City against the Cement Manufacturers' Protective Association; he followed this with a criminal indictment early in August.

In the fall, suits were filed against regional cement associations in other sections of the country. But when Fowler and Shale prepared to try the New York civil case, Hayward intervened, insisting that the criminal suit be tried first, and by his own staff. Fowler patiently refreshed Daugherty's memory as to the purpose and importance of the New York civil suit against the cement manufacturers. At stake was the question "whether or not those engaged in the same business may legitimately form an association and exchange information as to production, and to some extent the price, and in fact acquaint every competitor with his entire business." The equity suit could be appealed to the Supreme Court, where the vital issues at stake would be decided. If the government tried the criminal suit first and lost, it was lost for good as no appeal was possible, and the chances for successful trial of the civil suit would have been much diminished. "I . . . understand," Fowler commented of Hayward's insistence upon criminal prosecution, "that the Colonel thinks that he will soon have the psychological condition in New York so favorable to the Government that everyone against whom an indictment has been or may hereafter be returned will rush to the court, plead guilty, and take his sentence to jail." When that condition arose, Fowler quipped, he would consent to Hayward's insistence on prior criminal prosecution; but it was not likely to arise. "The fact is that Colonel Hayward is laboring under a very serious misapprehension as to the relative value of a criminal prosecution and an action in equity under the antitrust laws."

Fowler was disturbed at other aspects of Hayward's behavior. He was monopolizing the Bureau of Investigation's agents trained for antitrust work; of the twenty-two agents available, thirteen had been assigned to New York, leaving only nine for Fowler's nationwide investigation of building-materials cases and all the other matters before the Antitrust Division, "with the consequent result that the activities of the division have been greatly reduced, and this notwithstanding the fact that demands of the most urgent character are being made upon it." Daugherty intervened, after long hesitation, and decided in mid-December to settle the cement matter in Fowler's favor. The civil suit would be tried first, by Fowler, and the Department would get on with the task Hayward had delayed, of trying a case directed against the basic principles of the open price plan.[15]

As though in reward for this decision to place fundamental goals above expediency, the Supreme Court on December 19 handed down its decision in the Hardwood case, presenting the Department with a very impressive victory over an open price association. The issues in the Hardwood case were not as clear-cut as was necessary for a definitive statement of the legality of open price associations. The Hardwood Association had not merely circulated price statistics but accompanied them with interpretations and predictions of market trends and performed other acts which supported the government's contention that the association's open price system was a means for implementing a conspiracy. A precise definition of the Supreme Court's view of open price and of other forms of statistical reporting could not be divined from the Hardwood opinion, but Daugherty and his Antitrust Division decided at once to place as severe an interpretation upon it as it would bear. Preparation of the brief for the argument before the Court had received the Department's earnest attention. "I am aware," one of Solicitor General James E. Beck's assistants advised during the writing of the brief, "that the Supreme Court does not welcome argument on the 'disastrous consequences' which may ensue from an adverse decision." Nevertheless, the brief should contain references to the disclosures emanating from the Chicago investigations of open price associations. "These unsettled times are inappropriate for even that court to strike public opinion in the face." The Department's first impulse when the brief was accepted was to interpret the Court's opinion as a virtual prohibition of open price associations. Guy E. Goff, the Assistant to the Attorney General and head of the Department's Antitrust Division, informed a trade association executive two weeks after the Hardwood case was decided, "that the Department has rather pronounced views with regard to the practices of trade associations and that the systematic exchange of statistics relating to production, sales and prices is regarded as unlawful." This interpretation of the Hardwood ruling was not publicized, however, and the statement of policy toward trade association statistical work which Daugherty issued was a much more judicious document than the letter which Goff had written a month earlier.[16]

The Department would likely have attempted to enforce the hard line Goff had taken had it not been for Hoover's exertions in favor of a more moderate reading of the Hardwood decision. By mid-July 1921, Hoover had begun to reassess his position. By this time Fowler had filed the civil suit against the Cement Manufacturers' Protective Association, Hayward had begun his investigation in New York of open price associations, and it was becoming apparent that Daugherty would not accept the simple formula for determining open price illegality which Hoover had urged. In July 1921, Hoover began the publication of statistical data obtained from a few contributing associations as the *Survey of Current Business*. But this demonstration of support for statistical work was hardly enough to quiet the sense of unease developing among trade associationists. During July and August Hoover familiarized himself more thoroughly with the intracacies of the various types of open price reporting and discussed, with departmental advisers William E. Lamb and Frederick M. Feiker and with Nathan B. Williams, the NAM's associate counsel, possible methods for obtaining a clarification of Daugherty's interpretation of the law. Lamb, the Commerce Solicitor, at length broached the subject with Daugherty, and at the end of August believed that agreement virtually had been reached and that he and Daugherty would confer in the near future "and shortly thereafter a public expression of the views of the Attorney General and the Secretary [of Commerce] will be available to the public."

What further discussions there may have been with the Attorney General it is impossible to say. If, as Lamb believed, Daugherty had made an agreement to issue a joint statement with Hoover clarifying the legal rights of trade associations, then the Attorney General reneged on it. Hoover, seriously impressed now by the threat the Justice Department was posing, apparently dropped all attempts to influence Daugherty and awaited the outcome of the Hardwood case coming up for argument before the Supreme Court's fall term, hoping the result would strengthen the trade association position. In the meantime, realizing the potentially embarrassing position he had been placing himself in earlier, Hoover stopped proffering his own interpretation of trade association law, and even advised some associations that "the best thing to do" was to end the reporting of prices altogether.[17]

The weeks following the Hardwood decision were extremely trying for Hoover and the whole association world. Within days of the Justice Department's victory in the Hardwood case on December 19, 1921, Daugherty opened a spectacular investigation of price-fixing in the distribution trades, enhancing the reputation for severity and recklessness which he already had earned in business circles. The investigation was makeshift, ill prepared and poorly conceived, and far more revealing of Daugherty's motivation, in the attitude he was displaying toward organized business, than of the extent of price-gouging in distribution. The correspondence between the Special Assistant, G. E. Strong, handling the investigation and Daugherty's Antitrust Division head, Guy E. Goff, underlines the extent to which political as opposed to economic or legal calculations determined the moves of some of the Justice Department's decisionmakers, including, more than likely, those of its chief. Daugherty's announcement that certain retail trade associations were fixing prices at "unconscionable levels" and would be investigated came on December 22. For some time the work of his investigator, Strong, was largely confined to analyzing the flood of letters to the Department which the announcement provoked. "One writer says," Strong noted pointedly, that " 'this investigation is a better vote getter than the disarmament conference which seems to deal with the possibilities of the future rather than the present ills of society.' " But on the whole, the public's reaction was disquieting, Strong thought. The letters denoted "a general tone of suspicion, discontent, and unrest." The Wilson "regime left a bad taste in the mouths of the people and they question the good faith of this investigation, asking whether it is merely a repetition of Palmerism." He suggested "that greater publicity be given" to the results obtained in recent antitrust prosecutions "in an effort to allay the suspicion that the Administration is in league with the Trust and Combine."

But the "high cost of living" investigation had not progressed very far before the retail associations embarrassed the Department by offering to cooperate in the gathering of information on the condition that full publicity be given to the facts revealed. This created a serious dilemma, according to Special Assistant Strong. "If the Attorney General vindicates [the retailers,] he will lose prestige before the American people who will unreasonably conclude that the Attorney General is in collusion with the profiteer." If, on the other hand, Daugherty did not make his findings public, the retailers would "set up a clamor accusing the Administration of persecution, hostility to business and unfairness. I am not an alarmist," Strong concluded, "but this is the situation as I see it."

The Department's position was difficult because, despite Daugherty's accusations, it had no evidence that retail profits were excessive. Strong could suggest only one escape. Questionnaires would be sent to a few principal dealers in each city. This would give the Attorney General "an idea as to the causes of high prices and would permit the retailers to present their side of the case and thereby stop their present claims of political demagoguery, prejudiced testimony and misunderstanding." The Attorney General

> could then say that based on the statistics secured prices were entirely too high; that they were due to exorbitant profits, etc.; that the retailers explained these prices by high rental costs, etc., but that in the opinion of the Department their explanation was unsatisfactory and that further action or prosecution was contemplated. This would be fair to the retailers, would satisfy the great mass of them who are inefficient and poor business men and therefore making no profit and yet would secure beneficial results for the consumer by publicity.[18]

The case against the retailers was so weak and the volume of protest against the investigation so great that its political justification was problematical. As a Cincinnati clothing manufacturer informed Daugherty, "there was bitter complaint" about the investigation among businessmen, who felt it was threatening to ruin the economic recovery which had begun the previous summer. "The country was promised, under the present administration, relief from Government control of private affairs. Upon such pledges, loyal, partisan Republicans, such as I supported the party in its return to power. Since March 4th, 1921, we have been awaiting action, only to be handed fruit washed up by the sea."

Protests against Daugherty's policy toward trade associations were no less urgent. The Hardwood decision, the head of the American Trade Association Executives told Daugherty late in December 1921, had produced a " 'panicky feeling' among thousands of members of national trade organizations and in many lines general demoralization." Associations "that engage in statistical work of any character are greatly disturbed and uncertain as to the legal limitations now imposed upon them." There were similar pleas from other individuals highly placed in the trade association world; and from some businessmen protests which were somewhat more pointed. A Camden banker, for example, writing Daugherty on behalf of the New Jersey sanitary pottery manufacturers the Justice Department was threatening to indict, reminded the Attorney General that "all business men look for protection from a Republican Administration and if they believe they are not getting a 'square deal', they naturally will turn against our candidates for Senator, Governor and Congress at the coming fall elections." There was a "growing sentiment against the present administration on the part of big business, due to the apparent disposition to hamper them in every way by investigations, etc. on the part of the Department of Justice." Daugherty should realize that "the number of complaints and dissatisfaction is so great, that I really believe it my duty to let you know how the administration is being attacked and how our Party will suffer, unless something is done to appease the business man." [19]

The "high cost of living" investigation could be readily abandoned and was, during the latter part of January 1922. But the trade association campaign was a different matter. To judge from the readiness his Antitrust Division had shown immediately after the Hardwood decision to interpret it as severely as possible, Daugherty probably felt his efforts against associations were too popular to relax. Moreover, the influences which had originally set off the Justice Department's crusade were stronger than ever. In the weeks following the Hardwood decision, the FTC exerted continual pressure upon Daugherty to uphold the position, which the Commission deemed "manifest," that the Supreme Court had outlawed the "collection and dissemination of cost, price and production statistics in itself." Certain trade association lawyers were publicly arguing that the decision had not condemned most forms of statistical interchange so long as it was not practiced with the purpose and effect "of unduly restricting production or enhancing price." It looked to the Commission "as though a fight would have to be made to establish and maintain the full scope of that decision," lest "the substance of this decision . . . be lost and merely the shadow remain." [20]

During these same weeks, Hoover had been exerting a counter pressure; and Daugherty, at length, in the first week of February 1922, decided not to adopt the extreme position toward which his own inclination and the FTC's prodding had been leading him. Realizing, probably, that a general condemnation of statistical interchange would be premature on the basis of the Hardwood decision alone and might never receive a satisfactory underpinning from the Court, Daugherty accepted a compromise which Hoover offered in a letter of February 3, 1922. Daugherty assented to the proposition that it was not in itself illegal for an association to collect certain types of statistics, including statistics of prices on closed transactions, to average them and circulate the results to members, so long as all circulation was done through the Department of Commerce and full publicity for all data was provided for. The assent was grudging; the practice would be illegal, Daugherty warned, if "used as a scheme or device to curtail production and enhance prices." Daugherty, in fact, left the door open for a total retraction of his "tentative" agreement with Hoover's view that circulation of production figures and price averages through the Commerce Department did not necessarily lead to or constitute restraint of trade. But, though Daugherty largely retained complete freedom of action, the effect of his reply to Hoover's letter was to release a sigh of relief from trade associationists and to give them hope of further backtracking by the Attorney General. For him, the exchange with Hoover represented a maximum and rescindable statement of trade association rights. As for Hoover: he had in the first place established the legality of his existing program of publishing statistics in the *Survey of Current Business*, a program he intended to expand; but, more importantly, for the Secretary of Commerce, Daugherty's statements represented a minimum, a basis to build upon.[21]

NOTES

1. National Association of Manufacturers, *Annual Convention* (1919), pp. 134–56.

2. The fact of the tension alluded to, or instances of reluctance of political representatives of smaller business to support big business proposals for antitrust revision which looked toward greater government toleration of market agreements, are discussed in Robert H. Wiebe, *Businessmen and Reform: A Study of the Progressive Movement* (Cambridge: Harvard University Press, 1963), pp. 45–47, 79–81, 137–41; Arthur M. Johnson, "Antitrust Policy in Transition, 1908: Ideal and Reality," *Mississippi Valley Historical Review*, 48 (December 1961), 424–34; and Gabriel Kolko, *The Triumph of Conservatism* (New York: Free Press, 1963), pp. 65–89, 113–38, 255–78. Perhaps the two best general sources on prewar trade associations are H. R. Tosdal, "Open Price Associations," *American Economic Review*, 7, No. 2 (June 1917), 331–52; and National Industrial Conference Board, *Trade Associations: Their Economic Significance and Legal Status* (New York: NICB, 1925), pp. 7–24. For the experience of one industry, cotton textiles, with prewar associationism, there is an excellent guide in Chapter 4 of Louis C. Galambos' *Competition and Cooperation: The Emergence of a National Trade Association* (Baltimore: The Johns Hopkins University Press, 1966).

3. Two studies were made, one in the early, the other in the late, 1930s, of the date of the formation of extant trade associations. The Chamber of Commerce study, *Trade Association Activities: A Classification and Statistical Survey of the Activities and Services of 500 Associations* (Trade Association Department of the

Chamber of Commerce, 1932), gave the number of associations (of the 500 included in the study) founded during each of a series of five-year periods, beginning in 1900, as follows: 1900–04, 39; 1905–09, 34; 1910–14, 63; 1915–19, 83; 1920–24, 73; 1925–29, 87. In C. A. Pearce, *Trade Association Survey*, Temporary National Economic Committee Monograph No. 18 (Washington, D.C.: Government Printing Office, 1941), p. 369, the corresponding figures, beginning in 1915, are as follows: 1915–19, 143; 1920–24, 98; 1925–29, 151. Pearce's study included a far higher number of associations (1,167), but there is approximate agreement between the two surveys.

NAM, *Annual Convention* (1919), p. 285; on the NAM attitude, see, as well, James A. Emery, "Industrial Readjustment," *American Industries*, 19, No. 6 (January 1919), 12–15. Harry A. Wheeler, "Foundations for the Future," *Nation's Business*, 7, No. 6 (June 1919), 17–18. "Minutes of the War Emergency and Reconstruction Congress under Auspices of the Chamber of Commerce of the United States of America" (Chamber of Commerce Library, Washington, D.C.), pp. 229–231. Chamber of Commerce, *Referendum No. 26: On the Report of the Federal Trade Committee of the Chamber Regarding Trust Legislation. February 1, 1919.* The first two questions submitted were the important ones. To understand their full meaning, it is necessary to read the text of the accompanying explanations. The vote is recorded in the Chamber's *Special Bulletin: Referendum Number Twenty-Six, April 11, 1919.* For the solicitude of War Industries Board administrators for the preservation and strengthening of the industries, the best source is Robert Cuff, *The War Industries Board: Business–Government Relations During World War I* (Baltimore: The Johns Hopkins University Press, 1973), pp. 1–5, 149, 182, 219, 229.

4. These efforts to sway government policy are detailed in Robert F. Himmelberg, "The War Industries Board and the Antitrust Question in November, 1918," *Journal of American History*, 52, No. 1 (June 1965), 59–74, and *idem*, "Business, Antitrust Policy and the Industrial Board of the Department of Commerce, 1919," *Business History Review*, 42, No. 1 (Spring 1968), 1–23. For the revival of public and governmental concern over business behavior, see John J. Hanrahan, "The High Cost of Living Controversy, 1919–1920" (Fordham University diss., 1969), pp. 36–54, 131–34.

5. The FTC surveyed trade associations during 1921 at the request of the Joint Commission of Agricultural Inquiry of Congress. A brief reference to the findings appeared in the FTC's *Annual Report* for 1922, but details were not published. A copy of the statement of findings given to the Joint Commission early in 1922, titled "Statement of Secretary J. P. Yoder, Federal Trade Commission . . . On Open Price Associations . . . ," was given to the Commerce Department and is in the Trade Association file, Secretary of Commerce Papers, Herbert Hoover Papers, Herbert Hoover Presidential Library. (Hereafter cited as CP, HHL.) For Palmer's prosecution of the Hardwood Lumber Manufacturers' Association, and his statements regarding open price associations, see *New York Times,* March 18, 21, April 4, July 28, August 24, 1920.

Report of Illinois Building Investigation Commission (Springfield: Illinois *State Register*, 1923), pp. 9–10, 12–39, 97–98. The summary of the New York investigation is in New York State Assembly, *Final Report of the Joint Legislative Committee on Housing.* Legislative Document No. 48, 1923.

6. *New York Times,* September 8, October 14, 18, 21–27, 29, 31, November 1, 5–8, 10, 12–13, 16, 18, 20, 24, December 1–4, 8, 10, 12, 14–16, 18, 22, 24, 29, 30, 1920. *New York World,* October 21–22, 25, November 5, 9, 12, December 2, 8, 19, 1920.

7. Untermeyer to Palmer, October 16, 1920; Henry S. Mitchell to Untermeyer, October 22, 1920; to Caffey, October 26, November 2, 4, 1920; Caffey to Untermeyer, October 26, November 1, 1920; to Mitchell, November 3, 1920; Palmer to Caffey, December 13, 1920; Caffey to Palmer, December 13, 1920, January 14, 1921; Henry A. Guiler to Caffey, January 25, 1921; in file 60/12/0, Record Group 60, General Records of the Department of Justice, National Archives. (Hereafter cited as RG 60.)

Untermeyer later told Harry Daugherty (then Attorney General) that he had from the outset of his dealings with the Justice Department in 1920 offered to handle federal prosecutions. But the correspondence between him and the Justice Department officials belies this, as the narrative above makes clear. Untermeyer to Daugherty, March 17, 1921, *ibid.*

New York Times, November 16, December 8, 1920, January 6, 19–21, 26, 1921; *New York World*, January 19, 1921, for Untermeyer's polemic against Palmer and the latter's feeble efforts to reply.

8. Robert K. Murray's *The Harding Era: Warren G. Harding and His Administration* (Minneapolis: The University of Minnesota Press, 1969), has made it clear that the Harding Administration, though "permeated" with "that business thinking of the type identified with the middle class," was not "oriented toward big business" (yet Harding's economic ideas were compatible with Wall Street's) and that the Harding period "was more a time of conflict and testing," with "the laborer, the businessman and the farmer . . . constantly jockeying for preferential government treatment," than a "time of one-sided victory for any economic group" (pp. 170–71). See especially his Chapters 6, 7, 8, and 12.

Consult Hoover, *American Individualism* (Garden City: Doubleday, 1922) *passim*, for the observations above on the general outlines of his politico-economic philosophy. For a more detailed treatment and additional references, see my essay in *Herbert Hoover and the Crisis of American Capitalism*, edd. Joseph J. Huthmacher and Warren Sussmann (Cambridge: Schenckman, 1974), pp. 59–85. For Hoover's ideas concerning trade associations, see Secretary of Commerce, *Annual Report* (1922), pp. 138–40; (1926), pp. 11–14; (1929), p. xxx; Department of Commerce, *Business Cycles and Unemployment: Report and Recommendations of a Committee of the President's Conference on Unemployment* (Washington, 1923), pp. v–vi; Hoover, "A Problem in Distribution: An Address Delivered Before the National Distribution Conference," January 14–15, 1925; Hoover to Harding, June 9, 1921, Harding file, CP, HHL. See Ellis Hawley, "Herbert Hoover, the Commerce Secretariat, and the Vision of an 'Associative State,' 1921–1928," *Journal of American History*, 61, No. 1 (June 1974), 116–40, for a comprehensive survey of Hoover's efforts to apply the associative idea to a broad range of economic and social problems.

9. Important books, from the early 1920s, arguing for moderate forms of trade association practices and contending that such practices were compatible with traditional concepts of the competitive market, are: *Co-Operative Competition: A Discussion of the Acute Legal and Economic Perplexities Confronting Trade Associations* (reprinted from the New York *Post*, 1921); Emmett Hay Naylor, *Trade Associations: Their Organization and Management* (New York: Ronald Press, 1921); and Franklin D. Jones, *Trade Association Activities and the Law* (New York: McGraw-Hill, 1922).

Representative of such literature from the later 'twenties are NICB, *Trade Associations*, and Joseph H. Foth, *Trade Associations: Their Services to Industry* (New York: Ronald Press, 1930).

10. Hoover to Harding, March 16, June 9, 1921, Harding file; Nathan B.

Williams to W. M. Steuart, June 4, 1921; memo by Williams, June 7, 1921; "Memorandum for Dr. Surface" by Williams, July 6, 1921; "Memorandum of Conversation with Secretary Hoover" by Williams, July 7, 1921, National Association of Manufacturers file; Hoover to Elliot E. Goodwin, May 16, 1921, Chamber of Commerce file; memo for Hoover by Miller, May 23, 1921; Hoover to Edge, June 13, 1921; Senator Arthur Capper (Kans.) to Hoover, August 15, 1921; memo for Hoover by William E. Lamb, August 30, 1921, Federal Trade Commission file; Edge to Hoover, May 13, 26, 1921, Edge file; Hoover to Daugherty, March 22, 1921; Guy D. Goff to Hoover, March 28, 1921; Daugherty to Hoover, May 16, 1921, Justice Department file. All in CP, HHL.

11. Harding to Huston Thompson, March 21, 1921, box 150, Warren G. Harding Papers, Ohio State Historical Society. For the background of the Commission's reply, see the "Minutes" of the Federal Trade Commission, March 23, April 7, 1921. This record is held in the FTC building in Washington and was made available by permission of the Commission.

For the message to Congress, see Harding, *Speeches as President* (Columbus, Ohio, n. d.), pp. 3–19.

12. Untermeyer to Daugherty, March 17, 29, 1921; to Guy E. Goff, April 4, 1921; Goff to Untermeyer, April 1, 1921, file 60/12/0, RG 60.

Daugherty displayed intense concern with the Department's investigation of the building-materials cases stemming from the Lockwood Committee from the very beginning of the Harding Administration. Henry S. Matthews to Daugherty, March 14, 1921; Shale to Goff, March 28, 1921; to Daugherty, April 16, 1921, file 60/10/2, *ibid.* Fowler to Daugherty, December 14, 1921, file 60/12/0; Shale to Daugherty, April 23, 1932, file 89289/1/27; George T. Buckingham to Daugherty, June 1, 1921, file 60/10/5, *ibid.*

13. Senator William M. Calder (N.Y.) to Daugherty, May 18, 1921; Untermeyer to Daugherty, March 29, June 12, 23, 24, 1921; Daugherty to Untermeyer, June 24, 1921, file 60/10/0, *ibid.*

14. *New York Commercial*, May 24, 27, June 1, 3, 1921. *New York Times*, June 1, 3, 11, 1921. Press statement regarding Administration trade association policies [June 1921]; Hoover to Daugherty, June 15, July 27, 1921, Justice Department file; Hoover to Harding, June 9, 1921, Harding file, CP, HHL.

15. Hayward to Daugherty, November 23, December 27, 1921, file 60/55/12; Fowler to Daugherty, November 15, 23, 1921, April 29, 1922; Daugherty to Fowler, November 26, 1921; Shale to Daugherty, January 26, 1922, file 60/10/2; Fowler to Daugherty, December 14, 1921, file 60/12/0, RG 60.

Another conflict between Fowler and Hayward occurred when Fowler's staff in Washington conducting a national investigation of tile manufacturers appealed to Goff to prevent Hayward's agents from interviewing the manufacturers in connection with the New York investigation of tile dealers and setters, fearing the national case might be compromised. Fowler won this argument too. C. Stanley Thompson to Fowler, October 26, 1921; Goff to Hayward, October 26, November 2, 1921; David Podell to Goff, Hayward to Goff, November 1, 1921, file 60/55/12, *ibid.*

16. *American Column and Lumber Co.* v. *U.S.* 257 U.S. 377 (1921). Blackburn Esterline to Beck, n.d., file 60/160/14, RG 60. T. E. Cassidy to Daugherty, December 30, 1921; Goff to National Retail Monument Dealers Association of America, Inc., January 4, 1922, file 60/0, *ibid.*

17. Secretary of Commerce, *Annual Report* (1922), pp. 88–90. Hoover to Harding, July 19, 1921, box 5, Harding Papers. Memo, "Activities of Trade Associations," by Lamb, July 21, 1921; "Memorandum for the Secretary," July 21,

1921; W. H. Stackhouse to Hoover, August 8, 1921; Harry S. Matthews to Hoover, December 22, 1921, Trade Association file, CP, HHL. Williams to Feiker, August 13, 1921; memo for Feiker by Lamb, August 31, 1921, Feiker file, *ibid.* D. A. Skinner to Hoover, October 10, 1921, Chamber of Commerce file, *ibid.* J. R. Barnes to C. H. Huston, August 15, 1921; William Butterworth to Hoover, August 20, 1921; H. C. Meserve to Hoover, October 20, 1921; Hoover to Meserve, October 25, 1921; D. S. Hunger to Hoover, December 29, 1921; Richard S. Emmett to Hunger, January 6, 1922, file 81288, Record Group 40, General Records of the Department of Commerce, National Archives. (Hereafter cited as RG 40.)

18. *New York Commercial*, December 23, 1921. Strong to Goff, December 30, 1921, January 5, 11, 26, 1922; C. Bascom Slemp to Goff, January 14, 1922; Goff to Slemp, January 18, 1922, file 60/0/16, RG 60.

19. Roger W. Allen to Harding, December 31, 1921; Hamilton Kean to Harding, July 31, 1922, box 217, Harding Papers. Andrew W. Burkhardt to Daugherty, January 28, 1922; David A. Baird to Daugherty, January 25, 1922, file 60/0/16, RG 60. George D. McIlvaine to Hoover, February 4, 1922; Rush C. Butler to Hoover, February 8, 1922, Trade Association file, CP, HHL.

20. Nelson B. Gaskill's letter of January 12, 1922, to Daugherty describes a meeting shortly before that date between FTC representatives and the Attorney General and, probably, Hoover at the Justice Department. A second letter of the same date contains the second quote above. Both letters are reproduced in Senate, Select Committee on the Investigation of the Attorney General, *Investigation of Hon. Harry M. Daugherty, Formerly Attorney General of the United States: Hearings . . . Pursuant to S. R. 157*, 68th Cong., 1st sess., 1924, 3 vols., II 1930. Huston Thompson at the same time was explaining the significance of the "doctrine laid down" in the Hardwood decision: "Personally, I have made a constant attack on what is known as the open price association, which is definitely destroyed by the Supreme Court decision." Thompson to Woodrow Wilson, January 10, 1922, Woodrow Wilson Papers, Library of Congress.

21. Hoover to William E. Lamb, January 3, 1922, Trade Association file; Daugherty to Hoover, January 3, 1922, Justice Department file, CP, HHL. The February Hoover–Daugherty exchange is reproduced conveniently in Jones, *Trade Association Activities*, pp. 324–35. See "Nation's Business Observatory," *Nation's Business*, 10, No. 4 (April 1922), 50, for sampling of reactions to the correspondence.

2

The Hoover–Daugherty Controversy over the Rights of Associationism, 1922–1924

IN THE EXCHANGE with Daugherty early in 1922, Hoover had obtained a reaffirmation of the legality of the relatively uncontroversial trade association practices and vindication of a restricted form of statistical interchange. He now proceeded during the remaining three years of the Harding-Coolidge Administration to exploit this charter of rights, encouraging the practices which Daugherty had approved.

Many of the basic practices received little direct encouragement; trade associations were expected to develop uniform cost-accounting methods, cooperative advertising programs, and similar measures under their own steam. Hoover's speeches and departmental publications such as the 1923 *Trade Association Activities,* a vigorous apology for associations and a thorough survey of their activities, provided inspiration. To spur development of certain strategic practices, however, the Department of Commerce offered special services. The Division of Simplified Practice in the Bureau of Standards, established in January 1922, helped associations to work out the complexities of agreements for standardizing products and processes. By June 1928, some ninety-five standardization projects had been completed with its aid.[1]

The most important service the Department performed in the early 1920s was to provide facilities for the dissemination of trade statistics in accordance with the terms of the Hoover–Daugherty correspondence of February 1922. For many associations the *Survey of Current Business* was an adequate vehicle for disseminating trade information, and by June 1922, seventy associations were publishing their statistics through it—a total which grew, by mid-1928, to 117. For other associations, however—those wishing to circulate data more promptly or in greater detail than could be managed through the *Survey,* but still wanting to keep within the bounds of the Hoover–Daugherty agreement—Hoover worked out a special arrangement during the summer of 1922. The Department undertook to examine the form of the statistical data the association proposed to circulate to ensure that "information which lends itself readily to illegal use" was omitted. The association guaranteed that copies of its statistical compilation would be made available to non-members who requested it at the same time as it was to members, and that no supplementary information would be sent to members only. The Department agreed to accept file copies of the compilation and to make them available to inquirers. While the plan, as David Wing, the Hoover assistant who supervised the program, confessed, did not "follow the exact procedure specified in the correspondence with the Attorney General, in that the Department does not physically handle the distribution of the statistics," it was felt that "the spirit had been complied with." [2]

Keeping the spirit of the Hoover–Daugherty correspondence was taken equally seriously in all the other of the Commerce Department's relations with trade associations. Departmental publications encouraged the various association practices only in general terms, and only when the understanding with Daugherty clearly sanctioned them. And when an association applied, as not infrequently happened, to the Department for reassurance that the particular application of a practice it intended to make was legal, the response was uniformly non-committal. For a time during 1922 and possibly part of 1923, Hoover permitted Wing, who handled much of the Department's relations with trade associations, to act as intermediary between associations seeking advice and Nelson W. Gaskill, a Republican member of the FTC who was willing, as an individual, to give an opinion on specific questions. The procedure was for Wing to write to Gaskill, stating the association's problem, and to send a copy of Gaskill's reply to the association.[3]

But available evidence indicates that Hoover and his Commerce associates consistently refused to give any particular arrangement the color of Commerce Department approval. The case of Melvin Cassmore in 1924 is instructive. Cassmore was organizing the Pacific Coast plywood manufacturers into a trade association and found his work impeded by the refusal of several "most desirable" members to join. Some of these non-joiners were involved, as door manufacturers, in an antitrust suit; all had refrained from joining Cassmore's group "because they fear that a membership in any trade association will only invite further prosecution from the government." The plywood association's success depended upon a fuller membership, but this was "not possible unless some assurance can be had from an official source that membership in a trade association is not a dangerous entanglement." What could Hoover say, "in a signed letter," to reassure prospective members? "As you know," Hoover replied, "I am keenly interested in the development and progress of legitimate trade associations." But it would "be inappropriate for me to attempt to advise you or your association as to the legality of association activities" since the Secretary of Commerce had no such authority. Trusting that Cassmore would "understand my keen interest and position in this matter," Hoover could only enclose a copy of his correspondence with Daugherty.[4]

This circumspection in encouraging association activities and in advising individual groups was difficult for Hoover, as his letter to Cassmore suggests, but he accepted it as necessary. As Wing had warned Hoover late in 1922, "in view of the present difficulties in the statement of what definitely is legal or illegal . . . I feel that this Department should not put its official stamp on any construction of the legality or illegality of trade association activities." Pending litigation might "radically modify the present conceptions of the status of such activities." Furthermore, "this Department should hesitate to put itself in any position, whereby defendants in some antitrust suit" would be able to introduce the fact of Commerce Department approval "in justification or extenuation of acts charged against them by the Department of Justice."[5]

The trade association community imitated Hoover's air of circumspection. Ernest T. Trigg, an associationist of high standing, expressed the prevailing tone well when he explained to Hoover, in 1923, how "we are trying to do everything in our power in the Paint and Varnish Industry to make our associational work entirely without ground for any possible Governmental anxiety." Hesitation and uncertainty were expressed in behavior as well as in words. The rate of formation of new trade associations was somewhat lower from 1920 to 1924 than in either the preceding or succeeding five-year period. And if the common, though undocumented, belief of contemporaries be accepted, there was a sharp decline in the number of associations using the more extreme forms of cooperative practices during the Daugherty years.[6]

Attempts to influence antitrust policy were limited to a defense of traditional trade association prerogatives. Association attorneys rejected the implication of the Hoover–Daugherty correspondence that statistical interchange was legal only when done through the Secretary of Commerce as intermediary. They upheld the position that no practice was illegal unless it necessarily created, or was in fact used to implement, a market agreement. The common belief was that the doctrine of the correspondence was more severe than the Supreme Court's statement in the Hardwood opinion would support and that price-reporting plans were legal as long as the prices of individual firms were not disclosed, only past prices were reported, and interpretation and commentary upon the market implications of the statistics were avoided.

Official governmental affirmation of a moderate position such as this was the limit most trade association spokesmen and the major business organizations placed upon their efforts to influence antitrust policy during the remaining years of Daugherty's tenure in the Justice Department. When the NAM adopted, in 1924, a formal position on the issue of trade association rights, it emphasized its agreement with the basic antitrust doctrine that the use of statistics to "further the suppression of production, the control of prices, the division of territory, is reprehensible and inexcusable," and declined to support the open price system unqualifiedly. The Chamber of Commerce also took a moderate stand on trade association rights. In 1922 the Chamber's Board of Directors appointed a committee to deal with the association question, setting in motion the cumbersome machinery which would lead to a referendum by the Chamber's members on the issue. When the committee reported early in 1923, its conclusion was that associations should enjoy a clearly defined right to circulate statistics of prices on closed transactions if they were unaccompanied by interpretations which might foster collusion. But the report conceded that open price plans were inimical to the public interest.[7]

As an exception to this air of diffidence which trade associations showed to the traditional antitrust policy during the Harding-Coolidge Administration, one can point to the wave of interest in revision which broke out for a few months in 1922, in the months immediately following the Hoover–Daugherty correspondence. The correspondence had fixed, tentatively at least, a lower limit beyond which the Justice Department apparently did not intend to drive the scope of trade association activities. The fixing of this limit and the fact that during 1922 the Justice Deparment, though hardly quiescent, offered no serious new shocks to the association position, seem to have emboldened associations to hope for a few months, that an opportunity to take the initiative had appeared. In sharp contrast to the situation in 1919 when radicalism was ascendant, so much so that it controlled the policy aims of the business community's chief organizations, moderation prevailed during the discussion of antitrust revision in the early months of 1922.

Yet the discussion began on a radical note. The question of revision was first brought to the surface by the *New York Commercial* late in February 1922, in a series of articles addressed to the heavy concentration of business and trade association leaders in New York City, urging drastic change in the antitrust laws. The case was well argued, in terms familiar to a more modern era. The new business leadership was "free of the domination of the profit incentive and the instincts of greed," and should not be kept "busy in evasion of obstructive laws." Price administration was better put into the hands of the new businessman than left to the market. The inequity of a public policy which recently, in the Capper–Volstead Act, had granted farmers immunity from the antitrust laws, but which retained their force against business, was also stressed. The first series of articles provoked considerable interest, and a second series of ten articles appeared during the latter part of March.

A second newspaper, the *New York Evening Post*, joined the discussion during March. Editorially the *Post* argued the case for a purely regulatory policy for trade associations. The cooperative rights of asso-

ciations should expand, though not to the point of price-fixing, and the
FTC should be reorganized and given power to supervise asssociation
activities. Many of the articles which trade association spokesmen contributed to the series the *Post* ran were impeccably moderate, however,
and the effect of the discussion was to underline the diversity of opinion
among associationists and the relative weakness of the support for genuinely radical revision.[8]

The focus of the discussion of 1922 was a proposal for procedural, as
opposed to substantive, antitrust amendment, which Senator Walter Edge
of New Jersey brought before Congress early in April. Edge, a Republican who had held his seat since 1919, was sensitive to businessmen's
problems and had taken a significant part in the fashioning of several
pieces of landmark legislation affecting the operation of the business
system. In this case he was responding, it appears, to the theme often
recurring in associationists' commentary on the Hardwood decision and
on the Hoover–Daugherty correspondence: that the "twilight zone," the
area of association practice where the legal shaded into the illegal, was
too broad and that this uncertainty prevented associations from taking
up practices which might actually be innocuous before the law. Edge took
up this theme on April 3, 1922, when he introduced a resolution calling
for a Congressional investigation, through a special joint committee, "for
the purpose of recommending to Congress legislation defining the rights
and limitations of cooperative organizations as distinguished from illicit
combinations in restraint of trade." An accompanying bill offered what
Edge called one, but not necessarily the best, solution for the problem
which his resolution defined. The Edge bill provided for a procedure
under which associations would request and receive legal advice from
the FTC, but did not provide for immunity from prosecution in connection with acts performed supposedly in accordance with it.

There are grounds for the suspicion that Edge actually hoped the investigation he was requesting would provide an opening for the introduction of more thorough measures of antitrust amendment than his bill.
The *Commercial* claimed indirect paternity for Edge's measures since
they were addressed to the problems the paper had been presenting, and
declared that they were "really a starting point for a modification of
some of the drastic laws which are now hampering business and upon
which attention has been focused" by the recent Hardwood decision. "An
underlying thought also is that inasmuch as Congress has by a practically
unanimous vote agreed upon co-operative marketing for farmers, the
same principle should be extended to general business." Edge himself
said, when speaking at the NAM's annual meeting in May a few weeks
after introducing his resolution and bill, that his preference would be to
remove antitrust restraints from business altogether, to let business "go
unbridled." But he felt, as he told the NAM, "we will never return to a

position where business can go on without any restraint . . . you have passed those days." There is nothing to show that Edge thought that any form of antitrust revision other than procedural change was politically relevant in 1922 or that he planned to present a more radical bill if opportunity should arise, though Senate liberals, and the *Commercial*, believed he did.[9]

Few associationists, during the discussion of the Edge measure which went on during April and May 1922, revealed any hope, or even any wish, that the Congressional investigation would lead to anything more than procedural antitrust revision. Hoover, once Edge had provided an opening, enthusiastically supported a Congressional investigation of trade associations. "I have given a great deal of time during the past year to the study of Trade Associations and conferences with their officials," Hoover wrote Senator Wesley Jones, to whose Judiciary Committee Edge's bill had been referred, "and I believe that this Department is in a position to assist in the consideration and development of legislation that will make for the advancement of public interest through these Trade Associations, and at the same time eliminate from their organizations those destructive practices that have crept into a minority of them." If an inquiry should be held, he would "be able to present a great deal of information regarding the situation." [10]

Hoover, however, emphatically and repeatedly denied that his purpose was to achieve anything more than a guarantee to associations of traditional, limited rights of cooperation. At a mass meeting of trade association leaders held on April 12, Hoover pounded this theme home. The meeting had been scheduled some time earlier by the Department, not to discuss the Edge measures, but as an occasion for introducing and initiating the arrangements for the statistical interchange through the Department's facilities which the Hoover–Daugherty correspondence had called for. There is, in fact, no indication that Hoover knew anything of Edge's proposals until they were actually introduced in Congress. Now, however, the April 12 meeting became a rally in favor of Edge's resolution for a Congressional investigation of trade association requirements. Hoover categorically stated his refusal to establish any relations between the Commerce Department and associations using illegal practices or even practices "the legality of which has been questioned but not yet determined," including "open-price associations which are collecting data on prices and sales of their individual members, and circulating such individual data again to their members together with certain other activities." Whether such practices were "used in violation of the law or not," he did not "believe that these functions are in the public interest." He, and most of the trade association leaders who addressed the gathering, supported Edge's proposals as a step toward clarifying the legality of association, especially statistical, practices. When one speaker, the counsel for the National Lumber Manufacturers Association, suggested that relaxation, and not merely clarification, of the antitrust policy was necessary, Hoover contradicted any implication that he had "made any amendment to the Sherman Law. I have made some suggestions, but not amendments." Hoover's concluding remarks saluted the principle of enforcing competition. "The restraint of trade acts are based on the fundamental instinct of the American people," he said, "that they must preserve the competitive system and therefore do not wish groups to grow in our commerce and industry which can dominate the rest of us." His Department had never advocated "abrogation of the Sherman Act," he concluded, only "better interpretation" of its ambiguities.[11]

In mid-April the Senate refused to act upon Edge's resolution calling for a trade association investigation, but the Judiciary Committee's chairman agreed to appoint a subcommittee to consider the senator's bill when he was ready. For over a month Edge discussed his measure with associationists, seeking substantial agreement on the form it should take before asking for hearings. He found considerable sentiment favoring substitution of the Commerce Department for the FTC as the body empowered to advise trade associations. Hoover took no stand on this issue, but did advise Edge that stronger advisory powers were needed than those the senator's bill provided. Hoover would have had the advisory agency authorized to approve proposed trade association practices and give a limited immunity from prosecution to associations operating in good faith in conformity with the approved plan of cooperation. The Justice Department would have been able to challenge such approved plans and test them in court, but only after the association had been given an opportunity to abandon its practice.[12]

Trade association leaders, however, failed to reach agreement on the specific form Edge's proposed legislation should take, or even to agree that procedural revision was desirable in principle. By mid-June Edge was disgusted. "Frankly," he told Hoover, "the representatives of the Trade Associations are so divided in their view-point that I have simply permitted the matter to drift. I sometimes think that a great many of them prefer to try to evade or circumvent the Sherman Act rather than put themselves under even semi-jurisdiction of the Federal Trade Commission or for that matter, any other governmental tribunal." Edge's interest in the project was waning; he was "not going to try to press an important amendment to existing anti-trust laws" unless associations were "fairly well interested in securing such a change and have some concrete ideas of what they want." The hearings on Edge's proposal never materialized. But Hoover retained his interest; in the summer of 1922 his office submitted a draft bill to Edge, and in the fall Hoover was trying to interest Gilbert Montague and other legal experts in drafting still another version. Edge remained willing to sponsor a bill if enough trade association support could be aroused. But none of the major organizations, such as the NAM or the Chamber of Commerce, which might have stimulated consideration of the procedural amendment idea and brought it to a mature conclusion, made any effort in that direction.[13]

By the beginning of 1923, no one, not even Hoover, though he tried sporadically to revive the project, could have entertained a very firm belief that procedural revision would prove very useful until the Justice Department moderated its policies. In early 1922 these policies were relatively restrained. Trade association prosecutions continued with respectable frequency and success, but the Department's drive of 1921 to whittle down trade association prerogatives seemed in abeyance. It was this relative stability which had encouraged trade association spokesmen to raise the issue of antitrust revision and seriously to consider the desirability of the Edge–Hoover suggestion of procedural amendment. Later in 1922, however, Daugherty's lieutenants resumed their efforts to circumscribe the rights of trade associations, especially in the matter of statistical interchange. Procedural amendment, in the face of the Justice Department's renewed attitude of unbending hostility toward association activities, seemed a frail refuge. Genuine alarm spread through the trade association community during 1923 that this newly invigorated campaign actually would succeed in strait-jacketing association activities, and all available energy and resources were poured into the purely defensive task of halting Daugherty's aggressions.

The restraint which observers thought they saw in Justice Department policy during much of 1922 arose in part from hesitation in Daugherty's resolve, in part from circumstances. During the first months of 1922 Daugherty and Goff appear to have been uncertain whether to resume the Justice Department's effort of the previous year to limit or outlaw association statistical activities. In the spring Daugherty compromised himself somewhat by promising the counsel for the midwestern cement manufacturers association, against which Fowler had brought suit, that the Department would deal with the group by consent decree. Since the pledge was made before the association had bound itself to accept the government's wishes in a decree, and since its counsel happened to be a Kansas National Republican Committeeman, the suspicion arises that the arrangement stemmed from Daugherty's estimate of the politics and not of the law and economics of the situation. The counsel for the association made the most of the pledge, evading a settlement for months and causing Daugherty a good deal of embarrassment before his own men.[14]

Another instance of a tendency toward leniency occurred in April when Daugherty and Goff were on the point of making a significant concession to the American Hardwood Institute, an organization newly formed to replace the Hardwood Association the Department had destroyed a few months earlier. They agreed to review the institute's plan of cooperation and to give the Department's opinion of its legality. Whether Daugherty regarded the case as an exception, or was considering adopting as a policy the practice of advising associations on the legality of their programs, the Justice Department records do not make clear. This sort of consultation with associations would have greatly mitigated the Department's severity in dealing with those groups until then.

But moderation did not prevail. The pledge to the Hardwood Institute was not honored, and the Department continued on its former course. It was James Fowler who nipped off the tendency to moderation which Daugherty showed in his relations with the Hardwood Institute. When Goff informed him of the Attorney General's talk with the Hardwood counsel, Fowler responded by setting down a sterner objective than anyone in the Department had dared to entertain during the year-long struggle it had conducted against associations. During April and May Fowler was trying a criminal trade association prosecution in New York, and his "observation in the trial of [the] case," he said, had persuaded him "to consider these associations from a standpoint somewhat different from that from which I have heretofore viewed them. I have about reached the conclusion that there is a danger in any kind of organization of this kind." When men from the same business come together, even socially, Fowler wrote, paraphrasing Adam Smith, consciously or otherwise, "they can hardly refrain from taking advantage of the situation and will thereafter conduct their businesses in a comparatively uniform way and will charge uniform prices, although there may be no positive agreement to that effect." Fowler's conclusion—that the Department should not enter into friendly discussions with associations respecting the legal status of their proposed programs—was accepted. The Hardwood manufacturers received no advice from the Department.[15]

Not even Fowler, at least not immediately, concluded that the Department should attempt to suppress trade associations altogether. Yet he steadily maintained his position of the previous year—that the Department should, to whatever degree possible, curtail price and other forms of statistical interchange—and urged the expediting of appropriate test cases to the Supreme Court to obtain fresh statements of principle which would sustain the momentum the Department had gathered through the Hardwood decision. The Department's suit against the linseed manufacturers' open price plan, rejected by a district court in November, was in process of appeal to the Supreme Court. To complement it, Fowler argued for speeding up the civil suit which still pended against the Cement Manufacturers' Protective Association. During the previous year Fowler had insisted upon trying the case for the same reason he now gave: that it was a suitable vehicle for securing a Supreme Court decision bearing on the principles governing the legality of statistical activities. Against Hayward's opposition Fowler had persuaded Daugherty, late in 1921, to give the Department's civil suit against the eastern cement manufacturers priority over the criminal prosecution which also had been instituted. Not long after this decision, the Supreme Court had announced its opinion in the Hardwood case, and Fowler, convinced temporarily that it strengthened the government's hand so much that the need to secure immediate supporting decisions was not great, had agreed to accommodate Hayward by proceeding at once to prosecute the cement manufacturers under the criminal indictment, holding the civil suit in abeyance. Preparing and arguing the case against the cement association's counsel, Henry L. Stimson, had consumed much of Fowler's energy during the spring of 1922, and the case had ended disappointingly with the jury hung seven to five in favor of the government.

Fowler was convinced that the cement equity suit could be tried and won on the record compiled in the criminal trial and that the suit was especially likely to secure a narrow construction of trade association prerogatives from the Supreme Court. As in the previous year, Hayward tried to veto the plan, insisting on the immediate retrial of the criminal case. Once again Fowler prevailed. Priority would be given to obtaining the key requirement for the containment of trade association statistical activities, a clear and severe construction of the law. "It is very important," Fowler argued, "that the next case or two presented to the Supreme Court shall be in a large measure a typical association case but yet one in which their activities are of such a nature as to clearly indicate what their purposes were and what the result therefrom must be." By the late fall of 1922, the Justice Department's resolve to see its war against open price associations through to a finish had strengthened. Daugherty had agreed, over Hayward's protest, to allow Fowler to proceed with the civil suit against the cement association. Even Hayward, modifying his former stand for use of criminal proceedings exclusively, agreed by the end of the year to employ other methods, including the consent decree, in instances where they served the Department's grand strategy.[16]

Fowler's representations were one influence in revising Daugherty's determination to continue the Department's war against trade associations. But another, and no doubt the predominant, influence was the fact that public concern with prices and trade restraint remained high during 1922 and was available for exploitation by Daugherty's and the Republican Administration's critics. In the spring of 1922 Samuel Untermeyer tired of his long forbearance from public criticism of the Justice Department and openly attacked Daugherty for his failure to follow up the leads for antitrust prosecutions which the Lockwood Committee had furnished him. In a letter which Senator La Follette willingly read into the *Congressional Record* on May 25, Untermeyer pointed to information he had sent to Daugherty concerning alleged misdeeds by General Electric. That a prosecution had not materialized Untermeyer attributed to a political shield erected around G.E. by J. P. Morgan and Co. La Follette, already on the trail of a scandal elsewhere in the Harding Administration, commented gravely that it was "high time that the Senate take account of the conduct of the head of the Department of Justice."

The episode in the Senate was a forewarning of the charges of lax antitrust-enforcement which were made, in a more dangerous form, in the House in September when Representative Keller of Pennsylvania introduced a resolution for Daugherty's impeachment. Contemporaries regarded the impeachment attempt as a retaliation against Daugherty by the railway shopmen's union for the sweeping injunction against their strike which he had secured on September 1 in the Chicago federal court. This was undoubtedly the case; the attorney representing Keller at the hearings held on his resolution by the House Committee on the Judiciary in September and December 1922 admitted he was on the AFL legal staff. But the charges Keller made related chiefly to lax antitrust-enforcement. Samuel Untermeyer and the Democrat-controlled FTC furnished these allegations, nearly all of them specifying instances in which information of trade association misbehavior had been transmitted to the Attorney General without any result. The Harding Administration's friends controlled the hearings, and Daugherty, Hayward, and other witnesses were able to rebut the charges convincingly, pointing out that the number of cases the Department of Justice had started since March 1921 equalled or exceeded the number of starts during a similar period in other Administrations.

Without denying that there was some substance in the accusations which the FTC and the Lockwood Committee's counsel hurled at Daugherty through the Keller investigation, one must point out the ironical aspect of the charges. That the Department's campaign was poorly organized, that many cases went uninvestigated, Fowler himself had complained to Daugherty as early as December 1921. Even so, since the beginning of the Harding Administration, actions had been started— civil, criminal, or both—against nineteen different groups, most of them trade associations. Seven cases had ended in a decision for the government; of the remainder, most either were still awaiting trial or were in the process of being tried. More importantly—and in this lay the irony of the situation—the Department, under Fowler's direction, had mapped out and was proceeding with a plan of action which, if successful, would evoke judicial rulings drastically limiting association statistical activities and making successful prosecution of open price associations a simple task. Though the progress of this program lagged through the first half of 1922, it had not been abandoned. At a time when the trade association community was fearful of what harm Daugherty's policies might bring to it, the FTC and Untermeyer were somewhat beside the point in drawing mechanical comparisons between the number of allegations against associations they had forwarded to the Justice Department and the number the Department had acted upon.[17]

Daugherty's ambition, it appears, was to make a politically appealing record as Attorney General. How closely he watched the indicators of public opinion can be divined from Goff's comments, in September 1922, concerning public reaction to Daugherty's policies as Attorney General. "I have followed your course very studiously as reflected in the daily press," he said. "You are all right in everything you are doing. The country is with you, and with you stronger each day. Your critics belong to the class that would not convict a man who stole their dog." [18] The trade association crusade of 1921 was a direct response to public demand. If Daugherty was tempted to moderate the crusade during the early months of 1922, it was probably because he felt the time had come to mend his fences with the business community. Fowler's persistence, and the accusations aired at the hearings on the Keller resolution, persuaded him to resume the former policy with all vigor.

The immediate aim of the Department's renewed effort was to limit statistical reporting strictly to the forms outlined in the Hoover–Daugherty correspondence. It is probable that even more stringent restrictions on association activities, and not only with respect to their statistical programs, would have been sought had the first goal been firmly accomplished. The government's first move in the 1923 campaign was to force the Gypsum Industries Association to accept an extraordinarily severe consent decree which specifically enumerated the activities the association, after reorganization as a corporation, could perform. These included research, advertising, education, and credit bureau functions, but the most vital activities, cost accounting and statistical exchange, were entirely omitted from the list of permissible activities. The *Gypsum* decree was obtained by Hayward's office in New York and was represented by him as the expression of the Justice Department's attitude toward trade associations. The decree, he declared in a statement early in January 1923, "discourages the existence of a trade association as such because of the many opportunities at the regular meetings of the association for price fixing and other abuses." It favored as a substitute a non-profit corporation with strictly limited functions. Some activities of trade associations had proven beneficial to industry and the public, he said, but "most of these activities . . . such as the open price system, price fixing and numerous others, have resulted in gouging the public."

Whether Hayward accurately represented the government's fundamental attitude and ultimate aims in this statement is not entirely clear. Hayward stated that the decree, and presumably the policy interpretation he placed on it, had been approved at a conference in Washington with

Daugherty, but no record of such a meeting is available. Daugherty was "bedfast" at the time Hayward made the statement, trying to recover from a collapse following the strain of the Keller hearings, and A. T. Seymour, Acting Attorney General, was somewhat at a loss to interpret the decree for two urgent inquirers, Senator La Follette and Secretary Hoover. Hayward's office, to which Seymour turned for advice, replied, through David Podell, that the intent of the decree had been to signify that the Justice Department held all price-reporting plans illegal regardless of circumstances. If Hayward's newspaper statement and Podell's interpretation approximated a correct statement of the goals upon which Daugherty, Fowler, and Hayward had agreed, the outlook for trade association activities was bleak.[19]

None of the decrees the Department attempted to, or did, impose during most of the remainder of 1923 went to the extreme of the *Gypsum* decree. The leading aim of the decrees the Department sought to obtain was to prohibit the associations concerned from collecting any kind of statistics except those the Secretary of Commerce specifically requested them to gather, and to block dissemination of the results except through the Secretary's facilities and at his discretion. In May the Maple Flooring Manufacturers' Association refused to consent to such a decree, and the case went to trial. In June, however, the Supreme Court strengthened the Department's hand considerably when, for the first time since the Hardwood verdict in December 1921, it handed down a decision in a trade association case. The open price system of the Linseed Crushers' Council was struck down, and the government's leverage greatly improved, temporarily at least. "It might be advisable," as C. Stanley Thompson, a Special Assistant for Antitrust urged, "to bring pressure to bear on the Tile Manufacturers Association and the Southern Pine Association to have the decrees as submitted by us accepted before their attorneys have too much opportunity to decide that the Linseed Oil decision really means nothing because of fine distinctions that they can draw as to the facts concerned." In November, before the numbing effects of the *Linseed* decision had worn off, the Tile Manufacturers' Credit Association accepted a decree similar to the one the maple flooring manufacturers had rejected.[20]

The Justice Department's achievement in this case convinced associationists that a crisis in their relations with the government was at hand. The NAM's associate counsel, Nathan B. Williams, was the first leader in the association camp to recognize and try to meet the threat implied in the *Tile* decree. Learning of the decree's contents several weeks before the tile manufacturers had accepted it, Williams repeatedly protested its terms in interviews with A. T. Seymour, who had replaced Goff as head of antitrust enforcement early in 1923. When these representations accomplished nothing, Williams alerted other associationists in an evident attempt to bring pressure to bear on the Department. The fact that the decree permitted the Tile Association to engage in statistical work only to the extent of collecting and forwarding to the Commerce Department what data that agency might request meant, Williams asserted in a circular letter, that Daugherty's associates were committed to the view that association statistical work was "within the condemnation of existing law, and to be prohibited in so far as the Department of Justice was able to accomplish that end." Supported by the protests of other association spokesmen, which now began to bombard the Department, Williams kept up his fire, resorting finally to thinly veiled political threats. "For the business public to find," Williams wrote four days before the decree was entered, "that the administration, through its Department of Justice, insists that business must proceed without accurate knowledge, is to expect the impossible and if the mentioned decree is entered as drafted, the reactions will be most profound and distressing." [21]

Hoover, too, was distressed. If the *Tile* decree's rule that the association could collect statistical data, but only for transmission to a governmental agency for dissemination, was a principle of law in the Justice Department's view, then the Commerce Department was encouraging illegal practices. The Department had interpreted Daugherty's remarks in his exchange with Hoover of February 1922 to mean that association statistical work was proper if it avoided use of certain especially suspect types of data and full publicity be given to the data members received. To give associations an opportunity to make a public and emphatic showing of compliance with these principles, Hoover had worked out the arrangement whereby his Department undertook to review an association's statistical plan, and, if it appeared suitably moderate, to receive copies of its statistical publications. But the compilation and distribution of the publication were left entirely in the hands of associations. Had Hoover been mistaken in not taking Daugherty's remarks in their strict, literal sense? His assistant for trade association affairs, David Wing, believed so. Just as he opposed, Wing told his chief, certain "fundamental policies" of the Justice Department, "those responsible for such policies in that Department," he had learned, "look with disapproval on the work that I have been doing for you." [22]

On December 11, 1923, Hoover sought another exchange of opinion with the Attorney General on the legality of statistical activities. Was he to understand from the *Tile* decree that associations could collect only such statistics as a government agency might request and that associations themselves were prohibited from disseminating such statistics and compelled to rely solely upon the ability and willingness of the requesting agency to disseminate them? If this was the Justice Department's attitude, Hoover predicted, association statistical work would fall into decay. Many associations, he explained, desired statistical information promptly and would not accept the expense of collecting data if they could be circulated only through the slow and cumbersome mediation of the government. Daugherty's response was direct and severe, and clearly implied the impropriety of the program Wing had been overseeing for Hoover. Association statistics, he replied, should be disseminated "strictly through a responsible medium, like your department." Associations could collect information, "provided it be strictly guarded and the association be prohibited from distributing it among its members." [23]

Before this new Hoover–Daugherty exchange of mid-December 1923 was released early in January 1924, two more associations and their systems of statistical exchange fell victim to the Justice Department. The *Cement Manufacturers' Protective Association* case ended on December 14 with the imposition of a decree barring all statistical activities whatsoever; three weeks later, on January 4, 1924, Judge Sessions of the Western Michigan District Court imposed a decree similar to the tile decree upon the Maple Flooring Manufacturers' Association. Nathan Williams had correctly judged the Justice Department's intentions: to suppress trade association statistical activity insofar as it lay within the Department's power to do so. [24]

These decrees of late 1923 and early 1924 provoked a bitter reaction which surfaced when the second Hoover–Daugherty correspondence was published on January 10, 1924. Association spokesmen assailed Daugherty for attempting, as they said, to make law. If the ruling of the correspondence was "sustained," or if it was not made clear "that it represents only Mr. Daugherty's opinion," as one prominent association organizer and consultant told Calvin Coolidge, who had been elected to the presidency a few months earlier, the results would be extremely "harmful to legitimate trade associations." Daugherty's position was "a new and radical development in the construction of the Anti-Trust Law." It had to be withdrawn. [25]

NOTES

1. Secretary of Commerce, *Annual Report* (1922), pp. 138–40; (1923), pp. 17–19; (1924), pp. 136–37; (1925), p. 20; (1928), p. xxxiv.

2. *Ibid.* (1922), pp. 88–90; (1928), pp. 79–80. "Report on Cooperation Work for Distribution of Association Statistics" by Wing, August 5, 1922, Commerce Department file; memo for Hoover by Wing, October 20, 1922; Hoover to William H. Harrison, October 26, 1922; W. C. Mullendore to National Wholesale Lumber Dealers Association, September 14, 1922. Trade Association file, CP, HHL. Mullendore to Roy A. Cheney, September 7, 1922; to S. W. Cunningham, February 5, 1923 (mistakenly dated 1922); S. B. Davis, Jr., to J. M. Pritchard, May 24, 1923; to W. P. Fickett, June 1, 1923, file 81288, RG 40.

In setting up this program, however, the Department was interpreting Daugherty's ruling on the circulation of statistics liberally. For some months after the Hoover–Daugherty correspondence, the Commerce officials believed it would be necessary for the Department itself to distribute trade association statistical write-ups, either from Washington or through the Department's branch offices. Memo by Richard S. Emmett, [March or April 1922]; memo by Emmett, April 5, 1922, Trade Association file, CP, HHL.

3. "Report on Cooperation Work . . ."

4. Cassmore to Hoover, September 26, 1924; Hoover to Cassmore, October 7, 1924, file 81288, RG 40.

5. Memo for Richard S. Emmett by Wing, September 30, 1922, Commerce Department file; memo for Hoover by Wing, October 20, 1922, Trade Association file, CP, HHL.

6. Trigg to Hoover, May 29, 1923, file 81288, RG 40. I. L. Sharfman, "The Trade Association Movement," *American Economic Review Supplement*, 16, No. 1 (March 1926), 203–18. See Chapter 1, note 3, for comparative figures on trade association formation.

7. "Report of Committee on Regulation of Combinations," NAM, *Annual Convention* (1921), pp. 35–36; "Platform of American Industry," *ibid.* (1924), pp. 152–53. "Log of Organized Business," *Nation's Business*, 10, No. 5 (May 1922), 44–45; "What May a Trade Association Do?" *ibid.*, 11, No. 4 (April 1923), 98–99; George T. Buckingham, "Justice for the Trade Association," *ibid.*, 12, No. 7 (June 5, 1924), 15.

8. *New York Commercial*: the articles began on February 23 and ran intermittently through April 1922. *New York Evening Post*, March 18, 20, 21, 27, 28, 1922.

9. *Congressional Record*, 67th Cong., 2d sess., 1922, pp. 4901, 5389–91, 5493, 5618–31, 5663–68, 5700–01. Edge, "The Duty of Government to Business," NAM, *Annual Convention* (1922), pp. 210–20. *New York Commercial*, April 4, 1922.

10. According to Representative Clifton McArthur of Oregon, who sponsored the Edge bill in the House, Hoover had told him there was a "very urgent need for an investigation." McArthur to Representative A. J. Volstead (Minn.), April 10, 1922, file 67–A–D18, Record Group 233, Records of the House of Representatives, National Archives. (Hereafter cited as RG 233.) Letters from associationists to the House Judiciary Committee all spoke of the investigation as needed to clear up doubts about the legality of modern trade association practices. George D. McIlvaine to Volstead, April 15, 1922; Ernest T. Trigg to George S. Graham, April 18, 1922, *ibid.* Hoover to Jones, April 7, 1922, Trade Association file, CP, HHL.

11. Commerce Department press release, March 14, 1922; William E. Lamb to Hoover, April 1, 1922, *ibid. New York Commercial*, April 13, 1922. *New York Times*, April 13, 1922. "Official Summary of the Proceedings of the Conference of Trade Association Representatives held at Washington on April 12, 1922," file 711 General, Record Group 151, Records of the Bureau of Foreign and Domestic Commerce, National Archives. (Hereafter cited as RG 151.)

12. Edge to Hoover, April 22, May 5, 1922, Trade Association file; Edge to Hoover, May 16, 1922, Edge file; Hoover to Edge, April 15, 1922, Trade Association file; Hoover to Edge, June 12, 1922, with "Memorandum on Amendment of Anti-Trust Laws," Edge file, CP, HHL. "Address of Honorable Herbert Hoover," NAM, *Annual Convention* (1922), pp. 234–44.

13. Edge to Hoover, June 14, 1922, Edge file; Edge to Hoover, October 2, 1922, Trade Association file; "Report on Cooperation Work . . . ," CP, HHL.

14. Goff to Daugherty, September 15, 1922, file 16/10/5, RG 60, reviews these complications in the midwestern cement case, and there are many previous letters in the same file bearing upon them.

15. Goff to Fowler, May 4, 1922; Fowler to Goff, May 10, June 5, 1922, file

60/160/26, *ibid.* A. T. Seymour to Hoover, March 7, 1922, file 60/160/14, *ibid.*

16. Memo for Attorney General by Roger Shale, January 26, 1922; Hayward to Daugherty, April 3, 6, October 31, 1922; Daugherty to Hayward, April 1, 6, October 27, 1922; Fowler to Daugherty, April 29, May 27, October 19, 1922; to Hayward, October 14, 1922; file 60/10/2, *ibid.*

17. *New York Times,* May 26, 1922. House of Representatives, Committee on the Judiciary, *Charges of Honorable Oscar E. Keller Against the Attorney General of the United States: Hearings . . . on H. R. 425,* 67th Cong., 3d and 4th sess., 1922, pp. 1–4, 15–26, 28–29, 31–39, 40–41, 112–16. Harding felt Daugherty came out with "a wholly satisfactory vindication at the hands of Congress." Harding to J. Morton Howell, March 5, 1923, box 362, Harding Papers. The most convenient source reviewing the essentials of antitrust cases is *The Federal Antitrust Laws: With Summaries of Cases Instituted by the United States* (New York: Commerce Clearing House, 1949). Between June 1921 and March 1924, when Daugherty resigned, the Department instituted proceedings, criminal or both, against nineteen trade associations. See the following entries in *The Federal Antitrust Laws:* 237–46, 248, 250, 253–56, 259, 265, 268–69, 274, 276, 278–79, 282.

18. Goff to Daugherty, September 15, 1922, file 60/10/5, RG 60.

19. *New York Times,* January 4, 1923; "Government's Attitude toward Trade Associations Expressed in Gypsum Case," *Printers' Ink,* 102, No. 2 (January 11, 1923), 10–12. The *Gypsum* decree is conveniently reproduced in NICB, *Trade Associations,* pp. 350–53. Harding's letter to J. Morton Howell, cited in note 17, mentions Daugherty's condition. Podell's two letters to Seymour of January 23, 1923, are in file 60/144/1, RG 60.

20. The proposed decree which Thompson offered the Maple Flooring Manufacturers' Association is in file 60/160/9, *ibid. United States* v. *American Linseed Oil Company,* 262 U.S. 371 (1923). For Thompson's comments, see letters to James Fowler, June 1, 20, 1923, file 60/160/9, RG 60. The *Tile* decree is conveniently available in NICB, *Trade Associations,* pp. 354–58.

21. Williams to Seymour, October 20, November 3, 1923; Williams, mimeographed letter [for NAM members?], October 20, 1923, file 60/55/14, RG 60.

22. Wing to Hoover, December 10, 1923, Wing file, CP, HHL.

23. See *New York Times,* January 10, 1924, for the second Hoover–Daugherty correspondence.

24. The *Cement* decree is in NICB, *Trade Associations,* pp. 358–62; the *Maple Flooring* decree, in file 60/160/9, RG 60.

25. Some examples of business reaction to the second Hoover–Daugherty correspondence are "Common Sense on Trade Associations," *Iron Age,* 113, No. 6 (February 7, 1924), 452; *New York Times,* January 20, February 3, 1924; "Consent Decrees Not Decisions," *Nation's Business,* 12, No. 1 (January 1924), 36–37; "Trade Associations in Status Quo," *ibid.,* No. 3 (March 1924), 35; Ernest H. Gaunt to Edward T. Clark, January 31, 1924, file 511, Calvin Coolidge Papers, Library of Congress.

3

Exit Daugherty, Hoover Triumphs, 1924–1925

HAD ASSOCIATIONISTS ENJOYED only a minimal gift of foreknowledge, they would have shown less concern over the decrees of late 1923 and early 1924 and the Daugherty letter published early in January. The Attorney General's downfall was imminent. On March 28, 1924, Coolidge put his request for Daugherty's resignation in terms which precluded further procrastination. The evident cause for the dismissal was the charges of corruption and mismanagement which Senator Burton K. Wheeler and others brought against Daugherty during the hearings of a special committee to investigate the Attorney General which the Senate had authorized on March 1.[1]

In the preceding January the exhaustive efforts of Senator Thomas J. Walsh and other Democrats, and of a number of Republican progressives, to find evidence of impropriety in the leasing arrangements which Albert Fall, Secretary of the Interior during Harding's presidency, had made in connection with the government oil reserves at Teapot Dome, Wyoming, had met with sudden success. Fall, who had resigned from the Cabinet in March 1923, was now disgraced, as were his alleged accomplices in the oil industry. Accusations soon were made against the heads of the two other Departments, Navy and Justice, which could be plausibly implicated in the wrongdoing. The resistance of Edwin Denby, the Secretary of the Navy, to this pressure crumpled promptly. After his resignation in mid-February, Democratic scandal-seekers concentrated upon Daugherty. A parade of nondescript witnesses appeared at the hearings in March and, to the satisfaction of his investigators and of most of the historians who have written on the matter, successfully implicated the Attorney General in a number of corrupt practices which allegedly had gone on within the Justice Department. To supplement the charges of corruption, the special committee called upon the FTC, which rehearsed and brought up to date the accusations against Daugherty's supposed weakness in antitrust enforcement which it had made in 1922.[2]

As the committee's investigations blackened Daugherty's reputation, Coolidge pondered. He was slow in reaching the conclusion that Daugherty had to go. As one influential adviser warned the President, the danger was that if he yielded to the Democrats and dismissed Daugherty, the pressure for his removal might merely be transferred to another Administration figure, and then another. Many of the large number of communications on the problem which Coolidge received from businessmen agreed with this thesis or some variation of it. But an approximately equal number of businessmen's letters, it is interesting to note, urged simply that Daugherty was a liability and should be dropped unceremoniously. The customary view that Coolidge rid himself of Daugherty chiefly because it was the way to clear the Administration of scandal has much to recommend it. But to what degree was Coolidge influenced in his decision by the fact that, the question of scandal aside, Daugherty's antitrust policy had made him unacceptable to a large segment of the business community? There is little direct evidence that businessmen did exert pressure to have Daugherty removed for this reason. Most of the businessmen and business organizations writing to Coolidge to urge Daugherty's dismissal argued in terms of the harm the charges of his involvement in corruption were doing the Administration. It seems likely, though, that some business spokesmen, perhaps even Hoover, were working to persuade Coolidge to ease Daugherty out of the Administration even before the Senate investigation of his conduct began on March 12, 1924. A leading business periodical hinted at such maneuvers late in February. The Justice Department's trade association policy, the *Iron Age*'s editors commented, had been the result of "selfishness, malevolence and stupidity." While pursuing this policy, Daugherty had "let the matter of the oil leases pass without attention," and the "public recognition" of these facts was "inspiring the demand" for his removal.[3]

It is difficult to avoid the conclusion, in any case, that Coolidge could hardly have long tolerated Daugherty as Attorney General had Daugherty maintained the stand he had taken in the second exchange of letters with Hoover. The new President's fervor in currying favor with the business community is legendary. "Business" and "government" were distinct and separate entities in Coolidge's mind and, as he told the nation's businessmen in January 1926, "each ought to be sovereign in its own sphere." Could a President who believed as devoutly as Coolidge did that the "present generation of business" had shown "throughout its responsible organizations and management . . . every disposition to correct its own abuses with as little intervention of the Government as possible," long support the antitrust policies Daugherty was applying? [4]

The answer is suggested by the prompt and attentive way in which the Administration directed itself to the solution of the trade association problem once Daugherty was out of the way. During the months following Daugherty's departure, Hoover and the Chamber of Commerce shared the task of pressing for prompt redefinition of the trade association activities which the government would accept. Both Hoover and the Chamber contented themselves with the same minimal demands of the previous two years. At the Chamber's annual meeting in May, the members listened to George T. Buckingham, one of the counsel defeated in the *Cement* case the previous December, complain bitterly that "those who are assistants to the Attorney General . . . in charge of the so-called 'anti-trust' prosecutions" were making no distinction between proper and improper use of statistics. They were promoting the doctrine, which lower courts had sustained, he said, that the dissemination of statistics by associations was *per se* illegal; meanwhile, "the business community is in a state of unrest and uncertainty." Prompted by Buckingham, the convention delegates reaffirmed the Chamber's position expressed in the 1923 referendum on trade association practices and called for speedy vindication of the moderate forms of statistical interchange. In September the Chamber's president, Richard F. Grant, formed a committee, which he himself headed, to carry the organization's message straight to the Attorney General.

While the Chamber framed the need for clarification in terms of businessmen's rights, Hoover stressed that the prevailing uncertainty was wrong because it held up the advance of American economic welfare. "Just as 20 years ago," he argued in his *Annual Report* in the summer of 1924, "we undertook nation-wide conservation of natural resources, so now we must undertake nation-wide elimination of waste." American standards of living could be improved only by increasing industrial productivity. "The road to national progress lies in increasing real wages through proportionately lower prices. The one and only way is to improve methods and processes and eliminate wastes." Trade associations were the most effective tool for that task, but they were "fearful of proceeding with work of vital public importance." Hoover insisted therefore that "some definition . . . be made by which an assurance of legality in proper conduct can be had." But he admitted the need for strict limitation of association activities. "No one," he claimed, "would advocate any amendment to the law that would sooner or later create monopoly, price fixing, domination or unfair practice, or any of the category of collective action detrimental to public interest." But the fundamental and orthodox practices, including such statistical interchange "as will enable the industry and its consumers intelligently to judge future demands and supply," should receive an immediate and unambiguous acceptance by public policy.[5]

Coolidge's new Attorney General, Harlan Fiske Stone, was so readily impressed by these presentations, if one accepts the business-press rumors of 1924 and the pattern of his conduct as guides, that the only real question once he settled into his duties was how the desired clarification could be best and most quickly obtained. Earlier in the year when there was no assurance Daugherty would be enmeshed in scandal thoroughly enough to persuade Coolidge to rid the Administration of him, an appeal to Congress had appeared to many associationists the only way to override the Draconian principles of the *Tile* and *Cement* decrees and of the second Hoover–Daugherty correspondence. When, in February, FTC Commissioner Gaskill showed Hoover certain suggestions for antitrust reform which he had made to Coolidge, the Secretary of Commerce was enthusiastic. "I would like some time to have a session with you and such people as are like minded in the Administration, to see if we could not produce a real analysis and a proposition for an entire revision of the restraint of trade laws," he told Gaskill. But interest in legislation diminished when Stone took office and associationists learned of his willingness to clear up their legal problems through appropriately framed litigation. Business newspapers and trade journal accounts in May and June 1924 depicted "Administration officials" as working on a plan to institute a "friendly suit" against an association with a suitably moderate program, in the hope the Supreme Court would find it legal. As conferences with Hoover and association spokesmen continued through early June, Stone reportedly shifted to the view that a pre-existing case already in process of litigation would better serve the purpose.[6]

Evidently, Stone had no ambition, when he assumed his office, to achieve an outstanding record in the antitrust field. When a prominent Republican politician and banker, alarmed by rumors a business newsletter was circulating that the Justice Department's head, thinking of the impending national elections, was "looking about for violations of the anti-trust laws," told the Attorney General that "political suits" would lose rather than make votes, Stone deprecated an alarmist interpretation of his antitrust policies. In all the cases brought so far under his administration, he wrote at the end of June 1924, investigation had begun before he took office; and in each of them "the facts were such as to call for the institution of the suit so long as the anti-trust laws are on the statute books." Gradually Stone seems to have warmed to a more vigorous enforcement policy. In August he personally drew the attention of Abram F. Myers, a Special Assistant in the Antitrust Division, to reports of concerted curtailment of production by petroleum refiners. And by the time he left office a few months later, in January 1925, appointed to the Supreme Court, business gossip attributed the promotion to Coolidge's desire to cut off the "extensive anti-trust litigation" which "was regarded as probable if Mr. Stone had been given a free hand."[7]

Whether true or not that Stone was planning a campaign against serious antitrust violators, it is certain that he completed his term searching for the accommodation trade associations sought. During the fall of 1924, the Chamber of Commerce committee pressed its case with "the several Government Bureaus in a most forceful manner," as one business participant expressed it. Later in the year reports began to mention the *Maple Flooring* case, scheduled for hearing before the Supreme Court early in 1925, as the case businessmen hoped would produce the desired vindication of statistical exchange. By one of the more ironical twists in the development of antitrust policy, Stone participated in the hearing of the *Maple Flooring* case, in March 1925, as a justice of the Supreme Court rather than as a party; and the Court's opinion, handed down on June 1, 1925, came from his hand.[8]

The government's charge in the *Maple Flooring* case was framed perfectly for soliciting a basic statement of the legal status of association statistical practices. As the Court's opinion said, the government made no effort to prove that the maple flooring manufacturers had made a price agreement. The case turned, rather, on the government's allegation that the effect of an elaborate statistical plan such as the manufacturers had used "must necessarily be to bring about a concerted effort on the part of members of the Association to maintain prices at levels having a close relation to the average cost of flooring reported to members and that consequently there is a necessary and inevitable restraint of interstate commerce." The government was asking, in short, for a ruling that statistical interchange programs of any consequence were *per se* illegal. The Court rejected this doctrine and, in the course of vindicating the practices of the Maple Flooring Association, laid down, in effect, a comprehensive, positive statement of what forms of statistical exchange were legal. That this was the result the government wished to obtain seems entirely likely.

The effect of the Court's ruling in the *Maple Flooring* case, and in the *Cement Manufacturers' Association* case decided the same month was not to reverse the ruling in the Hardwood and *Linseed* cases—that illegal agreements could be inferred from the fact that supposed competitors joined together to use certain types of statistical exchange—but to distinguish between the practices of the two former and the two latter cases and to define practices which were regarded as, in themselves, blameless. The decision was that:

> trade associations or combinations of persons or corporations which openly and fairly gather and disseminate information as to the cost of their product, the volume of production, the actual price which the product has brought in past transactions, stocks of merchandise on hand, approximate cost of transportation from the principal point of shipment to the points of consumption, as did these defendants, and who, as they did, meet and discuss such information and statistics without however reaching or attempting to reach any agreement or any concerted action with respect to prices or production or restraining competition, do not thereby engage in unlawful restraint of commerce.

"What more," as a leading modern student of antitrust has irreverently inquired, "could businessmen who believe in competition want?" [9]

During Stone's tenure in 1924, the Justice Department policymakers who had caused so much trouble for associations in former years had been shorn of their influence. Now staffed, in 1925, in its key positions by men sharing Coolidge's ostentatiously pro-business attitude, the Department promptly accepted the Supreme Court's ruling. Petitions for a rehearing of the *Maple Flooring* and *Cement* cases were filed, but their purpose was not to challenge "as the test for legality of trade association activities the principles laid down by the Court in its decisions." The principles were expressly accepted; the petitions related only to the interpretation of matters of fact. "The significance of these petitions is not generally realized by the bar of the country," the Department's new Antitrust Division chief, William J. Donovan, asserted as he explained them in September 1925. They were significant "because they evidence a decided change in the attitude of the Department of Justice towards trade associations and their activities." In the context of Donovan's complete discussion, the words asserting a "change in attitude" were neither alarming for friends of antitrust policy, nor especially encouraging for trade associations, for they seemed merely to reiterate the Department's acceptance of the *Maple Flooring* and *Cement* decisions. Later in the same discussion, Donovan carefully cautioned associations that the recent decisions had validated only moderate forms of statistical interchange and that the Court had reaffirmed its condemnation, given in the Hardwood and *Linseed* decisions, against abuse of the practice. "These condemnations," he warned, included such practices as "secrecy in the use of information; . . . concerted action based upon such data; distribution of identified information—that is, identifying the figures of each competitor; the interchange of current price quotations and other information leading up to sale," as well as others. The right granted to association members to meet and to discuss statistical information was "particularly susceptible of abuse." [10]

But the phrase "change of attitude" was, as events soon would disclose, a prophetic one. Donovan, who shaped antitrust policy with little perceptible interference from John G. Sargent, Stone's successor as Attorney General, was one of the few forceful and creative figures of the Coolidge Administration. Better known as Colonel Donovan, a thrice-decorated veteran of the Fighting 69th, who would become chief of the oss during World War II, he proved an energetic and inventive head of the Antitrust Division. That these qualities were employed so largely in discovering a method for expanding the recognized cooperative rights of trade associations under the law—that he regarded *Maple Flooring* as a starting point rather than as a limit for association privileges—is one of the enduring losses of antitrust administration.[11]

Coolidge also accomplished transformation of the FTC by mid-1925. The change has frequently been analyzed, with stress laid upon the changes in procedure which the Commission adopted early in 1925 immediately after William E. Humphrey, a former Republican lobbyist, congressman, and Washington state politician who had been an early and influential Coolidge supporter in the Northwest in 1924, took up his appointment as commissioner. Humphrey's appointment gave the Commission a majority composed of three Harding-Coolidge Republicans. That Humphrey was appointed as a reward for political services and that he could be trusted with the two other conservative Republicans, Hunt and Van Fleet, to make the Commission's policies as agreeable to the business community as possible are eminently true. But it appears mistaken to emphasize the importance of the 1925 procedural changes. Under these new rules the Commission ceased to give publicity to its accusations against suspected offenders until the case had reached a fairly mature stage; declared its unwillingness to entertain any complaints unless the public interest, not merely the interest of an individual business, was at stake; and established the policy of ending a proceeding when deemed appropriate, upon the stipulation by the accused respondent of his intention to end the unfair practice of which he had been accused.[12]

These rule changes have been interpreted, variously, as weakening the protection the Commission would give to small as against big business or as betokening a general shift in attitude by which "the Commission no longer viewed business as an actual or even potential enemy to be investigated suspiciously and regulated stringently, but rather as a friend and partner to be assisted and encouraged in pursuit of common aims." Certainly the appointment of Humphrey brought a shift in the Commission's policies, but the significant changes were the result of other moves. No evidence has been presented to show that the procedural changes of 1925 led to any important substantive results of the type alleged. Inasmuch as nearly all the complaints against companies for unfair behavior which the Commission had received and continued to receive were lodged against concerns of small or middling size, very rarely against big corporations, it is difficult to see how these changes in processing complaints could have substantially favored big at the expense of small firms. Moreover, the fact that business enthusiastically applauded the rule changes need not imply that they were the basis for a reorientation by which the Commission slowed its efforts to protect small business. The Commission would continue to receive and act upon complaints from any firm charging a competitor with unfair tactics. It was probably only the tone which changed in this area. As Arnold Joerns, head of a leading advertising agency and much favored by businessmen for the slot on the Commission which Coolidge eventually gave to Humphrey, explained to the President after promulgation of the new rules, "It [was] gratifying that the so-called radical influences are curbed, that the Commission no longer enters into minor disputes between competitors, but confines itself to the larger issues, and that the majority of the Commissioners are opposed to dealing in half-baked and damaging promiscuous publicity." [13]

Domination of the Commission by Coolidge-Republicans did, however, have serious policy implications for other branches of its activities: economic investigations and trade practice conferences. The Commission's economic investigations policy probably became more cautious and conservative, though it would be impossible without lengthy analysis to conclude to what degree this occurred. Thomas Blaisdell's study of the FTC, now obsolete but still a valuable guide in many respects, shows how, in the immediate postwar period, the Democrat-controlled Commission adopted an imaginative and bold investigations policy, attempting directly to influence prices in certain industries by continuous surveillance and reporting of their behavior. This policy of what Wilson had once termed "pitiless publicity" evidently fell into abeyance before 1925, partly because of blocks thrown up by the courts. But the significance of the policy, when and why it was revised, remain only partially explained.[14] There probably was not a sharp and clearly defined policy change in this area of the Commission's work as a result of Humphrey's appointment. But there are many indications that the members of the new Republican majority, especially Humphrey, wished insofar as possible to avoid investigations which might offend businessmen.

Humphrey made no effort to conceal his desire to restrict the number and scope of the Commission's investigations. He was quoted in March 1926 as being opposed to the Commission's decision to send questionnaires to all trade associations, in conjunction with the investigation of open price associations, because, he said, it was not made clear that the agency had no power to compel a reply. A few weeks later he wrote the President's secretary, Edward T. Clark, protesting what he called the enormous total cost of FTC investigations since their beginning ($3,382,593.75). They had been "of very little public benefit," he wrote, and he hoped that the President might act to forestall as much future expense of this kind as possible, in particular that called for in a pending resolution Senator Thomas Walsh was sponsoring. "Certainly it cannot be contended that these resolutions as a general rule are introduced by friends of the administration or have for their primary purpose the public interest," said Humphrey. Somewhat later he wrote to tattle on one of his Republican colleagues who, during the summer of 1927 while Humphrey was absent on vacation, had voted with the minority to initiate investigations into resale price maintenance, stock market practices, and basing-point pricing. These investigations were "doing the Administration harm with the business interests and I think there is a general feeling that any concern that obeys the law should be free from the annoyance . . . of investigation," wrote Humphrey, who evidently regarded himself as the President's chosen instrument to make the FTC popular with businessmen rather than a cause of complaint. "I sincerely trust that you begin to see some effect of what we ["I" is crossed over] have been doing," he had written to Clark in 1925 shortly after his appointment, adding, a few weeks later in a letter explaining the new procedures the Commission had adopted, that "I hope that my record will be such to justify, at least in some degree," Coolidge's confidence.[15]

How much consequence Humphrey's attitude had in checking an aggressive use of the Commission's investigating power is a difficult question. Certainly the revival of the vigorous policing of the behavior of selected industries which Blaisdell attributes to the Commission of the early 'twenties was completely obviated. But the Commission's Economic Division executed, both in response to Congressional and presidential requests, and at its own initiative, investigations of many of the most pressing questions of the period concerning certain business structures and practices and their impact upon competition. The investigation of open price associations, published in 1929, was only one of several inquiries which were thorough, workmanlike, and of enduring value.[16]

A more important change in Commission policy and one more relevant to the trade association issue was begun when the Trade Practice Conference Division was set up in 1926, with Humphrey again playing an influential role. Trade practice conferences, in which specific industries drafted rules of fair competition which, when approved by the Commission, had the force of law, had been resorted to occasionally before 1926. Now the popularity of such conferences rose spectacularly. "The general effect," one authority has noted, "was to introduce an atmosphere of cooperation and common effort into relations between business and the Commission and to promote a tendency toward less governmental interference on the one hand and more corporate independence on the other." [17] True, but the meaning of the trade practice movements was more far-reaching than this description. They had, in fact, a sinister quality, and were (as will be shown) the means through which the Commission, following a policy parallel to the Justice Department's, was attempting to warp the meaning of the antitrust laws almost beyond recognition in encouragement of cartelistic practices.

NOTES

1. Burl Noggle, *Teapot Dome: Oil and Politics in the 1920's* (New York: Norton, 1962), pp. 126–29.

2. *Ibid.*, pp. 124–29. Senate, Select Committee on the Investigation of the Attorney General, *Investigation of Hon. Harry M. Daugherty, Formerly Attorney General of the United States: Hearings . . . Pursuant to S. R. 157*, 68th Cong., 1st sess., 1924, 3 vols., II 1692–1738, for the FTC allegations.

3. Noggle, *Teapot Dome*, pp. 125–26. The businessmen's letters referred to are in the 10–Misc. file, Coolidge Papers. "More Respecting Trade Associations," *Iron Age*, 113, No. 9 (February 28, 1924), 661–62.

4. "An Editorial Article by Mr. Coolidge," *Nation's Business*, 14, No. 1 (January 1926), 30. See Chapter 29, "Coolidge and Business," of Donald McCoy's *Calvin Coolidge: The Quiet President* (New York: Macmillan, 1967), pp. 314–21.

5. Buckingham, "Justice for the Trade Association," *Nation's Business*, 12, No. 7 (June 5, 1924), 15. For resolutions adopted by the delegates, *ibid.*, 26–28. Secretary of Commerce, *Annual Report* (1924), pp. 22–23.

6. Gaskill to Stephen P. Davis, January 30, 1924, enclosing Gaskill's letter of January 25, 1924, to Coolidge; Hoover to Gaskill, February 8, 1924; Gaskill to Hoover, February 11, 1924, Federal Trade Commission file, CP, HHL. *New York Commercial*, May 16, 1924; "Trade Association Work," *Iron Age*, 113, No. 23 (June 5, 1924), 1658.

7. Edward C. Stokes to Stone, June 23, 1924; Stone to Stokes, June 30, 1924, file 60/0, RG 60. Stone to Myers, August 8, 1924; Myers to Stone, August 14, 1924, file 60/57/0, *ibid*. *New York Commercial*, January 7, 1925.

8. American Trade Association Executives, Executive Council, "Minutes," October 22, 1924. (These typescript minutes were made available to the writer at the ATAE office in Washington, D.C.) "To Decide the Statistical Rights of Trade Associations," *Printers' Ink*, 129, No. 1 (October 2, 1924), 10–12. "Trade Associations: Renewed Effort to Clarify their Status," *The Index* (December 1924), 7.

9. For expert discussion of the legal and economic issues in *Maple Flooring Manufacturers' Association et al.* v. *U.S.*, 268 U.S. 563 (1925), and *Cement Manufacturers' Protective Association et al.* v. *U.S.*, 268 U.S. 588 (1925), see John Perry Miller, *Unfair Competition* (Cambridge: Harvard University Press, 1941), pp. 49–53; George W. Stocking, *Workable Competition and Antitrust Policy* (Nashville: Vanderbilt University Press, 1961), pp. 39–70.

10. Donovan, "The Legality of Trade Associations" (a part of his address of September 25, 1925, before the Association of Attorneys General), *Proceedings of the Academy of Political Science in the City of New York*, 11, No. 4 (January 1926), 19–26. James True, "Legal and Illegal Trade Association Activities" (interview with Donovan), *Printers' Ink*, 133, No. 8 (November 19, 1925), 89–98.

11. A brief biography is contained in James L. Wright, "The Law a Guide, Not a Hangman" (interview with Donovan), *Nation's Business*, 16, No. 6 (June 1928), 31–33, 103, 106–107.

12. G. Cullom Davis, "The Transformation of the Federal Trade Commission, 1914–1929," *Mississippi Valley Historical Review*, 49, No. 2 (September 1962), 437–55, and Thomas C. Blaisdell, Jr., *The Federal Trade Commission* (New York: Columbia University Press, 1932), pp. 83–85, have the two most significant accounts of the rule changes. The changes are detailed in FTC, *Annual Report* (1925), p. 111. The new rules actually were suggested before Humphrey's appointment, notably by FTC Commissioner Nelson B. Gaskill, who wanted but could not obtain reappointment from Coolidge, owing perhaps to Senator Edge's objections. Gaskill, a New Jerseyan, had "never been of the slightest use to me politically," Edge told Coolidge, and was regarded by the organization in New Jersey "as a Wilson Republican." Edge to C. Bascom Slemp, September 3, 1924; to Gaskill, September 3, 1924; Gaskill to Coolidge, December 5, 1924, file 100, Coolidge Papers. Contrary to Edge's assertion that he was "a trifle too hard on business," Gaskill actually had earned many friends in the trade association community and would become one of the leading advocates of more tolerant policies for trade associations in the later 1920s and early 'thirties. See the letters of endorsement for Gaskill from business groups in file 100–A, *ibid*.

The background of Humphrey's appointment is given in revealing detail in the Coolidge Papers. Humphrey pleaded that he needed a high federal post to avoid financial ruin. A bank in Seattle had pledged to support him during a crucial lawsuit if he obtained such a position (evidently because of the steady income this would mean, not because the bank expected favors, since Humphrey was willing to accept any well-paid post). Humphrey to Slemp, July 18, 1924; to Fred W. Stearns, July 18, August 5, 1924; also, on the appointment, C. B. Blethen to Coolidge, July 24, 1924, Charles W. Burke to Coolidge, December 30, 1924, all in *ibid.*

13. Blaisdell, *Trade Commission*, pp. 83–85; Davis, "Transformation," 450. For the statement regarding the type of firms involved in complaints see Myron W. Watkins, *Public Regulation of Competitive Practices in Business Enterprise* (New York: NICB, 1940), p. 275. Joerns to Coolidge, May 4, 1925, file 100, Coolidge Papers. There is an extremely interesting letter dated May 28, 1925, from an FTC employee, James S. Brinson, to Senator Thomas J. Walsh, box 270, Thomas J. Walsh Papers, Library of Congress, contemporary with the rule changes and defending them, and testifying to an improvement in the tenor of the Commission's work since the new Republican majority had taken charge. "It used to be under the old crowd almost as much as our jobs were worth to have the presumption and temerity to recommend dismissals before taking testimony. It was a reflection on the infallibility of the Commission." Under the new regime, "We can now consider our cases as lawyers and make recommendations accordingly." Brinson, who owed his job originally to Walsh, was writing to defend himself against criticisms he feared Huston Thompson might make about him to Walsh, and the letter is therefore open to self-serving imputations. It is nonetheless very convincing. Brinson felt Thompson aspired to the 1928 Democratic presidential nomination and had been using the FTC as a springboard for personal publicity.

14. Blaisdell, *Trade Commission*, pp. 117, 121–78. Information on the FTC's investigatory work in progress, including by whom initiated, is given for each year of the 1920s in the Commission's *Annual Report*. A convenient summary of FTC investigations, in the form of a complete bibliography of published investigatory reports, is provided by Watkins, *Public Regulation*, pp. 300–17.

15. *New York Times*, March 26, 1926. Humphrey to Clark, March 30, April 6, 1925, April 27, 1926, file 100, Coolidge Papers. Humphrey to Clark, March 1, 1928, Edward T. Clark Papers, Library of Congress.

16. FTC, *Open-Price Trade Associations*, 70th Cong., 2d sess., 1929, Senate Doc. No. 226. Other examples would be the investigations reported in *Resale Price Maintenance*, 2 vols. (1929–31), and in *Report on Price Bases Inquiry, The Basing-point Formula and Cement Prices* (1932).

17. Davis, "Transformation," 449–50.

4

The Republican Trade
Association Policy, 1924–1929

To JUDGE, the *New Republic* commented in the spring of 1928, "by the frequency with which proposals for modification of the anti-trust laws are turning up," the revision issue bids fair to play "a prominent part in the 1928 campaign." Though early by four years in its prediction the journal was correct in its observation, for the ink of the *Maple Flooring* decision had scarcely dried, and the new, more friendly Justice Department and FTC policies which Coolidge appointees had instituted had barely commenced, when a revival of interest within the trade association community in securing additional antitrust relaxation through legislation became evident. But placed beside the 1919 campaign for revision, the movement of the Coolidge years, though of substantial proportions, appears relatively anemic and confused. In 1919 trade association demands for radical Sherman Act revision had been so strong that both the major business organizations had accepted it as a policy goal and labored outspokenly to achieve it. The support for revision among associationists which developed in the later 'twenties, though extensive, was far from universal, a fact reflected in the failure of militant revisionists to commit either the NAM or the Chamber to their cause by the end of 1929. Revisionists, moreover, divided sharply over what form of relief to seek.

That antitrust revision was revived as a political issue clearly is attributable in the first instance to the sympathetic environment businessmen found themselves in during the Coolidge era after 1924. Just as they had been during the early 'twenties, so the trade association policies of the Justice and Commerce Departments and of the FTC were a major influence in the shaping of trade association attitudes toward the antitrust question during the latter part of the decade. Before any discussion of this revision movement itself, an account of Republican trade association policies in the later 'twenties is indispensable.

The most striking occurrence in the government's relations with trade associations during the Coolidge years was that the Justice Department's Antitrust Division supplanted the Commerce Department as the leading influence encouraging associations to extend the scope and effectiveness of their cooperative activities. To an experienced trade association attorney such as William E. Lamb, Hoover's Commerce Solicitor during the Harding Administration, the shift which had occurred in 1925 stood out sharply when he reviewed, from the vantage point of 1929, the course of antitrust administration during the preceding decade. During the early 'twenties, as Lamb knew from first-hand experience, the Department of Justice had harbored "numerous Special Assistants who had the firm and fixed idea that any trade association agreement was upon its face unlawful because in the very nature of things it must be an agreement in restraint of trade." Until the *Maple Flooring* decision, the Department had "run riot with this theory." But, after 1925 under Donovan's direction, the encouragement given trade association practices by the character of the antitrust "policy of the Department of Justice was way beyond anything ever advocated by the Department of Commerce." [1]

Though Lamb's observations were correct, and though it is true that under Donovan the state of antitrust enforcement encouraged associations to experiment with practices which a more severe standard would have condemned, it would be mistaken, and unjust to Donovan, to suppose this result to be the product merely of lax or inefficient administration of the law. On the contrary. Antitrust enforcement under Donovan was more efficient and orderly by far than it had been in the early 'twenties; and, more significantly, it very likely compared favorably with any earlier period of enforcement with respect to upholding, through successful prosecution, the basic antitrust prohibition against out-and-out price agreements.

Donovan was, in fact, proud of his enforcement record and sensitive to the criticisms of his Antitrust Division's performance which sometimes were lodged. On at least two occasions, he took pains to rebut them publicly. Reviewing, in mid-1928, the Division's record during the preceding four years, Donovan pointed out that more fines had been collected as a result of successful prosecutions then than during any other preceding four-year period, and that the number of cases instituted had been surpassed during a like period only under Taft. In 1930, after leaving office, he could even boast that the eighty-four suits begun during the Coolidge Administration of 1925–29 had actually surpassed by a margin of four the old record set during Taft's presidency. [2]

Though Donovan's figures were correct and are undeniably impressive, it is, of course, true that such facts as he offered fall short of providing the basis for valid comparison of the relative importance of antitrust-enforcement records. Such comparisons depend upon analysis of the economic importance of the successful prosecutions contained in each record. Analysis of this sort would undoubtedly greatly reduce the relative stature of Donovan's record below the implied claims he made for it. Nonetheless, it is true that under his direction the basic rule against definite, explicit agreements among competitors to fix prices or limit production was upheld in numerous cases brought against conspiratorial combinations.

Illustrations of this element in Donovan's enforcement record are plentiful. Arthur H. Vandenberg, for example—later a leading Republican senator but in 1926, when he crossed swords with Donovan, the editor and publisher of the *Grand Rapids Herald*—would have derided the suggestion that antitrust enforcement was lax during the Coolidge years. In 1925 Donovan initiated a criminal prosecution on a price-fixing charge against a large number of individuals and corporations engaged in the furniture industry. Since furniture making was centered in Grand Rapids and most of the defendants were of that community, Vandenberg and a number of other Michigan notables, including the state's governor and one of its senators, journeyed to Washington in the spring of 1926, after the first trial of the case had ended in a hung jury, to seek concessions from the Coolidge Administration. The Michigan delegation wanted the criminal prosecution dropped and the matter settled with a civil suit and a decree. The President was "extremely gracious," as Vandenberg described the visit to Edward Clark, Coolidge's secretary. The Attorney General was "the soul of hospitality and graciousness," and promised them a reply to their petition. But they had received none; instead, as Vandenberg explained it, Donovan bypassed the Michigan delegation and delivered "the Government's verdict" to the furniture makers' counsel. His offer was to drop the criminal proceedings against the individuals who had been indicted if the corporation defendants would agree to plead *nolo contendere* and take their fines. Since the jury in the first trial had been hung, Vandenberg and his associates believed Donovan might well have had to take this step before attempting retrial in any case and regarded his offer as no concession. Unwilling to accept the onus of guilt implied in a *nolo contendere* plea, the furniture manufacturers were prepared to fight in spite of the great expense defense would mean to an industry, as Vandenberg said, "already staggered by its fateful experience with the Government," if Coolidge failed to intervene to prevent Donovan from retrying the criminal suit. No record of Vandenberg's reaction when Donovan retried and won his case against the furniture industry in the fall of 1926 has come to light, but his previous view that antitrust enforcement under Coolidge was quite sufficiently vigorous must have been confirmed.[3]

Similar cases were instituted and won against combinations in a number of other industries during the Donovan period, but in other ways, too, the Antitrust Division upheld, under his leadership, the antitrust ban against price agreements. An extensive sampling of the Division's records indicates that complaints of price-fixing conspiracies usually were duly investigated, if they appeared to have any substance, oftentimes by a Bureau of Investigation agent in the field. It was during the period of

Donovan's tenure, too, that the Justice Department secured from the Supreme Court a decision, in the *Trenton Potteries* case, which commentators, then and since, have regarded as definitively stating that price-fixing is *per se* illegal, regardless of circumstances. The Court's ruling, constituting a formal refusal to apply the rule of reason to price-fixing agreements, was a timely and effective bolstering of the antitrust policy's traditional prohibition of overt cartel arrangements.[4]

If Donovan's policies discouraged overt price agreements, in keeping with the fundamental rule of the Sherman Act, they nevertheless encouraged competitors to experiment with cooperative practices and agreements which clearly were more extreme than those which the Supreme Court had validated in the *Maple Flooring* and *Cement* decisions. The encouragement was active, not merely passive, for Donovan not long after assuming his post established the policy of inviting associations to submit their cooperative plans to the Department for consideration and comment. The practice served in many instances to forestall the adoption of practices which the Department would have felt bound to proceed against had they been taken up. Representatives of the American Cotton Manufacturers' Association, for example, were told in 1928 that their plan for eliminating night shifts in textile plants by agreement "would be attacked by the Department" if adopted; and the leader of a group of New York yarn jobbers was advised, when he explained his group's plans by letter to Donovan, that a conference would be in order. "In view of some of the statements in your letter," Donovan warned, "I think this course would be especially desirable in this case before adopting the proposed plan finally." [5]

Often, however, consultation between an association and the Department resulted in the assurance that the group's program of activity was blameless. For some time Donovan appears to have made these assurances cautiously and during an interview. By the latter part of 1926, however, he had warmed to his innovation enough to conclude a consultation with a written comment. In nearly every case this comment consisted of little more than the formula that, after consideration of "the situation as at present disclosed, there does not appear to be a basis for any proceeding by this Department," but that this finding "must not be understood, however, as in any way restricting the Department's freedom of action, should subsequent developments indicate the necessity for action by it." [6]

Despite the tentative quality of the formula of approval, even the most cautious use of it would, as was intended, serve to advertise the Justice Department's sympathy for association activities and to stimulate the range and pace of their development. By 1927 the consultation–approval system was serving an even more important purpose; it was being used directly to stimulate remarkably advanced cooperative schemes whose legality was patently doubtful in terms of traditional antitrust concepts.

The Department's relations with the Sugar Institute furnishes a clear illustration of the practice. The institute's program consisted essentially of a pledge by each refiner to notify competitors immediately, through the institute, when he changed his prices and to refrain from granting discounts from list prices under any circumstances. Donovan's letter of comment on the plan, following its submission to the Department in December 1927, contained the usual formula that the scheme appeared blameless. Yet he must have realized then what one of his Special Assistants pointed out some months later when the Department was reviewing the institute's workings after receiving complaints about them: that both of the organization's leading practices, the no-discount rule and the agreement to circulate statistics of current prices, were legally suspect. The suggestion of Horace Lamb, the aide to whom the investigation had been entrusted, that the institute's practices might require a testing in court, had no immediate result.

Toward the end of 1928, however, Donovan sent an investigator to examine the institute's files and to report further on the legal and economic implications of its program. The investigator's report is an extremely interesting document and sheds some light, perhaps, on Donovan's rationale for encouraging practices which, on strictly legal grounds, he probably ought, instead, to have prosecuted. The report found, first, that sugar prices, though they had increased during 1928, were not really unfair, especially in view of the price wars and low profits which had dominated the history of the sugar industry in preceding years. The higher prices were the result not of explicit agreement but of tacit understandings made possible by the statistical program and the newly awakened cooperative spirit among producers which the institute had engendered. "Suppose" the investigator wrote, describing hypothetically the way sugar prices were set, "the margin [between raw and refined sugar prices] to be high but not so that the public protest is aroused. A mere informal remark that the price is about right, assented to by the others, is all that is necessary to have each man feel certain that he will not lose any trade by sticking to his price. In addition, it must be remembered that past experience has shown in this, as in all industries with heavy capital investment, that price-cutting leads easily to a real price war, and that price wars are ruinous." What was going on in this industry, with its few competitors and effective trade association was

similar to what is going on in many other industries. Broadly speaking, it represents the business man's idea of the proper and reasonable solution of the universal problem of over production. It represents probably in most cases a very slight extortion of the consumer, but it is by no means proved that the benefits, first of all to the producer, both employer and worker, and, later even to the consumer from the stabilization of industry, do not outweigh this.

Should the Department take action against the sugar industry and others exhibiting similar behavior? The investigator suggested that the criteria for deciding this question should be economic, not legal. "If the Government could find some way of watching the prices of important commodities to make sure that this 'extortion' does not go beyond very reasonable limits, it would be a saner plan than to try to prevent it, especially in case the agreement is, as it is here, totally tacit and informal." Since the Sugar Institute's program had aroused relatively little complaint and evidently was moderate in its effect, action was unnecessary.[7]

Another example of Donovan's disposition to allow practices of radical tenor to develop under the aegis of Justice Department approval arises from his dealings with the Bolt, Nut & Rivet Manufacturers' Association. In this case the leading element in the cooperative plan was an agreement by the bolt manufacturers to solicit wholesalers only, leaving to them the distribution of the product to industrial consumers and retailers. Charles J. Graham, the association's president, represented the plan, when he discussed it with one of Donovan's assistants on December 21, 1927, as merely a method for reducing packaging costs since it would promote sales only in large lots. A more wary listener might have recognized ulterior purposes in this Graham Plan, as it was known in association circles, but the Special Assistant, Russel Hardy, to whom Graham described his scheme, entered into a friendly discussion of it. "I said," Hardy recorded in a memorandum written immediately after the interview, "that if the plan in mind left each member of the Association free to sell in retail quantities according to his own circumstances and his own independent judgement, without any restraint, even by way of criticism for failure to follow a policy generally concurred in, the plan would, as a general proposition, be free from criticism." Appropriately, however, Hardy warned that his explanation of the principles the Department would regard as applying to Graham's case did not constitute approval of it.[8]

In a technical sense, Hardy's statement of relevant legal principles was perhaps accurate. Nonetheless, the tenor of this conference with Graham was questionable. The line between agreements not to solicit orders from certain classes of buyers and agreements not to sell except to designated wholesalers was rather thin, and the latter the Supreme Court had found illegal years earlier. Moreover, the scheme, even as Graham described it to Hardy would, for obvious reasons, simplify price-fixing among the bolt manufacturers if they were minded to use it for that purpose.

Even so, it would be an exaggeration to regard the Department's dealings with Graham's association, had they ended with the interview of December 1927, as an instance of the encouragement of radical cooperative practices. But the interview marked only the beginning of these dealings. Some months after the meeting between Hardy and Graham, evidence reached the Department that Graham, in reporting to his association, had placed an extraordinary construction on Hardy's remarks. In Graham's version, Hardy had been contemptuous of pettifogging lawyers who interpreted the antitrust laws too stringently. "The trouble," Hardy had said according to Graham, the Department was "having with a great many attorneys these days was the fact that they did not realize that industry had to have some place to start from." In response to Graham's question whether it would be legal for him to go to a manufacturer who was "disturbing our industry and attempting to break down our effort" and "show him the error of his ways and the great danger he is creating not only for himself, but to industry generally," Hardy had, as Graham recounted it, "advised that I was entirely within my province to do so at any time." [9]

From these comments two conclusions were evident. The Graham Plan as the Bolt, Nut & Rivet Manufacturers' Association actually operated it was a very questionable scheme, and the association was claiming that the Justice Department had approved a form of the plan which, in fact, it had not. The circumstances called for an investigation of the association's activities to determine how the Graham Plan operated and quick action to rebut or obtain a withdrawal of Graham's claim concerning his conference with the Department. No effective action on either score was ever taken, however, while Donovan remained in charge of the Antitrust Division.

What action was taken seems to have been a response to the steady pressure for an investigation of the Graham Plan which Felix Levy, a well-known trade association lawyer, applied to the Department beginning in May 1928. Levy believed that the Graham Plan was illegal on its face and that eventually the Justice Department, under the current Administration or the next, would be forced to proceed against it. Many associations, Levy asserted, accepted Graham's claim of Justice Department approval of his plan, and therefore were considering adopting it. If this occurred, Levy warned, the trade association movement would be thrown into confusion when, as he claimed was inevitable, the plan came under attack.[10]

Following Levy's insistent protests in the early summer of 1928, Graham was called to the Department, questioned about the operations of his association, and asked not to repeat any claims concerning Justice Department approval which he might have made. But he was not asked to retract anything he had already claimed. Nor did the Department seem unduly troubled that the Graham Plan actually amounted to an agreement on the part of the manufacturers to sell only to designated wholesalers. The Antitrust Division staff which succeeded Donovan's would find the plan clearly illegal under long-standing Supreme Court decisions: Donovan's staff, through an analysis which avoided a direct comparison with existing case law, justified the scheme, largely on the ground that it had eliminated what was pictured as wasteful forms of competition which supposedly had previously pervaded the industry. Despite Levy's allegations, made repeatedly during the summer and fall of 1928—that Graham was actively proselytizing other industries as converts to his plan, that he still was claiming Justice Department support for it, and that the Bolt, Nut & Rivet Manufacturers' Association's practices included not only the plan itself but price-fixing too—the Department, as far as its records indicate, made no serious investigation of them. It is clear, however, that by the late fall of 1928 the Department had become uneasy over its relationship with the Bolt Association. In November steps were taken to learn more about the association's activities, but these consisted only of inquiries addressed to the committee chairmen who administered the Graham Plan in the different market districts. Finding that the FTC was investigating the association because it had applied for approval of its trade practices, the Department decided to hold further investigation in abeyance but to take the matter up again at some indeterminate date, after "a disposition of the question before the Federal Trade Commission and in the light of its decision and the facts in the business at that time." Meanwhile the Department refused, despite Levy's insistent requests, to state whether it had ever or then approved the Graham Plan. When the management of the Justice Department changed with the end of the Coolidge Administration, the Bolt, Nut & Rivet Manufacturers' Association continued its operations unhampered by any serious prospect of interference.[11]

Again, as in the Department's relations with the Sugar Institute, there are indications in this case that the rationale of the tolerant, encouraging attitude toward radical cooperation was the belief that, except for practices the Supreme Court had definitely condemned, association activities should be judged by the flexible yardstick of economic effect rather than of the more rigid traditional test of whether they appeared to indicate agreement in restraint of trade. That such a reorientation was desirable Donovan stated, obliquely, at least once when he was the Assistant to the Attorney General, in an article prepared for the Chamber of Commerce's *Nation's Business*. The Justice Department, he explained, felt, "with reference to the present controversy concerning the necessity for repeal, modification, or increased stringency of the Sherman Law, that we are now passing through a period of economic transition, and because of that fact further legislation at this moment would be uncertain in result." The Department's intention, moreover, was, "by the employment of a sane and intelligent administration of the law, to make evident that the law as construed by the Supreme Court is effective enough to deal with violations, yet elastic enough to meet changing economic conditions."[12]

But how could Donovan hope to formalize and make permanent the reorientation he experimented with? He answered this not long after leaving the Department when he began to publicize his conviction that the Supreme Court, if approached properly, could be expected to relax the rules it had traditionally applied in determining the legality of co-operative practices. Even agreements among competitors fixing the volume of production, he believed, might be legalized. "So far as production is concerned," Donovan told the members of the American Petroleum Institute in 1930, "the legality of any agreement must be determined by its purpose and effect as disclosed by the surrounding facts and circumstances." If agreements were made "in good faith for the purpose of maintaining a stable condition, and for the purpose of overcoming the business disasters and depressions which come from periods of excessive production," the Court would probably be led to apply the rule of reason to them, to hold that their "effect upon prices charged in transactions in interstate commerce is indirect and remote, and that the agreement does not fall within the prohibitions of the anti-trust laws." The Court, of course, could not be expected to take the initiative; businessmen had to have the "intelligence" to put their schemes in forms likely to be acceptable, and the "courage" to put them into effect so they could be tested by the court.[13]

These remarks in 1930 were as much an explanation of the purpose of the policies Donovan had followed from 1925 to 1929 as they were advice to the business community with reference to future conduct. Donovan's lenient application of the antitrust policy to radical practices which fell short of actual price-fixing agreements was intended to accomplish a great deal more than a lull in antitrust enforcement. The conclusion is inescapable that the intention was to entrench such practices in the fabric of association activities so firmly that the Court, impressed both by the supposed reasonableness of such practices and by the sheer extent of their use, would be persuaded to validate them.

Meanwhile the FTC followed a parallel course through its trade practice conference procedure. Originally the FTC had conceived and employed these conferences as a means for securing the agreement of an industry's members to eliminate unfair practices which, because of their widespread use within the industry, the Commission, using its ordinary methods could have suppressed only with great difficulty. Soon after the reorientation of the Commission which Coolidge achieved in 1925, however, trade practice conferences assumed a broader significance. Industries now presented, and the Commission approved, complete codes of fair practice. During 1926 a new division was established within the Commission's organization to oversee the new program, and the number of trade practice conferences held annually increased rapidly, from six in 1927 to fifteen in 1928, and to fifty in 1929.

The explanation the FTC gave for sponsoring these conferences, and for approving the codes which resulted from them, seemed unimpeachable. Each of the codes was a statement of how the law of fair competition and the principles of proper business ethics applied to a specific industry. Each code was written in the idiom of the industry to which it applied and dealt specifically with the problem which characterized that industry. A code, therefore, the argument ran, provided every member of the relevant industry with an unambiguous guide to proper conduct; and, since to win approval a code was required to enjoy the support of most of an industry's firms, the code-making process encouraged respect for, and voluntary compliance with, the law of fair competition. Rules were divided into two categories. Those in Group I defined practices which the Commission regarded as unfair in the legal sense and against which it would take action. Rules placed in Group II had no binding legal status; although the Commission approved them, they represented, legally, merely the judgment of the industry that certain practices were undesirable and unethical.[14]

Had these really been the only purpose of the trade practice codes, it is unlikely they would have generated the immense interest trade associations showed in them after 1926. Actually, by 1928 at least, the Commission was permitting the inclusion of rules in the codes which were intended to suppress competition, not merely make it "fair." Especially important in this respect were two Group I rules dealing with price-making which appeared routinely in many codes by 1928. One of these prohibited price discrimination, the other selling below cost. Under certain conditions, "where the effect may be to substantially lessen competition or tend to create monopoly," the Clayton Act had prohibited price discrimination; selling below cost had been found illegal by the courts under the Sherman Act when it was done maliciously, with the intent of injuring competitors. The intention in both instances had been to prevent strong firms from using price discrimination or sales below cost as a means of injuring or eliminating competitors as would happen when, for example, a large firm cuts prices in one area to drive local rivals out of business. In the FTC codes, however, price discrimination and selling below cost were prohibited without adequate reference to these vital tests, and the appearance given that the Commission was prepared to treat the practices as unfair competition regardless of circumstances.

The result was that the codes became potential instruments for limiting competition. The blanket prohibition of price discrimination would have the effect of preventing a seller from shaving prices to win a new customer, and thus eliminate one of the leading inducements for price competition. And as an economist has remarked of the no-selling-below-cost rule, "it requires no prophetic vision to state that in the business world" it would "be accepted as an authoritative disapproval of forthright price competition." [15]

In approving these rules and the many other suspicious provisions which found their way into the codes, the Commission has been found by commentators to have been negligent, but nothing more. It seems likely, however, that the Commission was no more the dupe of the associations than Donovan was, but, rather, that it was consciously bent upon eroding the antitrust laws.

Officially, the Commission continued to picture the codes as merely clarifying the law and intensifying its enforcement. But businessmen, and even commissioners, sometimes acknowledged the fact that the effect of the Commission's policy would be to create new interpretations of price discrimination and below-cost selling and to give trade associationists new rights of cooperation, if the courts supported the codes. The most outspoken commissioner was Abram F. Myers, who had held his post for about three years—between January 1927 and November 1929—when he resigned. Myers gave two speeches late in 1928 which stated quite openly that the Commission's intention was to establish new legal interpretations of price discrimination, selling below cost, "dumping" outside a firm's normal market territory, and so on. The result would be, he claimed, the "rationalization" of competition, not its destruction. Myers was somewhat more restrained in his appearance at a round-table discussion of trade practice conferences held during the Chamber of Commerce's May 1929 meeting. He nonetheless emphasized that the codes would gradually liberalize the antitrust laws.

Myers seems also to have been the leading promoter of the so-called "clandestine violation" rule. Beginning in October 1928, the Commission allowed the incorporation into the codes of a rule which provided that secret violations of Group II rules (rules not otherwise enforceable by law) by companies which had agreed to them constituted unfair practice within the meaning of the law. Thus the Commission devised a way to enforce Group II rules, another tactic for expanding the scope of cooperative agreements. The clandestine violation rule was so blatantly designed to serve this purpose that it was rescinded in May 1929. William Humphrey had opposed the rule from the outset and overturned it as soon as Myers left the Commission, with the aid of votes from Garland Ferguson and Myers' replacement, Charles H. March.[16]

Occasionally the Commission approved a code which appeared so perfect an instrument for enforcing a price-fixing agreement that even the Justice Department regarded it as improper. Late in 1928 the Department became aware of a code of ethics which the American Petroleum Institute was in the process of formulating and offered to discuss its legal implications with the institute's leaders. "The representatives of the Institute," when they came to the Department for a conference early in January 1929, "frankly conceded that [certain] provisions [of the code] might go beyond existing law," but they argued they should be given an opportunity to submit it at an FTC trade practice conference. If the Commission approved the code, they argued, and undertook "to have the various competing companies agree to abide by this code, then the companies cannot be prosecuted for the violation of the federal anti-trust laws, for the reason that they are acting under the authority of a federal agency." The argument was patently defective. "While advancing this position," as Horace Lamb, who interviewed the oil spokesmen, noted, "counsel frankly conceded that they knew of no law by which immunity from prosecution could be obtained merely because the acts done had been approved by the Federal Trade Commission." Yet the argument produced the desired effect. Upon the understanding that the code would be held in abeyance, Lamb "stated that I did not believe the Department would take any action, and that especially we would do nothing to interfere in any way with the plans of the Institute and the Commission for the holding of a trade practice conference." Further Department consideration might be necessary, Lamb said, after the FTC made its decision; but, as is evident, the Department was eager to avoid interfering with the FTC's legal experiments which closely paralleled its own.[17]

What relation did Hoover and his Commerce Department have to these policies of the Justice Department and the FTC? During the early 'twenties, as he championed the trade association community in its struggle with the Justice Department, Hoover limited his goal to legitimization of the fundamental trade association practices. He had taken the ideological position that proper limited use of cooperative practices would result in "intelligent" competition; that such competition, in turn, would enhance industrial stability and efficiency; and that none of this would conflict with the antitrust laws as traditionally construed. When the *Maple Flooring* decision was handed down and it was apparent that the effort had succeeded, the association community praised Hoover unstintingly for his aid. "I feel," wrote one association leader, "that your wise handling of trade association matters and your clear understanding of the real issues involved and the real effect on the public interest, must have had a great influence on the formation of correct economic opinion in Washington." American industry was grateful for Hoover's "wise, energetic and constructive leadership in American industry and commerce." [18]

But would the limited, orthodox practices approved in *Maple Flooring* seem a sufficient acknowledgment of cooperation to Hoover or, in company with the Justice Department and the FTC, would he encourage associations to experiment with more advanced practices and join them in planning for the erosion of the antitrust tradition? At the level of official dealings with associations, the answer is definitely no. In its official publications, certainly, the Department of Commerce continued to caution trade associations against using radical cooperative practices. The revised edition of the Department's *Trade Association Activities*, for example, issued in 1927, reasserted the refusal Hoover had made in the early 'twenties to cooperate with associations whose statistical activities included the circulation of current prices or the prices of individual firms, and warned that the circulation of cost averages was a dubious practice. The Department's formal programs for encouraging association development remained limited, much the same as before 1925. The Division of Simplified Practice continued to help associations work out agreements for the standardization and simplification of products and techniques. The Bureau of the Census continued publication of the *Survey of Current Business*. As for the Bureau of Foreign and Domestic Commerce, the largest and most impressive branch of the Department, organized into commodity sections and closely in touch with businessmen and trade association leaders from every segment of industry: its programs remained geared, as before, to stimulating the flow of American exports. There was a Domestic Commerce Division within the Bureau, a Hoover innovation dating from 1924, but the connection between it and the increased use trade associations made of radical practices after 1925 was remote. Pinched in its early years by limited staff and funds, the new Division had little contact with trade associations until the later 'twenties when the program and services it had evolved began to attract attention. Market research was the Division's specialty, and it included studies of the characteristics of regional markets, the marketing problems of particular commodities, and studies of the "cost of distribution." These latter investigations—studies of how companies could increase profit margins by knowing which items and markets were excessively costly—were attracting substantial attention from business by the end of the 'twenties.

The only Domestic Commerce Division program which directly influenced trade association cooperative practices was its "attempt to simplify trade terms and trade practices" in the same way the Division of Simplified Practice attempted to eliminate unnecessary sizes and styles. The program dealt with such problems as "whether it is possible to arrive at a standardized definition of the term 'F.O.B. shipping point, freight allowed,' " and was evidently innocuous in terms of effects upon competition.[19]

In its formal, official relations with associations, then, the Commerce Department's circumspect policies contrasted sharply with those of the Justice Department and of the FTC. Hoover, too, continued in the same absolute terms used in defending associations during the controversy with Daugherty to draw a sharp line between moderate and radical associationism. He had "no patience," he said in 1925, with those who confused his efforts to foster "co-operation in waste elimination with price-fixing and restraint of trade. . . . Any intelligent person," he asserted, could, with a little study, convince himself that the association practices he advocated were in the public interest "and free from trade restraint." [20]

Yet it seems doubtful that Hoover's distinction between proper and improper cooperation was really so sharply defined, and likely that he would have welcomed a somewhat more flexible standard for judging the appropriateness of given activities than the antitrust tradition provided, if this could have been done without creating political problems. Early during his Secretaryship of Commerce, Hoover's concept of permissible cooperation was quite broad. When he took over the Commerce Department in 1921, he was inclined to give a generous latitude to association use of the open price system. It was only as a result of the Justice Department's challenge that he came to make a careful and realistic distinction between moderate and excessive use of statistical interchange. An even more significant circumstance revealing the extent, during this early period, to which Hoover thought cooperation permissible under certain conditions was his endorsement, on two separate occasions during his first year as Secretary of Commerce, of trade association programs which, if implemented, would have amounted to virtually complete cartel agreements. The endorsement took the form of a sympathetic presentation to the Attorney General of the acute problems of the two industries, the plans they had worked out to solve them, and their hope that the Justice Department would allow them to proceed.[21]

The meaning of these overtures is probably not that Hoover's insistently claimed loyalty to the principle of competition and the antitrust laws was false. It would be more reasonable to regard Hoover's statements that he thought competition should be limited only to the extent which followed from moderate cooperative practices as genuine but incomplete. What really was in Hoover's mind, it appears, was that competition, modified and mitigated by moderate cooperative practices, was the appropriate principle of discipline and organization for industry except in cases where it failed to produce the stable and orderly operation which, as Hoover always stressed, should and could result from it. When "intelligent competition" appeared really inadequate for introducing stability and order, Hoover was prepared to entertain the possibility of exceptions.

The nature of the argument for permitting cartel arrangements which Hoover made to Daugherty in the cases referred to above illuminates this aspect of Hoover's thought. In both presentations, the argument was from economic necessity. In the case of one of the industries, the corn products manufacturers, the dozen or so independent companies which between them shared the half of the market not controlled by the Corn Products Refining Company claimed that a price-and-production-control agreement among themselves was absolutely required. With the cooperation of the giant firm, which had agreed not to increase its share of the market at the expense of its smaller rivals if their plan became effective, "the independents," Hoover wrote approvingly, "wish to agree among themselves as to the distribution of the other half and upon prices. They want to limit their profit to some figure—say 12 cents a bushel. Subject to the correctness of their statements—which I have no reason to doubt—this may be the only thing that will save them from bankruptcy." The economic case for the plan was clear, Hoover seems to imply. But, as he concluded, "It is, however, a matter of law. Can you suggest anything?"

Hoover's attitude toward the coal industry in the early 'twenties also suggests that poor performance under competitive conditions, if long protracted, qualified an industry for an exemption from antitrust. It suggests, too, that the more endemic the instability of an industry, and the more its difficulties threatened to injure other areas of the economy, the more urgent Hoover regarded the need for exemption. Hoover identified productive overcapacity and labor underemployment as the root causes of the coal industry's problems and the reason why satisfactory labor–management relations could not be worked out in it. During 1922, the year of a long UMW strike which again presented the threat of a coal famine, Hoover felt the industry's problems were so deep-rooted that permitting the operators to effect stability of production and price through a cooperative marketing association would be justified. And late in 1923 when it appeared another strike might occur at the expiration of the UMW contract in April 1924, Hoover urged Coolidge not only to ask in his Annual Message for stand-by emergency legislation in the event of a strike, but also to advise that the "intermittence of operation of the bituminous coal industry with its resulting part time employment of a greatly excessive amount of labor and capital," could be remedied by amendment of the "restraint of trade acts, modification of which under control" was necessary.[22]

Even in the case of a greatly overdeveloped, overcompetitive, and distressed industry like coal, however, Hoover was wary of the principle of selective antitrust relaxation. Even a moderate application of the principle, which would leave independent operators outside the combine to act, at least in some degree, as a check on prices, would probably bring "an outcry from the demagogues," as Hoover dubbed them, "that this is the formation of a coal trust." To still criticism and satisfy the public, regulation of the industry's prices probably would have to be installed. And if thoroughgoing cartelization with government enforcement of the combine's policies proved necessary to effect stability, then regulation could not be avoided. To Hoover these considerations raised grave difficulties because he did "not like control of either price or profit because both tend to break down initiative." [23]

Perhaps it was this consideration—namely, the difficulty of showing public opinion that selective antitrust liberalization was not necessarily inconsistent intellectually and programmatically—which persuaded Hoover to refrain from publicly discussing his view that economic need could sometimes justify such action. There was also evidently an increasing awareness on his part that advocating interference with competition implied a willingness to accept the accompanying regulation the public would demand. And he was resolutely opposed to the growth of bureaucratic controls. Even the coal industry, after 1923, he tried to fit into a frame of reference in which competition provided an adequate remedy for all difficulties. "The real cure," for the coal industry's overdevelopment, Hoover told the operators in June 1924, in urging them to reach agreement with the union, "is a period of continuous operation under free competition and full movement of coal." This too was what he advised in 1926 when Congress was making one of its recurring studies of the coal problem.[24]

Hoover continued to speculate, however, on whether a milder form of antitrust revision might be feasible in both political and economic terms. In 1923, he had proposed the establishment of a system under which an advisory body would have approved trade association plans, giving them, until approval was withdrawn, immunity from prosecution. Conditions were so trying for trade associations at that time that it seems possible to accept Hoover's statement that the purpose of the system he proposed would have been to facilitate clarification of the antitrust laws and to allow associations to proceed with their work without undue fear of prosecution. By the later 'twenties, however, the idea which Hoover had proposed and then put aside after the *Maple Flooring* decision had taken on another connotation and become very popular among associationists. Many lawyers, believing the *Maple Flooring* decision had signaled the beginning of a trend, predicted a progressive relaxation in the Court's interpretation of the antitrust laws. It was a not-very-well-kept secret that "administrative amendment" was regarded as a method for encouraging and hastening this trend. That Hoover could have been unaware of the implications now attached to the proposal he had originally brought into prominence seems unlikely. It is, therefore, significant that Hoover's interest in administrative amendment revived, too, in the later 'twenties and that he seriously considered, for a time early in 1927, renewing his support for the proposal.[25]

Hoover then felt not only that a condition of severe instability justified exemptions from the antitrust policy, but, perhaps, also that even better functioning industries required some degree of antitrust relaxation to deal with their problems successfully. What degree of relaxation he regarded as appropriate for such industries—whether he agreed with Donovan that it should extend as far as the legalization of production agreements—is uncertain. Certainly his uniformly unfavorable reaction to price-fixing in the literal sense suggests this ultimate form of cooperation was entirely inconsistent with the concept of the stable but progressive industrial order he prophesied so frequently in his addresses. "I do not think I would go so far as to suggest," Hoover replied to a businessman who had expressed his hope that a trade practice conference would give his industry the conditions it needed to raise its profits, "that the Federal Trade Commission should interpret what a fair price is, because I am not in favor of price fixing in any particular." Reminded during his presidency, when the FTC codes were under fire, that he had met with the commissioners in the spring of 1927 and explained to them the desirability of their developing industrial self-government through a more energetic trade practice conference procedure, Hoover replied similarly. "We did not in these discussions," he maintained, "carry it over to . . . price-fixing." [26]

Whatever the degree of antitrust liberalization Hoover thought was appropriate for industry generally—and it seems likely it was a rather moderate degree—the question arises again at this point whether he translated his sympathy for liberalization into action during his later years as Secretary of Commerce. While the Department's formal, official dealings with trade associations avoided encouragement of radical practices, the status of the many informal contacts Hoover and his aides had with associations is not so clear. It was not uncommon for associations seeking a solution for their industry's problems to solicit the Department's advice and encouragement, and to receive it. In 1926, for example, when a group of southern cotton manufacturers began the organizing of the national trade group which became the Cotton Textile Institute Hoover met with, encouraged, and advised them. And when the Rubber Institute was founded in 1928, the organization's director-general appears to have sought the advice of E. G. Holt, Chief of the Rubber Division, as soon as he took up his duties. [27]

Information on the nature of the advice associations received through these contacts is difficult to find. Hoover apparently preferred to keep such meetings as informal and unrecorded as possible. "The Chief wants to know," Hoover's secretary informed the Textile Division's head in 1927, after an association had approached the Department for advice on its plans, "if you can find some way for him to have a personal contact with Mr. Franklin W. Hobbs, President of the National Association of Wool Manufacturers. . . . He feels that this is not a matter that should be taken up through correspondence." Did the advice given in these informal meetings sometimes belie the very correct attitude the Department maintained in its formal relations with trade associations? In some small degree this may have happened, for Hoover appears occasionally to have lent his moral support and prestige to associations which were applying at the Justice Department for approval of highly developed cooperative plans. Hoover seems to have encouraged the leaders of the CTI to ask Colonel Donovan to approve an agreement one of the organization's commodity groups had made to shorten the production week. Hoover's attitude, as the CTI leaders quoted it to Donovan, was that the "Department regarded what was being done as sound economics . . . ," and that he would be willing to discuss the question with Donovan. There is a hint of the same kind of service, helping associations to build an economic case for cooperative plans they intended to submit for Justice Department approval, in the circumstance that, on one of his visits to the Department to discuss his plan in 1928, Charles Graham was accompanied by a Commerce Department division chief.[28]

Hoover probably left the responsibility for giving legal advice to associations with questionable plans entirely to the Justice Department. And it is likely that he was extremely cautious even when he discussed problems and possible remedies with an association's representatives and advised them to seek an accommodation with Donovan. It is clear that Hoover had a horror of finding himself or his Department identified publicly with trade association wrongdoing. Following a near-miss in 1926, when it had been discovered only just in time that an association, to which a message of endorsement and encouragement was about to go out from Hoover, was on the point of undergoing indictment by the Justice Department, a special procedure was established to ensure that an association's status was checked before it received so much as a message of good wishes from the Department. It is notable too that trade association gossip regarded the Commerce Department as confined, in the services and solutions it offered, to the safe side of the line between legality and illegality. Some industrialists, such as Otto Falk, president of Allis–Chalmers, grew disgusted, "convinced that anything practically effective, or even helpful, through co-operation with the Department of Commerce . . . cannot be expected," in the way of the development of a stronger brand of associationism.[29]

Hoover may have felt that there was a case for selective relaxation of the antitrust laws, but both intellectual consistency and practical difficulties made this hard to acknowledge and to act upon. And he may have yielded in some cases, in some degree, to the climate of the late 'twenties in which associationists and antitrust-enforcement officials alike were bending the law toward liberalization. But even though his concept of what constituted a competitive market was vague and somewhat elastic, his acceptance of competition as the organizing principle of the economy was genuine enough. It was an important part of his political philosophy, which stressed equality of opportunity and fluidity of class lines—a philosophy he enlarged upon continuously during the 'twenties and during his presidency.

NOTES

1. "Revising the Anti-Trust Laws," *New Republic*, 59, No. 697 (April 11, 1928), 234–35. Lamb to Wheeler P. Bloodgood, July 23, 1929, General Correspondence, National Civil Federation Papers, New York Public Library.

2. James L. Wright, "The Law a Guide, Not a Hangman" (interview with Donovan), *Nation's Business*, 16, No. 6 (June 1928), 31–33, 103, 106–107; Donovan, "Some Practical Aspects of the Sherman Law," *Report of the 35th Annual Meeting of the Pennsylvania Bar Association* (June 1929), pp. 332–50.

3. Vandenberg to Clark, July 6, 1926, Clark Papers.

4. For an example of investigations, C. W. Cederberg to Department of Justice, July 16, 1927; Donovan to Cederberg, July 20, 1927; Joseph V. Machugh to Donovan, July 26, November 4, 28, 1927, file 60/138/25, RG 60. For summaries of the most important cases against associations under Donovan, including the *Trenton Potteries* case, see *The Federal Antitrust Laws*, entries 305, 307, 310, 311, 315, 318–22, 324, 326–27, 329, 332, 335–36, 347, 352, 358.

5. Memo for Donovan by H. B. Teegarden, September 5, 1928; Donovan to Teegarden, September [5?], 1928, file 60/147/0, RG 60. Julius Schwartz to Attorney General, May 15, 1926; Donovan to Schwartz, May 22, 1926, file 60/0, *ibid.*

6. Examples reflecting this early reluctance to commit the Department in writing, or even to give an oral evaluation, are in Donovan to E. K. Cormack, November 3, 1925, file 60/12/0; Fayette B. Dow to Attorney General, April 5, 1926; Donovan to Dow, April 10, 1926, file 60/57/0; E. T. Brown to Justice Department, January 20, 1926; Donovan to Brown, January 23, 1926, file 60/0, *ibid.* Early examples of approvals are in Charles M. Best to Attorney General, June 5, 1926; Donovan to Best, July 15, 1926, file 60/138/21; Donovan to Secretary, Hardwood Trim Manufacturers Association, January 18, 1927, file 60/0/17, *ibid.*

7. Donovan to Wilbur L. Cummings, January 26, May 4, 1928; "Memorandum Re Sugar Institute" by Horace R. Lamb, May 7, 1928; "Memorandum for Col. Donovan: Re Sugar Institute" by Simon N. Whitney, June 14, 1928; "Memorandum for Col. Donovan Re Sugar Institute" by Lamb, June 15, 1928; "Memorandum on the Sugar Institute, Inc." by Whitney, December 1, 1928; Donovan to Cummings, January 5, 1929, all in file 60/104/13, *ibid.*

8. Memo by Hardy, December 21, 1927, file 60/126/13, *ibid.*

9. Graham's "Report" to his association of January 5, 1928, reached the Department through Abram F. Myers in a letter to Donovan of April 27, 1928, *ibid.*

10. Levy to Donovan, May 9, 1928; to Justice Department, May 26, 1928; to Russel Hardy, June 8, 29, 1928, *ibid.* Perhaps it is needless to add that Levy's insistent attacks on the Graham Plan were motivated in part by personal grievances. Certain of his own trade association clients were restive because he would not advise them to adopt the Graham Plan principles.

11. Donovan to Graham, June 12, 1928; memo by Russel Hardy, June 15, 1928; memo for Donovan by Porter R. Chandler, July 2, 1928; Donovan to Levy, July 3, 1928; Levy to Donovan, July 3, 1928; Graham to Donovan, July 3, 1928; memos by Hardy, July 10, September 27, December 7, 1928, January 3, 1929; Graham to

Hardy, September 19, 1928; Samuel P. Bush to Donovan, October 18, 1928; William E. Lamb to Donovan, December 16, 1928; Donovan to Lamb, December 31, 1928; memo for Hardy by Breck McAllister, February 13, 1929, all in *ibid.* Levy was correct in alleging that Graham was actively proselytizing for his plan. See "Unite to Cut Distribution Costs," *Iron Age*, 122, No. 1 (July 5, 1928), 16–19, 62, an account of a so-called National Distribution Conference held under Graham's auspices.

12. "Memorandum: The Graham Plan" by Russel Hardy, September 27, 1928, file 60/126/13, RG 60. Wright, "The Law," 106.

13. Donovan, "The Anti-Trust Laws," American Petroleum Institute, *Bulletin*, 11, No. 75 (December 31, 1930), 11–14. See also Donovan, "Trusts Within the Law," *World's Work*, 61, No. 5 (May 1932), 52–55.

14. Watkins, *Public Regulation*, p. 242; Foth, *Trade Associations*, p. 103; Miller, *Unfair Competition*, p. 268; Blaisdell, *Trade Commission*, pp. 92–94. William E. Humphrey submitted the resolution creating the new division. Huston Thompson was absent the day the Commission acted upon it, but the other Democrat, John F. Nugent, was present and voted no. See FTC, "Minutes," April 19, 1926.

15. Watkins, *Public Regulation*, pp. 243–44.

16. For Myers' 1928 speeches, see Warren C. Platt, "How the Commission Would 'Make Law': The A. P. I. Code of Ethics," *National Petroleum News*, 21, No. 3 (January 16, 1929), 28–30. For his remarks at the Chamber round-table, see the typescript volume "Trade Practice Conferences" (1929) in the Chamber of Commerce Library, Washington, D.C.

For the clandestine violation rule controversy, see Foth, *Trade Associations*, p. 115; "The Trade Commission Rescinds an Important Rule," *Printers' Ink*, 147, No. 10 (June 6, 1929), 93–94; and FTC, "Minutes," October 1, 5, 1928, April 5, May 8, 15, 27, 1929.

An especially important source concerning the purposes of the Commission and its trade practice conference clients is the record of the meeting of the Congress of Industries in September 1930, published in ATAE, *Proceedings* (1930). Fred W. Swanson, chairman of the Congress, made it clear that the aim of the trade practice conference industries (which made up the membership of the Congress) was to secure complete prohibition of price discrimination, of deviation from price lists, and of selling below cost.

17. Memo by Lamb, January 4, 1929; William R. Boyd to Donovan, January 7, 1929, file 60/57/32, RG 60. Donovan informed the Commission in a letter of January 8, 1929, of the oil men's position; FTC, "Minutes," January 16, February 4, 1929.

18. Ernest H. Gaunt to Hoover, June 5, 1925; Jacob Newman to Hoover, June 10, 1925; C. H. Sherrill to Hoover, June 22, 1925, file 81288, RG 40.

19. Irving S. Paull, *Trade Association Activities*, Bureau of Foreign and Domestic Commerce (Washington, D.C.: Government Printing Office, 1927), pp. 33–36. Secretary of Commerce, *Annual Report* (1928), pp. xxxiv, 80–81. A good account of the work of the Division of Simplified Practice, which expanded during the 'twenties to include commercial practice standardization, is given in R. M. Hudson to Hoover, February 6, 1928, Commerce Department—Simplified Practice file, CP, HHL. The activities of the Domestic Commerce Division are reviewed in a lengthy memo, written apparently about June 1928 by Frank M. Surface, Assistant Director of the Bureau of Foreign and Domestic Commerce, in Bureau of Foreign and Domestic Commerce file, *ibid.* See also, Secretary of Commerce, *Annual Report* (1929) pp. 106–27; (1930) pp. 98–114.

20. Ray Lyman Wilbur and Arthur M. Hyde, *The Hoover Policies* (New York: Scribner, 1937), pp. 110–12, quoting a Hoover speech of January 14, 1925.

21. Hoover to Daugherty, March 22, 1921; Daugherty to Hoover, March 28, 1921, Justice Department file; Hoover to Daugherty, January 16, 1922; Daugherty to Hoover, January 25, 1922; William G. Irwin to Hoover, January 28, 1922; Hoover to Irwin, February 4, 1922, Corn and Corn Products file, CP, HHL.

22. Hoover commented upon the 1922 plan in letters to Harry A. Garfield, May 2, 1922, and to Julius Barnes, July 22, 1922, box 1–I/354, Coal file, *ibid.* Hoover to Coolidge, November 17, 1923, *ibid.*

23. Hoover to Garfield, cited in note 22.

24. Hoover to C. J. Goodyear, January 26, 1924, *ibid.* House of Representatives, Committee on Interstate and Foreign Commerce, *Coal Hearings*, 69th Cong., 1st sess., 1926, pp. 525–42. Hoover's comments on the necessity of regulation if competition be suspended can be found on p. 542. See also Ellis W. Hawley, "Secretary Hoover and the Bituminous Coal Problem, 1921–1928," *Business History Review*, 42, No. 3 (Autumn 1968), 247–70.

25. Hoover to James F. Burke, January 24, 1927, Burke file, CP, HHL.

26. Hoover to W. A. Vincent, October 31, 1927, Trade Association file; to Coolidge, September 26, 1926, Federal Trade Commission file, *ibid.*; to Abram F. Myers, May 4, 1931, Federal Trade Commission file, Herbert Hoover Presidential Papers, Herbert Hoover Presidential Library. (Hereafter cited as HHPP.) The letter to Coolidge cited above indicates, as does the correspondence with Myers, that Hoover's role in encouraging the FTC to develop its trade practice conference work was considerable.

27. W. J. Vereen to Hoover, May 27, 1926, Textile file; Holt to Director, Bureau of Foreign and Domestic Commerce, May 23, 1928, Rubber file, CP, HHL. See Galambos, *Competition and Cooperation*, pp. 102–103, for details of Hoover's role in the formation of the CTI.

28. George E. Akerson to Edward T. Pickard, February 23, 1927, National Association of Wool Manufacturers file, CP, HHL. Galambos, *Competition and Cooperation*, pp. 126–27. Memo by Russel Hardy, July 10, 1928, file 60/126/13, RG 60.

29. Two exchanges preserved in the Commerce Department archives indicate that the normal practice was simply to refer all questions about the legality of cooperative activities to the Justice Department without comment. O. M. Stafford to Hoover, October 18, 1926; Stephen Davis to Stafford, November 5, 1926; Clancy M. Lewis to Hoover, February 15, 1926; Davis to Lewis, March 16, 1926, file 81288, RG 40. Stafford, a wool manufacturer, asked: "Can we frankly discuss with one another our costs? Can we discuss with each other the requirements of the trade as to value in the effort to stop over-production?" He was referred to the Justice Department.

Thomas R. Taylor to Klein, February 20, 1926, file 711 General, RG 151. Wheeler P. Bloodgood to Ralph Easley, March 24, 1928, General Correspondence, NCF Papers, quotes from a conversation with Falk.

5

The Coolidge Era and the
Rise of the Revision Movement

THE TRADE ASSOCIATION POLICIES of the Coolidge era overfulfilled by a considerable margin the demands for a more moderate antitrust policy which business organizations had made in 1924 and 1925. The new policies tolerated, even encouraged, trade associations to use radical cooperative plans and constituted a more thoroughgoing relaxation of antitrust than associationists had dared to hope or ask for earlier in the decade. The business community's response to the new departure in Washington took two forms. Many industries seized the opportunities for more effective trade association organization and practice which the new legal environment permitted. The history of Graham's Bolt, Nut & Rivet Manufacturers' Association and of the Sugar Institute, recorded in the previous chapter, provide illumination on this point, and additional light is available in the observations of contemporary economists and other commentators upon the business scene. The rapid emergence, after 1925, of closely knit and powerful trade organizations in a number of basic fields—including sugar, cotton and wool textiles, rubber, certain metal industries, and a number of others—was a much-discussed phenomenon. Often terming themselves institutes, these new, reorganized, or simply newly strengthened trade groups were better led, had a wider range of activities, and enjoyed a higher status and greater degree of influence within their industries than the traditional trade association. Under the relaxed antitrust standards administered by Donovan's Antitrust Division and the Coolidge-dominated FTC, it was possible openly to use cooperative devices denied to associations earlier in the decade. Under the new dispensation, "institutes" and associations in many industries attempted with a new sophistication, as one business journalist put it, to "control the market and obtain prices which will make it possible for everyone to survive and make some profit." [1]

This greater latitude allowed associations had the effect, however, of arousing more discontent with the antitrust tradition than it succeeded in quieting. Many industries responded to the more sympathetic government attitude by demanding an ever-more-extensive relaxation of antitrust policy or by demanding outright repeal or radical revision of the antitrust laws. The political agitation which led to the American lapse into governmentally approved cartelism, the NRA, began, not during the years of the Great Depression, but during the later 'twenties, a period known, and properly so, as one of overall growth and prosperity for the nation's economy. This may seem paradoxical, but it appears less so when the specific individuals and industries which led the movement are identified. They tend to come from the segments of industry which shared least in the prosperity of the 1920s. As Ralph C. Epstein demonstrated long ago, the profitability of the different industries varied greatly in the later 'twenties, and many, including some of the largest and most important of them, made relatively poor profit-showings. Industries rating low on Epstein's profit scale often appeared in the forefront of the movement for revision.[2]

Leaders of these disadvantaged industries coined a term, "profitless prosperity," to describe their condition and endlessly sought explanations and remedies for it. "Profitless prosperity," it was generally accepted, had engulfed the old, basic industries. Only, as a leading business-economist, Virgil Jordan, told the National Founders Association in 1928, in "industries catering directly to the new wants and consumptive habits of the population, providing the luxury goods and services that make the high standard of living about which we talk," were satisfactory profits being earned. Most businessmen in the low-return fields no doubt agreed with Jordan that these enviable profits came "in part at the expense of the older industries furnishing the basic materials and the fundamental services." How the profitable industries had gained their advantage was disputed. The burden of the excessive production capacity in the basic industries which wartime expansion had created was a favorite explanation. Another answer cited a supposed superiority of skill and chicane in bargaining ability which enabled the automakers and other key consumers' goods producers to lord it over steel and other basic industries. A more sophisticated explanation argued the hypothesis that unprofitability arose when an industry, after proceeding through certain stages of development, had reached maturity. In the earlier stages, when an industry was young, high profits for some firms in it were available by reason of patent advantage, superior managerial performance, and other factors. But as an industry matured, each of its firms acquired much the same capabilities, and profits were squeezed out by competition.

Another version of this "maturity" explanation stressed the factor of expanding and then stabilized market opportunities during the early and later stages, respectively, of an industry's history. Whatever explanation they accepted, businessmen from industries such as coal, lumber, oil, rubber, and textiles joined in envying their more prosperous cousins in the auto, electrical appliance, toilet goods, cigarette, and other fields. "Must the steel industry go in rags so that the automobile industry may

wear diamonds?" The question, posed before the National Association of
Flat Rolled Steel Manufacturers in 1928 was echoed, with appropriate
modifications, at the meetings of many other associations in the waning
years of the 'twenties.[3]

It was the efforts of these discontented industries which brought the
question of antitrust revision to the level of open discussion within the
business community. The members of the American Supply and Machinery Manufacturers Association, for example, producers of the basic
equipment and machinery used in the nation's factories, set up a propaganda committee on the antitrust laws in 1925, charging it with the
task of persuading all the other national trade associations to meet together to "consider ways and means of bringing forcibly to the attention
of Congress the necessity of amending the Sherman and other so-called
anti-trust laws so that business can function fearlessly along legitimate
and sensible lines." By the time the ASMMA met again, in May 1926, the
committee's chairman, Dixon C. Williams, could report that his group
had been in contact with more than 400 trade associations. Whether the
endeavors of this particular committee, as its chairman claimed, actually
"contributed in no small degree to a favorable change in the sentiments
of people generally" respecting antitrust revision is debatable. But it is
clear that it was the cumulative effect of the agitation of industries like
this one, which had for years bitterly complained of the "state of ruthless,
uneconomic and wasteful competition" into which the antitrust laws
supposedly forced it, which brought about a reopening of the business
community's case against the Sherman Act tradition of maintaining
competition.[4]

The hand of such industries was always discernible as the influence
which persuaded the major business organizations, in the later 'twenties,
to admit the revision question to their deliberations over policy formulation. When the Board of Directors of the Chamber of Commerce voted in
May 1928 to establish a committee to investigate the antitrust laws to
determine whether they were consonant with "modern economic requirements," they were acting at the insistence of the Natural Resources
Product Group, which comprised such interests as lumber, petroleum,
and mining. Similarly, representatives of the textile, steel, and factory
machinery and supply industries clearly had much to do with making
a major place for the revision question on the agenda of the NAM's annual
meeting in 1928, for it was men from these fields who read the papers
and dominated the discussion on the topic.[5]

To judge from the attention the revision question received in the late
1920s from the most important organizations representing business opinion, a large proportion of the industrial community was prepared to
support a political movement aimed at getting legislation for promoting
a cartelized economy. The same record shows, however, that an even

larger proportion either opposed political meddling with the existing antitrust laws or felt that a head-on legislative clash with the Sherman Act was inadvisable. Majority opinion among businessmen in general and evidently within the ranks of industrialists as well, held that if there was to be an attempt to change the substance of antitrust law, it should be through indirect means.

A struggle between groups inclined to more and less radical courses of action or to no action at all took place within each of the three most influential national organizations acting as spokesman for business interests. In each case the radicals lost. Within the American Bar Association, the forum in which corporation lawyers debated the merits of proposed legislation affecting their clients, partisans of radical revision showed an early strength. The initial reports of the Association's Commerce Committee, which began to study the antitrust question in 1926, clearly favored outright amendment of the substance of the Sherman Act so as to soften its pronouncement that "every contract in restraint of trade" is illegal. In determining whether to ban a given kind of collective business activity, according to one typical formula the committee suggested, the courts would not merely be concerned with determining the fact of restraint. Rather, they would judge the legality of a particular restraint only after taking into account "the interests of producers [and] workers" as well as the interests of the "consumers" whom, as the revisionist argument claimed, the existing law favored exclusively. Between the 1928 and 1929 ABA conventions, however, the Commerce Committee fell under moderate influence. Its 1929 report shied away from the substantive-revision approach and, instead, came down for "procedural" or, as it was sometimes titled, "administrative" amendment.

The committee's proposal called for creation of an agency with "jurisdiction to determine in advance at the request of industry whether or not a given agreement should be permitted to take effect without incurring the penalties of the Sherman law." It was, in principle at least, familiar to the Bar Association's members, just as it was to most of the businessmen whose interests they represented. The substance of the committee's plan dated back at least as far as 1913–14. At that time, when the Wilson Administration and Congress were preparing new antitrust legislation, a number of influential business groups had tried to persuade the politicians to equip the FTC with power to approve trade association activities. In the early 'twenties during the critical struggle with Daugherty over antitrust policy, Senator Edge and then Hoover had renewed the proposal by urging creation of a body empowered to advise trade associations of their rights and, in Hoover's version, to grant immunity to acts performed in accordance with that body's approval.[6]

Supporters of this procedural amendment proposal had traditionally represented it as having no effect on the substance of antitrust. Such assurances also sheathed the proposal when it was brought forward in the late 1920s, but they clearly were not genuine. By adopting the extremely tenuous legal position that, under standing Supreme Court rulings, agreements among competitors regulating the rate of production were legal, the ABA committee could claim both that its proposal would not tamper with antitrust law and that it would pave the way for effective production agreements. The reason, so the argument ran, why no lawyer would advise associations to take advantage of this freedom to control production was that the scope of control which the Supreme Court would accept could not be determined in advance. The new government body the commerce committee envisioned, by freeing associations from the danger of criminal and civil liability, would allow them to explore and locate, through litigation, the boundaries the Court had in mind.[7]

The 1929 ABA convention accepted the committee's proposal and recommended it to Congress for immediate action. As Rush Butler, the committee's chairman, confidentially explained after the convention to a small group of antitrust-revision enthusiasts, the proposal the convention had accepted was a "conservative" one, "one which we think can be put through [Congress] without much delay." But, as he emphasized, it was intended to achieve a break-through for trade associations into the forbidden area of cartel practice. In principle, he remarked, "I haven't any objection to going further"; but the politics of the matter dictated his "conservative" and limited effort at antitrust revision. The more radical forms of revision which interested many lawyers and businessmen were unwise, in Butler's view, only because they had little chance of winning acceptance.[8]

Evidently there were additional factors counseling businessmen to prefer a moderate form of antitrust revision. When the NAM first turned, in 1928, to a consideration of the antitrust problem, radical revisionists made a strong showing, just as they had initially within the ABA. The NAM's president, John E. Edgerton, himself a textile manufacturer, opened the association's 1928 convention with an alarmist address upon the "ominous problems" resulting "from the general loss of balance between production and distribution" which the regimen of competition was creating. Moreover, the program of the afternoon session devoted to exploration of the antitrust question was conspicuously loaded in favor of speakers who were identified with the cause of direct, substantive, Sherman Act revision. But by the time the NAM's members assembled again, in October 1929, their leaders evidently had determined to turn the organization toward a commitment to procedural amendment. John C. Gall, the NAM's associate counsel, in the only address at the convention directly concerned with the revision issue, urged the membership to support the concept of a government agency with power to rule in advance upon trade association activities and confer immunity upon them. The convention followed this lead, endorsing a resolution for the creation of a study committee to outline a specific position for the association to adopt. In the wake of the convention, Edgerton and the other NAM officers addressed a general letter to the membership requesting an expression of opinion for the guidance of the committee which shortly would be established. The letter, by way of suggesting the nature of the proposed revision, repeated the substance of the argument for procedural amendment which Gall had made at the convention a few weeks earlier. There was no reference to the existence of serious alternatives to Gall's proposal; the general letter revealed the determination of the NAM leaders to limit the proposed study merely to a consideration of the variations which could be made upon the procedural revision theme.[9]

The Chamber of Commerce of the United States, though it numbered nearly 600 industrial trade associations among its members, lagged behind both the ABA and the NAM in its response to the men and groups who were stirring up interest in the antitrust question in the later 1920s. While the ABA actually had thrown its weight behind revision and the NAM was fast approaching the same position by the end of 1929, conservatives within the Chamber were able to hedge the revisionists in their organization within narrow bounds. In the record of the Chamber's activities, one can read ample evidence of the intense interest in the antitrust problem which many of its members felt. But this interest was allowed to express itself only with difficulty, and it received no encouragement from the Chamber's established leaders. Although the Chamber's monthly publication, Nation's Business, occasionally opened its pages in the later 'twenties to outspoken partisans of radical changes in antitrust policy, it dissociated itself from any implied editorial endorsement of such views. Moreover, discussion of the antitrust question had almost no part in the Chamber's annual meeting in 1927, 1928, or 1929. During the Chamber's 1928 meeting, the Board of Directors did establish a committee to study and report on the necessity for antitrust revision, but it appears this was done more to prevent the subject from reaching the floor of the convention for discussion than to hasten a definition of Chamber policy. The board acted on the second day of the convention, after the Natural Resources Production Group had passed a resolution, which it wished to have submitted at a general meeting of the convention, asking for creation of a Chamber committee to deal with the problem of antitrust revision. After first acting to send the resolution to the convention floor, the board at another session the following day reversed its decision and voted to establish the committee itself, obviating the need for letting the resolution go forward for consideration by the membership. The committee appears never to have been appointed. If appointed, it left no visible traces in the available Chamber records and certainly never filed a report. It may well be, therefore, that the board's purpose in 1928 was to side-track a measure which would have brought the antitrust question before the Chamber membership for open discussion.[10]

The history of the revision question before these three business organizations reveals a complex pattern. Clearly, large elements within the business community wanted to commit these groups to an active effort to secure antitrust liberalization. Established leaders counseled moderate, indirect means to that end and urged so-called administrative amendment as the vehicle of change. Substantial sentiment seems to have been indifferent to the issue altogether. Some further elaboration and interpretation of this pattern can be obtained from a fourth organization which participated in—and, in fact, sought to lead—the movement for antitrust revision in the late 1920s, the National Civic Federation. The NCF was not a business organization in the usual sense. It was an artifact of the Progressive era. Before the World War, it had garnered considerable prestige as the leading spokesman for the theory of the underlying harmony of the interests of capital and labor and as the major institution through which moderates from both camps came together to propagandize for the acceptance of trade unionism and inveigh against labor radicalism. In the 'twenties, an era of decline in AFL strength and the rise of corporate welfarism, the NCF rapidly became an anachronism. Ralph Easley, the NCF's energetic executive director since 1898, tried to enhance its relevance by making the Federation one of the most prominent anti-radical groups of the decade. In 1927, in an effort to revive the original purposes of the organization, the Federation's annual meeting directed the appointment of an Industrial Commission to investigate "certain industrial questions which are disturbing the relation between capital and labor in this country today." There were four questions, the most interesting being antitrust-law revision; the others dealt with labor problems, principally injunctions in labor disputes, yellow dog contracts, and company unions. The Industrial Commission met for the first time in March 1928 with Matthew Woll, the conservative AFL vice president, in the chair and with a substantial number of the prominent figures who had agreed to sit on the commission in attendance. These included such notable men as Owen D. Young, the chairman of G.E., and James W. Gerard, the former ambassador to Germany. Woll in his address before the commission explained that the AFL favored antitrust revision in order to secure higher standards for workers. Many important industries were "oversupplied with producing units and overmanned with labor." When prices rose and decent wages were paid, marginal producers entered, "depressing prices and thereby driving wages down to unsatisfactory levels. Thus, industry founders in the quicksand of overproduction and excessive competition." Though labor suffered from the Sherman Act in a different way, when it was used as a basis for injunctions in labor disputes, the two issues were separable, Woll said. Labor was prepared to consider the need for a more profitable industrial system apart from the injunction issue. Present at the commission meeting was Wheeler P. Bloodgood, a Milwaukee attorney active in corporate and trade association affairs and a long-time participant in NCF programs. He now was to become chairman of the commission's committee to study the antitrust question. Bloodgood reviewed the current proposals for antitrust revision and prophesied chaotic competition for industry and depressed standards for labor unless there was liberalization.[11]

Though Woll portrayed it in his speech as only one of several problems "which are the cause of much of the bitterness between . . . capital and labor," Easley expected the antitrust question to benefit from most of the commission's attention. There would no doubt be a recommendation for abatement of the use of labor injunctions but, Easley told Bloodgood, "emphasis will not be placed upon company unions and 'yellow dog' contracts but upon the amendment of the Sherman Anti-Trust Act," with Woll and William Green ready to back revision strongly.

Bloodgood and Easley soon formed the Committee on Anti-Trust, securing the willing participation of several of the most-noted protagonists of revision from the business and legal world. Rush Butler, a Chicago attorney, numbered many trade associations among his firm's clients. In 1918–19 he had headed the Chamber of Commerce committee which had reported in favor of radical antitrust revision. Currently, he was chairman of the Commerce Committee of the ABA, whose attention to the antitrust question antedated the NCF's. Gilbert Montague, who, though not a member, worked closely with Bloodgood's Committee, was a prominent New York attorney who had specialized in antitrust law since the turn of the century. He was adviser to several trade associations and enjoyed the confidence of leaders of the New York financial community as well. J. Harvey Williams, a third recruit, was a Buffalo tool manufacturer. Working from a base in the American Supply and Machinery Manufacturers Association and other trade groups, Williams had in recent years developed through publications and speeches a widespread reputation as a militant and effective proponent of radical antitrust revision. With leaders of this caliber on their antitrust committee, with the support of such figures as Charles Schwab, Bethlehem Steel chairman and president of the American Iron and Steel Institute, Bloodgood and Easley were confident of success. Easley even believed that the Republican presidential candidate was in sympathy with the committee's aims. Reporting, in June 1928, to Hoover, with whom he fancied he enjoyed a confidential relationship, on a conversation with

Woll, Easley told how the AFL had, as expected, obtained no concessions from the Republican platform committee as a result of a recent
appearance before it. Nevertheless the AFL was "sure that you are in
sympathy with" the demand that the Sherman Act be amended to allow labor and industry to "develop along normal, constructive lines." [12]

The antitrust committee's work proceeded more slowly than Bloodgood and Easley had hoped. Opposition of employers associations and
indifference from the major business organizations, especially the Chamber, exerted a drag during 1928. The National Metal Trades Association, the League for Industrial Rights, and other open-shop groups
besieged Bloodgood, protesting that Sherman Act revision, though intended to relieve business, might remove the legislative basis for labor
injunctions, especially against the secondary boycott. The NAM leaders
took this position for a time, "so bitter against the unions," Easley
claimed, "that they would rather suffer the ills they now bear as a result
of the Sherman Act than see anything done with it" which might help
the unions surmount the injunction problem. The Chamber of Commerce indifference was attributed to the sway of what J. Harvey Williams
called the "consumer philosophy." The Chamber would never move toward antitrust revision, Williams thought, "as long as department stores
and chain stores retain their influence" within it. "Those are the interests
which thrive upon the present legal restrictions." Relief would be won
only by mobilizing the industrial trade associations. [13]

Another source of concern was the Graham Plan of the Bolt, Nut &
Rivet Manufacturers' Association. Alerted to the situation by Felix
Levy, the NCF committee agreed that Graham's scheme was illegal and
that his open attempts during 1928 to have other associations adopt it
would result in "unfortunate publicity" and "have a most unfortunate
effect upon the entire trade association movement." At one point Bloodgood felt compelled to attempt to persuade Graham to cancel one of the
meetings he held during 1928 to propagate his ideas. But there was little
the committee could do to amend the problems presented by the Graham
Plan for the time being. [14]

Despite these distractions the committee set its executive secretary,
Arthur E. Foote, a former associate of Hoover's in the Commerce Department, to work making a survey of business opinion on the revision
question. By March 1929, a preliminary tabulation of opinion gathered
during the previous months demonstrated, the committee believed, solid
support for antitrust liberalization and spurred the readying of a concrete
proposal. [15]

The returns to the Federation's questionnaires are very helpful for
testing the impression, discussed earlier, that it was the industries suffering from "profitless prosperity" which were responsible for the pressure
for antitrust revision which the major business groups felt in the late

'twenties. It was such industries the Federation relied upon to establish the existence of widespread trade association support for the revision movement it was attempting to initiate during 1928 and 1929. The Federation's own tabulation was simply a totaling of replies, but it is possible to use Foote's work materials to discern, with rough accuracy at least, which trade associations (industries) showed the most active interest in the investigation during 1928 and early 1929. Seeking names and addresses of potential respondents, Foote approached apparently at random, a large number, probably 200 to 300, trade association secretaries,

TABLE I

Trade Associations Supporting
NCF Revision Movement, 1928–1929

Above Median	*Below Median*
American Bakers Council, Inc.	Am. Brush Mfrs. Assoc.
Associated Trade Papers	Am. Ceramic Society
Assoc. of Am. Soap and Glycerine Producers, Inc.	Am. Inst. of Steel Const.
	Am. Paper and Pulp Assoc.
Assoc. of Cocoa and Chocolate Mfrs.	Am. Supply and Machinery Mfrs. Assoc.
Assoc. of Knit Underwear Mfrs.	
Bolt, Nut & Rivet Mfrs. Assoc.	Am. Zinc Inst.
Greeting Card Assoc., Inc.	Assoc. of Collar Mfrs.
Institute of Carpet Mfrs.	Casket Mfrs. Assoc. of Am.
Motion Picture Producers and Distributors of Am., Inc.	Common Brick Mfrs. Assoc.
	Copper and Brass Research Inst.
Natl. Boot and Shoe Mfrs. Assoc.	Cordage Inst.
Natl. Coffee Roasters Assoc.	Cotton Textile Inst.
Natl. Gas Appliance Mfrs. Assoc.	Dry Color Mfrs. Assoc.
	Gummed Industries Assoc.
	Gypsum Inst.
	Industrial Alcohol Inst.
	Machine Knife Statistical Assoc.
	Motor and Equipt. Mfrs. Assoc.
	Natl. Assoc. of Steel Furniture Mfrs.
	Natl. Assoc. of Wood Turners
	Natl. Coal Assoc.
	Natl. Crushed Stone Assoc.
	Natl. Fertilizer Assoc.
	Natl. Lumber Mfrs. Assoc.
	Natl. Pipe and Supplies Assoc.
	Natl. Slate Assoc.
	Pressed Metal Inst.
	Rubber Mfrs. Assoc.
	Rail Steel Bar Assoc.
	Steel Barrel Mfrs. Assoc.
	Sugar Institute
	Wirebound Box Mfrs. Assoc.
TOTALS 12	32

requesting their assistance. About fifty of these cooperated in some measure: some sending a list of members; some offering to mail the questionnaires to their members; some answering the questionnaire themselves, but giving no further help; and some expressing interest, promising to cooperate and then failing to do so. On the basis that any of these responses is a display of a positive attitude—an active interest in revision—the associations which these secretaries represented have been listed in Table I. Because a second NCF questionnaire has been analyzed in considerable detail for similar purposes in a later chapter, here the associations are examined from only one viewpoint: whether they belonged to the "profitless prosperity" class so much lamented by contemporaries. As the table indicates, thirty-two of the forty-four associations listed represent industries which Epstein ranked below the median rank of profitability for all industries in the period from 1919 to 1928. Most of the industries above the median rose only slightly beyond it. Even though it is a crude index indeed, Table I reinforces the impression that industries which deemed themselves in the throes of "profitless prosperity" were most receptive to the agitation for antitrust liberalization which got underway in the closing years of the 1920s.[16]

NOTES

1. There was a very well-informed series in the *Annalist* on these matters in 1929: Edward S. Meade, "Adjusting Excess Productive Capacity to Closed Markets —The 'Institute,'" *Annalist*, 34, No. 861 (July 19, 1929), 97–98; "Lawful Restraint of Trade through Education—How the 'Institutes' Do It," *ibid.*, No. 864 (August 9, 1929), 251–52; "The Wool Institute: A Successful Cooperative Control of an Industry," *ibid.*, No. 866 (August 23, 1929), 347–48; "Cotton-Textile Institute: A Demoralized Industry Saved by Cooperation," *ibid.*, No. 872 (October 4, 1929), 637–38. Galambos, *Competition and Cooperation*, pp. 101–12, 113–38, 291–95, has given full-scale treatment to the evolution of associational forms in the cotton textile industry. Associationism progressed in this industry from the "service association" type, which predominated between 1900 and 1925, to the institute, the "policy shaping" association (the Cotton Textile Institute), which guided the industry between 1925 and the mid-1930s. The main distinguishing mark of the institute, according to Galambos, was the relatively high prestige of its leaders and their relative freedom from immediate pressure by disgruntled members. This permitted the institute to build up cooperative progress through education and persuasion, to exert some pressure upon recalcitrants. Simon N. Whitney, *Trade Associations and Industrial Control: A Critique of the NRA* (New York: Central, 1934), describes several of the new, powerful associations which emerged in the late 1920s.

2. Epstein, *Industrial Profits in the United States* (New York: National Bureau of Economic Research, 1934), pp. 75–78, 122–23, for the basic tables.

3. Charles J. Graham, "Let Railroads Buy Bolts and Nuts," *Iron Age*, 116, No. 13 (September 24, 1925), 831–32. Alexander C. Brown, "Prosperity but no

Profits," *Nation's Business*, 15, No. 9 (August 1927), 15–17. Nearly all the thirty-seven executives queried in a survey replied that "overproduction" threatened their industries' prosperity according to "The Power and Production Program for 1927," *Industrial Management*, 52, No. 6 (December 1926), 337–48. During the summer of 1929 the NAM, impressed by the greatly differing rates of profit in different industries, arranged for a survey by an engineering firm of opinion on the causes. The results were summarized in two papers: Leon V. Alden and E. L. Woolworth, "The Problem of Depressed Price Level," and A. A. Hadden, "Can a Manufacturer Get a Fair Price for his Products?" *American Industries*, 30, No. 1 (October 1929), 3–14, 15–34. Gilmore Iden, "Business Leaders Voice Their Sentiments on the Anti-Trust Laws," *Magazine of Wall Street*, 43, No. 8 (February 9, 1929), 636–38. O. H. Cheney, "Whose Steel Industry Is It?" *Iron Trade Review*, 82, No. 24 (June 14, 1928), 1531–33, 1547. "[Virgil Jordan] Sees Strength in Flexible, Elastic, and Mobile Production System," *Iron Age*, 120, No. 18 (November 3, 1927), 1231–32.

4. *Mill Supplies*, 15, No. 3 (June 1925), 37, 43, 67; *ibid.*, 16, No. 3 (June 1926), 47, 69, 71, 73; *ibid.*, 17, No. 4 (July 1927), 98, 126b. "Demand Revision of Anti-Trust Acts," *Iron Age*, 115, No. 20 (May 14, 1925), 1419–21; "To Organize 500 Trade Bodies," *ibid.*, 117, No. 21 (May 27, 1926), 1502–04. "Supply Dealers Attack Competition," *ibid.*, 119, No. 25 (June 23, 1927), 1830–31.

5. Chamber of Commerce, Board of Directors, *Minutes*, May 8, 9, 1928. Charles Cheney, "Opening Presentation"; Robert J. Adams, "An Affirmative Law for Business"; George M. Verity, "Should Anti-Trust Laws Be Amended?"; J. Harvey Williams, "Remarks"; Samuel P. Bush, "Competition, Co-operation and the Law"; all in NAM, *Annual Meeting* (1928), pp. 211–17, 218–25, 228–34, 235–38.

6. *Report of the . . . Meeting of the American Bar Association* (1927), p. 251; (1928), pp. 373–74; (1929), pp. 104–105, 310–12.

7. *Ibid.*

8. Butler's comments from transcript of "Luncheon Conference, Committee on Study of Anti-Trust Legislation," December 10, 1929, box 134, NCF Papers.

9. Edgerton, "Annual Address of President," in NAM, *Annual Meeting* (1928), pp. 18–30; other relevant speakers at the 1928 meeting are cited in note 5. Gall, "Prevention or Punishment in the Administration of the Anti-Trust Laws," *ibid.* (1929), pp. 95–102; NAM, Board of Directors, "Minutes," December 12, 1929.

10. Brown, "Prosperity," 15–17; O. H. Cheney, "The Answer to the New Competition," *Nation's Business*, 15, No. 11 (October 1927), 15–17; "The Anti-Trust Laws," *ibid.*, 30; Julius Kahn, "A Plea for More Government Regulation," *ibid.*, 16, No. 2 (February 1928), 20–22. Chamber of Commerce, Board of Directors, *Minutes*, May 8, 9, 1928. E. W. McCullough to George S. Barnum, April 30, May 22, 1928, box 66, NCF Papers. McCullough was head of the Chamber's Trade Association Department. The letters indicate that the Chamber's staff opposed serious revision and did not believe the Chamber would support it.

11. Marguerite Green, *The National Civic Federation and the American Labor Movement, 1900–1925* (Washington, D.C.: Catholic University of America Press, 1956) is the standard work on the Federation in its role as intermediary between capital and labor. Chapters 9 and 10 offer some general information on the Federation in the later 1920s. The perusal of Easley's voluminous correspondence for this period shows he had great difficulty in maintaining the contributions which supplied the Federation's budget. The antitrust investigation has all the earmarks of a desperate attempt to bring his organization into the limelight, as were his many ventures into anti-radicalism, including an episode in which he was hoodwinked by the most celebrated rogue of the 'twenties, Gaston B. Means.

The record of the Industrial Commission meeting of March 16, 1928, is in box 65, NCF Papers.

12. Easley to Bloodgood, February 2, 1928; Bloodgood to Williams, June 4, 1928; Easley to Hoover, June 19, 1928, General Correspondence, *ibid.*

13. Williams to Arthur E. Foote, February 2, 1928; to George S. Barnum, May 25, 1928; Bloodgood to Foote, November 18, 1929; to E. R. Burton, November 19, 1929, all in box 66, *ibid.* Bloodgood to Easley, March 8, 1928; Easley to Hoover, June 16, September 15, 1928; to Bloodgood, December 21, 1928; to George E. Akerson, February 18, 1929; Williams to John A. Topping, June 8, 1929, all in General Correspondence, *ibid.*

14. Bloodgood to Williams, June 15, 1928, file 60/126/13, RG 60. Anonymous memorandum, sent to Easley by Bloodgood, December 5, 1928, General Correspondence, NCF Papers. Memo, Meeting of Federation Committee on Anti-Trust "to discuss the Graham Plan," July 25, 1928, box 66, *ibid.*

15. Easley to Bloodgood, April 10, 1929, General Correspondence, *ibid.* Easley to Butler, March 22, 1929, box 65; "Work of the National Civic Federation— Industrial Commission," September 1929, box 66, *ibid.*

16. Table I is based upon the work materials in box 98, *ibid.* I do not present a detailed justification here for the steps involved in constructing this table because such a justification has been given in Chapter 7 for Table II. The procedure and the sources described there for determining what industry a given trade association represents and to which of Epstein's "industries" it corresponds were followed in constructing Table I.

6

The Hoover Administration's
Antitrust-Enforcement Policy, 1929–1931

ANTITRUST POLICY proved an extremely troublesome problem for the Hoover Administration. The problems owed little to presidential initiatives. They were largely unavoidable, in part a legacy of the Coolidge Administration, in part the result of the Great Depression. Coolidge-era policies had encouraged trade association experimentation with practices an orthodox enforcement of the law would have challenged. By March 1929 these policies had raised many hopes, entwined the government in many commitments. Whether to continue this line of development or arrest it was an inevitable and difficult question for the new Administration. A second, complicating factor was the rising intensity of demands for antitrust relaxation when prices and production turned in a seemingly unending sweep downward after the stock market crash in October 1929.

Hoover's own contribution to the problems he experienced in forming an appropriate and consistent antitrust policy arose from his effort to apply certain concepts for reform which he had worked out earlier. The attitudes toward antitrust policy Hoover brought to the presidency were, of course, those he had held as Secretary of Commerce. He had found the *Maple Flooring* definition of the limits the Sherman Act placed upon industrial cooperation acceptable and had given no indication he felt further moderation of the law, in its general bearing, was necessary. But Hoover had never held in doctrinaire fashion that competition was necessarily and always the life of trade. If competition led irreversibly to an industry's impoverishment, then some more or less drastic mitigation of competition was in order. This reasoning had led him at one point to suggest the desirability of the organization of the bituminous coal industry into regional sales agencies and to assist in the formulation of the Federal Oil Conservation Board's proposal of 1926 for oil conservation through unitary operation of oil pools. Unitary operation was to be accomplished through uniform state conservation laws and an interstate compact. This remedy involved a relatively moderate departure from the competitive norm. The proposal provided for no relaxation of the antitrust laws for oil producers, for no production quotas, whether through state authorities or business agreements. Unitary operation of oil pools was primarily a conservation measure designed to maximize recovery of oil reserves. But it also contained, as the FOCB had long recognized, and as Hoover explained in a press release of April 2, 1929, "a certain economic phase in that with regulated drilling it would be possible, to a remote extent perhaps, to prevent periods of intense over-production." [1] The new President's advocacy of this approach to correcting what oil men called the "chaotic competition" and "overproduction" of their industry made it difficult for Hoover not to cooperate with the state-regulation–interstate-compact approach when it was used during the depression for the direct regulation of production. Issues of general significance for antitrust policy arose during this involvement and complicated the Hoover Administration's attempt to maintain an orthodox and consistent policy of antitrust enforcement.

When he entered the White House, however, Hoover gave no indication that he thought antitrust policy would offer his Administration any special challenges. What evidence is available concerning his consideration of antitrust affairs in the early stage of his term indicates an initial ignorance of the difficult legacy which the Coolidge-era policies constituted and an assignment of a relatively low priority to general antitrust policy as an area requiring his innovating energies. It is true that William J. Donovan was refused appointment as Attorney General. This gave rise to considerable gossip in political circles and to a more limited extent in the press; and it offended and angered Donovan deeply, though not to the point of permanent estrangement. Hoover's action apparently was linked to a certain, but probably not profound, knowledge of the dubious nature of Donovan's enforcement of the Sherman Act. However, Hoover had known of and approved Donovan's practice of reviewing and commenting upon the legality of trade association programs. There are some indications that Hoover intended the practice to continue, but it seems unlikely he was informed how far Donovan had gone with his advice and to what problems his practice was leading. As to whether Hoover had in mind major new departures in antitrust policy: there are signs he had certain plans, but they appear to have been vague and indefinite, and they came to nothing. Some discussion of Hoover's "purpose to bring the Anti-Trust Laws into line with the public interest" took place with Judge Thomas D. Thacher when the latter was offered, in April 1929, appointment as the Assistant to the Attorney General. With the appointee who accepted the post, John Lord O'Brian, Hoover in August considered a similar purpose. A letter to O'Brian refers to Hoover's hopes of continuing "discussion on the whole question [of antitrust policy] leading to the determination of some definition of an economic as well as legal program." In referring to "what steps should be taken to reorient the Sherman and Clayton Acts to deal more particularly with the situation that has now developed," Hoover seemed to intimate that important changes were under consideration, but his conclusion—that such consideration "would make no consequential difference in the action the Department is to take but might enable us to drive more to an ultimate point of view"—seems to contradict this. The subject of these discussions may have been, at least in part, administrative revision of the antitrust laws. In the 'twenties Hoover had at times supported in principle the proposal that an arrangement be made for government approval of proposed agreements with suspension of criminal penalties while the approval was in force. In April, Rush Butler, a major protagonist of such a measure, discussed a number of matters with Hoover and found that "the one in which he was most interested was the Sherman Law situation." Butler came away believing that the proposal of the ABA's Commerce Committee, which he chaired, met with "the President's approval." [2]

There is little indication, however, that Hoover was inclined seriously to support administrative, let alone substantive, antitrust amendment. Rather, he displayed that same sensitivity and defensiveness toward possible criticisms that he was too lenient with businessmen's agreements which he showed in later stages of his presidency. In the early months of his term, this sensitivity took the form of repeatedly jogging his Attorney General, William D. Mitchell, who had been Solicitor General under Coolidge, to look into possible antitrust violations which Hoover had noted in the newspapers. In March 1929 he drew Mitchell's attention, long before their representatives reached Washington, to the "meeting of oil producers held in Texas recently where proposals were put forward as to unity of action in control of production." Hoover was "somewhat anxious about this" and felt "that these activities should be closely scrutinized to see if they are being kept within the law." In September he asked Mitchell, on at least two occasions, to look into the legality of well-publicized mergers.[3] In a similar vein he told Will Hays, the movie "czar" since 1923, of his concern over the West Coast Theatres case then pending. The case involved relations between independent-theater owners who felt threatened by the movie producers. "I was impressed," Hays assured Hoover, "with your suggestion that you were yourself getting the reflexes, and I meant exactly what I said when I said that I would go the limit to relieve you and the Administration and to aid in removing any burdens growing out of any overreaching on the part of this business." [4]

The clinching proof of Hoover's eagerness to cover himself against charges of lax antitrust-enforcement standards, however, was the episode which alerted his Administration to the problems it had inherited from Donovan's tenure at the Antitrust Division. During the summer of 1929, events forced Hoover's new Justice Department appointees to forge a new and less liberal stance toward trade association programs. Neither Mitchell nor O'Brian shared Donovan's purpose of bringing about antitrust liberalization, and O'Brian, at least, appeared at times to feel personally committed to the orthodox concept that enforcement of competition was the only valid alternative to full-scale government regulation of business and, therefore, that consistent enforcement according to the Supreme Court guidelines was desirable public policy as well as his duty.[5]

It was the NCF's Committee on Anti-Trust which forced the new Administration into an early reconsideration of the Coolidge-era policies. The committee's leaders entertained great hopes of securing the Administration's support for their efforts to revise the law but, as in the previous year, believed a revival of traditional antitrust-enforcement standards was a necessary first step for mobilizing business concern for change. The committee's contacts with Cabinet members and the President himself were good, quite sufficient to transmit effectively the message that the recent practice of the Antitrust Division and the FTC needed reconsideration, but not influential enough, as it turned out, to secure any significant support for the Federation's revision proposal. The committee's best contact was through Robert P. Lamont, former president of American Steel Foundries who now held the post through which Hoover himself in the 'twenties had risen to political leadership, the Secretaryship of Commerce. Lamont was, until his resignation in August 1932, the Cabinet member Hoover relied upon most in the formation and execution of general economic policy. Lamont's new prominence was the NCF's good fortune for, until shortly before entering the Cabinet, Lamont had been associated with Wheeler P. Bloodgood, the chairman of the Federation's antitrust committee, in a venture called the Howard Finance Company, and the two were friends as well as former business partners. In answering the committee's antitrust questionnaire the previous year Lamont, as head of American Steel Foundries, had acknowledged that revision was necessary in order to provide that "contracts and combinations restraining trade are lawful if in the public interest when considered from the view of capital, labor and the consumer." By mid-April 1929, Bloodgood was busy corresponding with Lamont sounding out prospects for the Commerce Secretary's cooperation with the committee's plans. Another newly acquired committee asset was the assistance of William E. Lamb. Closely associated with Hoover as Commerce Department Solicitor during the battle with Daugherty in the early 'twenties, Lamb was now a partner in Rush Butler's Chicago law firm and willing to assist the committee.[6]

Before quiet and patient promptings through these contacts had any time to have effect, however, circumstances abruptly presented themselves which enabled the Federation to press the issue of defining antitrust-enforcement policy as one requiring immediate solution. In June, Bloodgood learned that Felix Levy, who had been closely in touch with the committee's work during the previous two years and who shared the view that revival of enforcement was a necessary prelude to revision, but also had personal reason for wishing to see the Graham Plan attacked, was being pressured by the "New York *World* to assist in furnishing data to be used as a basis for the [newspaper's planned] attack upon the Department of Justice." Bloodgood acted promptly to forestall Levy's cooperation with the *World*, alert the Administration to the situation, and enhance his committee's influence in Washington. Bloodgood spoke to Lamont and received through him assurances, which he passed on to Levy, from Attorney General Mitchell that the Justice Department would investigate the whole issue of trade association relations with the Department as soon as O'Brian had been confirmed. Lamb, through Bloodgood, agreed to arrange a personal interview with Hoover if that proved necessary. Levy was dissuaded, Lamont grateful, the Administration eager to have Bloodgood explain the Federation's charges concerning Donovan's policies to O'Brian immediately. Bloodgood was elated, believing that the Administration's gratitude for the committee's warding off the newspaper attack was such that it would support "any program that may be approved by the full Committee." This estimate proved delusive, but the Justice Department promptly studied the committee's complaints, which Lamb had presented in an ably drafted memorandum, and then moved at once to reform former policies.[7]

Initial study of the committee's findings led to an almost immediate decision on O'Brian's part to abolish the former practice of reviewing and approving trade association proposals. Justice Department files for August 1929 provide a glimpse of the new Antitrust Division chief as actually somewhat resentful toward Donovan who had left behind him the problem which O'Brian now had to clear up. Donovan was already established as a much-sought-after trade association specialist, a "lawyer's lawyer." In early August Donovan wrote to the Department asking for comment upon a code of ethics and articles of association shortly to be signed by the members of the Cement Institute. O'Brian was angered, penciling his pique on the correspondence. Had the Supreme Court not neglected certain facts in the celebrated *Cement* case of 1925 (a case similar in import to *Maple Flooring*), he wrote, it would have been decided otherwise. "My inclination is to decline to express any opinion whatever upon these articles. In view of what I have heard second hand of the operations of this group, the submission of their plans seems like audacity." The letter to Donovan was curt: "The policy of the Department . . . [is] to make no ruling on so-called codes of business ethics . . . and therefore we have no comment to make." Other associations met the same refusal. In October the Attorney General, speaking before the annual meeting of the ABA, formally terminated the previous practice of ruling in advance upon association plans. Requests for the customary review and approval were turned down. More importantly, the Department had realized that only affirmative action could reassert traditional antitrust standards. In a conference with Bloodgood in late October, O'Brian explained that Mitchell's speech meant that the Department would no longer allow such mechanisms as the Graham Plan to function in defiance of established principle. Alert associations received the message promptly. The Law Committee of the National Electrical Manufacturers Association, for example, decided, after hearing an account of their counsel's discussion with O'Brian in November 1929, that "the present attitude of the Department of Justice is somewhat different from the attitude of the Department of Justice under the previous Attorney General and that any extension of trade association activities beyond the limits of the decision in the Maple Flooring Case involved the willingness of those concerned to stand prosecution, either by indictment or by suit in equity." [8]

The NCF leaders were jubilant. Enforcement in these terms would shake the feeling of security which pervaded much of the trade association world and bring into sharp focus the need for antitrust revision. Now was the time, Bloodgood told Lamont, to bring "conservative leaders in both business and labor together and to agree upon some program of constructive legislation which will help to ameliorate the conditions that are bound to follow through enforcement of the Anti-Trust laws." [9] This forecast that a more orthodox standard of enforcement would stimulate a more widespread demand for antitrust revision from businessmen was correct. The effect was not immediate, however, partly because, despite the occasional scares of an impending "trust-busting" crusade which, reflected in the business press, rippled more than once through the New York trade association community, the Justice Department proceeded very deliberately if not cautiously, following Mitchell's address in October 1929, against cartelistic trade associations. [10] The cumulative effect over the next three years was profound, however, as one by one—often with long intervals between the public initiation of a new case—many of the most notorious of such organizations (some of whose programs had, initially at least, been approved by Donovan) were attacked, in nearly every case with prompt success. Even more upsetting for trade associations was the conflict between the FTC's trade practice code and the Justice Department which broke out in the fall of 1930. The clash ended in wholesale revision of the codes during 1931 and a mounting realization among associationists that hopes of antitrust relaxation from this quarter had been destroyed.

The Justice Department's caution and deliberation were reflected in the slow development of the Bolt, Nut & Rivet Manufacturers' Association case. Allegations against this association and its Graham Plan had precipitated the Department's rejection of the Donovan policies; yet when O'Brian, in December 1929, had in hand the conclusions of the investigation he had ordered, additional months were consumed in determining what remedy to use. O'Brian found the Bolt Association protected by a web of protective obstructions. In the first place, the Department had approved the Graham Plan in 1927. Although the Department's present analysis found the Bolt Association's program illegal, partly on the basis of practices which had not been revealed at the time of the approval, still it was clear that the program's key element had been revealed: the practice of agreement between manufacturers not to sell except to approved wholesalers. Nevertheless, in the Attorney General's mind, the fact of prior approval formed a barrier to strong action. Mitchell initially questioned whether the association's members should simply be given an opportunity to withdraw from the plan upon notification of the Department's attitude. To O'Brian, the finding that the association was "notorious and apparently has given considerable encouragement to other similar organizations" was controlling, and Mitchell's objections were overridden.[11]

Next came the fact that the Bolt Association had already been investigated by the FTC over the preceding year; in fact the Justice Department simply used the facts compiled in the FTC investigation in determining the Bolt Association's illegality. Though helpful in this respect, however, the FTC's prior involvement meant a conflict of jurisdiction. And since the FTC could settle the matter only by stipulation—in essence a promise unenforceable through injunctive proceedings and enforceable in any way only in roundabout fashion—the Bolt Association and the forces within the Commission friendly to it struggled tenaciously to move that body to assert priority. The association's counsel was James F. Burke, during the early months of the new Administration a White House aide, but now general counsel to the Republican National Committee and not at all reluctant to exercise any leverage his position might give him. Working, as O'Brian discerned, through William E. Humphrey, the staunch pro-associationist Coolidge had appointed to the FTC in 1925 to change its policies, Burke sought to pressure the Commission to assert priority. Burke and Humphrey both argued strenuously that a Justice Department action against the Graham Plan would be impolitic. "Such action," Burke urged, "would reflect both on the members of the Association and upon their counsel." It would also, Humphrey asserted, "put this Association in the position of having been investigated by the Federal Trade Commission and prosecuted by the Department of Justice and would give rise to the feeling that they were being persecuted." Both Humphrey and Burke, the latter accompanied at one point by eleven members of the association, argued finally the thesis which became a pervasive business refrain: "that the Department must permit business men to stabilize industry, and . . . that in the present state of business the Department should cooperate with the Administration in preventing any disruption of existing arrangements." [12]

Meanwhile, Charles J. Graham remained unreconstructed, was still informing his members that no proceedings would eventuate, still preaching to other industries the virtues of his plan and claiming it had government approval. Other associations were still enviously eying the Graham Plan and planning to adopt it. Finally securing agreement with the FTC, O'Brian proceeded to dissolve the Bolt Association through a consent decree, the method least painful for the businessmen. Burke was still unappreciative and obstructive, and the decree was not worked out and entered until June 1931. Of course, the proceedings were well-known to the business community during 1930 and conveyed the unpleasant message that the Justice Department was dissolving one of the most promising of the Coolidge-era experiments.[13]

In June 1930, another widely-publicized association, the Wool Institute was dissolved through an equity proceeding. In this case, the period between the initiation of investigation and the imposition of the decree was short and the impact of the decision clear. The institute's counsel commented that the Department had "gone further" in construing Sherman Act limitations upon associations than in the past, while *The New York Times* recorded the conviction of "legal circles" in New York that the *Wool* decree signaled a tightening of enforcement. Associations would "be subjected to a much closer scrutiny," and "many of the practices" which they believed "to be entirely within the law and in step with the spirit of co-operation in business would go by the board." [14]

The evaporation of the "new spirit" of the later 'twenties proceeded farther in September 1930 with the finalization of the decree in the California oil refineries case. The case for a time interfered with the market-control practices of the industry, but the real casualty was the trade practice codes of the FTC. Numerous complaints in 1930 convinced the Department that the West Coast refineries had agreed to restrain trade and were using certain provisions of the trade practice code of the API to implement the conspiracy. Ringleaders were leading filling station operators to believe "that the Federal Trade Commission has affirmatively approved both price fixing and the allocation of customers." The FTC had approved the existing code in August 1929, but closely similar models had been under consideration for several years and, in the case of the California refiners, in use. In the approval of the code, the Justice Department had played only a minor role. Early in 1929, in fact, Donovan's assistants had told the API representatives that certain provisions of the code would have to be tested in court if adopted. Told of the industry's plans to present the code to the FTC in a trade practice conference, the Justice Department had agreed to take no action until after the conference, and then not until after discussing the situation further with the industry. In separate contacts with the California refiners, the Department had been assured the code would not be put into effect. Only with the flood of complaints which came in the fall of 1929 did the code again come to the Department's attention.[15]

O'Brian responded to his investigator's findings by authorizing presentation of the case before a grand jury, implying a criminal prosecution would be used to break up the conspiracy. O'Brian and John Harlan Amen, the Special Assistant in charge, believed there had been blatant price-fixing and an element of fraud in that, a year earlier, counsel for the California refiners had told the Department the code would not be used. At this point occurred the first of a series of interventions by the Attorney General which progressively tied O'Brian's hands. Overriding O'Brian's objections, Mitchell agreed to let the oil men defend themselves in conference. According to their representations, Mitchell said, the chief officials of the companies had not known of the wrongdoing; besides, the Department had to keep in mind that the Administration was working with the West Coast oil men, as well as others, to secure an oil conservation program. Though this did not justify law-breaking, "it does form a reason why we should give careful consideration to any contention by the oil interests that they should be given an opportunity to correct any illegal practices they may have developed" before indicting them. This conference of January 23, 1930, resulted, not in the dropping of the case, but in the substitution of civil for criminal proceedings. The oil men probably had some influence, too, upon the decision made shortly after the conference to redraft the bill of complaint in the case to eliminate explicit reference to the national trade practice code of the API. A wish not to clash too publicly with the FTC, however, was probably the operative factor in the decision.[16]

Privately O'Brian was less tender of the Commission's sensibilities. Three times during the coming year—in conference with the full Commission in February; in a talk with its chairman, Garland Ferguson, in June; and in a strongly worded letter in December—O'Brian protested that certain articles of the approved code could readily be, and were being, interpreted as sanctioning practices which actually were illegal. Realizing that many other codes contained articles open to the same criticism, a majority within the Commission favoring a general review of codes took shape in March 1930. William E. Humphrey, appointed in 1925 to consolidate Republican control, evidently now feared the Commission had gone too far, and pressed his colleagues for a prompt review and revision of the codes. The Commission's announcement of its intention to inspect and revise codes dismayed the associations which had already obtained or planned to secure the benefits of a trade practice conference. An organization calling itself the Congress of Industries, composed of trade associations which had received FTC approval for a code, immediately formed for defense. The group's meeting in late September 1930 revealed clearly that such associations believed the Commission already had approved rules which limited competition far more than traditional concepts of "fair competition" allowed, and definitely had been expected to move toward establishing these concepts in court. Outspoken warnings of demoralization and disaffection among associationists if the plan should be carried out reached Hoover immediately. "The central points which I desire to emphasize with the President," wrote an attorney for several associations, seeking a meeting which was granted, "are that any attempt . . . to recall or to revise the Trade Practice Conference Rules would be a source of much disturbance and discouragement in trade and industrial groups and that any publicity concerning such an attempt would be most unfortunate for his Administration." Abram F. Myers, chairman, in the fall of 1930, of the Standing Committee of the Congress of Industries, insisted that the threatened revision had "plunged the whole question of industrial cooperation through trade association activity into hopeless confusion." Myers as a Commissioner in the late 'twenties had probably played the key role in moving the FTC's code approvals in the liberal and legally questionable direction they had taken. He regarded himself as a Hoover confidant. Politically, he wrote, "It seems a pity that so many *unnecessary* things should happen at a time like this." Even though the FTC was an independent agency and Hoover could not logically be held responsible for its new policy, the effect had "not been to make lighter the burdens of the Administration." [17]

The Commission seemed paralyzed. During the summer of 1930 most of the codes received an initial revision, but division within the Commission and pleas from the Congress of Industries for hearings and postponements forestalled issue of even one revised code during 1930. If there had been any inclination to stall the revisions indefinitely, perhaps O'Brian's continued protests against the oil code stiffened the Commission's resolve. O'Brian was discouraged to find in the fall of 1930 that the decree the Department had imposed upon the California refiners was defective. The failure openly to condemn the relevant articles of the FTC-approved code and the decision instead merely to specify the refiners' illegal activities in general language had left open a way for them to continue the practice through which they maintained their market agreement. This practice was the concerted refusal to sell gasoline to dealers who failed to observe refiners' posted prices. Forbidden in general terms under the decree, the practice was in effect re-established indirectly by the refiners' invoking of Article Four of their approved code. O'Brian's pressure forced the Commission's hand. On January 30, 1931,

Garland Ferguson, whose term as FTC chairman had just ended, and one of the agency's two Democrats, suddenly pushed hard for a new and more thoroughgoing theory of revision—the Commission should not approve any rule which it could not enforce under the law of fair competition. Approval of unenforceable rules, even though seemingly innocuous, must "inevitably result in the approval of some agreements that under the circumstances are illegal." Without accepting Ferguson's procedure in principle, the Commission applied it by adopting a new code for the petroleum industry, completely gutting the old code O'Brian had complained of so bitterly.[18]

The oil men proved impregnable, however. First winning directly from the FTC a stay of the effective date of the revised code, API representatives then obtained intervention from higher authority. The Department of Commerce was anxious, institute representatives learned in March, to serve "as friendly intermediary to adjust [the] Institute's differences with [the] Trade Commission code of practice for marketing refined petroleum products." This mediation probably decided the fate of the code, though the oil men fought resourcefully on their own, at one point arguing so persuasively that the Justice Department had originally approved the code that Commissioner Humphrey hurried to O'Brian to ask whether the Justice Department would be embarrassed if the code were revised! In June the Commission restored the original code with minor changes. O'Brian was furious. "Rule 17," he told the Attorney General, "has been systematically used as a disguise for the violation of the Sherman Act in California and the Coast states, in Texas, Florida, New York, Massachusetts, and probably elsewhere." All this had repeatedly been told to the Commission, and yet the code had been restored. "In my judgement it will be impossible in a criminal prosecution to convict the companies of violating the Sherman Act if they make a pretext of acting under Rule 17 and Rule 4, and that as a practical matter it is impossible to enforce the Sherman Act by civil suit on complaints against price fixing while these rules remain in force." Mitchell vetoed O'Brian's plan to protest the FTC's decision. The Commission could hardly shift again, he noted, and in any case one of the rules had been changed slightly making it a little less offensive. "However," he concluded with what must have been his compelling reason for inaction, "the oil industry is in such a deplorable condition, and the prices at which oil is being sold are so excessively low, that I have serious doubt whether it is advisable to pay any attention to approval of these rules at this time." If strong evidence of a refiners' conspiracy turned up, prosecution might be in order. But O'Brian felt his hands tied by the code, as he had said. Despite continued complaints and investigations, there was no further attempt to enforce the Sherman Act in this industry. Meanwhile, according to a Department attorney, the code prevented unfair competition in California (and probably elsewhere) as the refiners defined it: "all that competition which takes business away from the major companies, or hinders them in maintaining *their* price schedules, or is carried on contrary to their policies and practices." [19]

The fact of Commerce Department intervention, and of Attorney General Mitchell's restraint of O'Brian, implies that the decision to treat the API code liberally was made by the President himself. Other codes had been handled less gently. In the weeks before and after the oil code restoration, member associations of the Congress of Industries received back their codes, all significantly revised, with the most useful sections, from the business viewpoint, excised or expressed in carefully guarded and legally appropriate language. Stung by the favoritism for the oil code which they perceived in the Commission's actions, leaders of other trade practice code industries blamed Humphrey and promised to fight his confirmation for a new term, to which Hoover had announced his appointment on June 30, when the Senate convened. Through him, it was alleged, Hoover was responding to the oil industry's plight. Opposition to Humphrey's appointment already was intensive. Arthur Fisher, a representative of a Chicago law firm which managed the affairs of many trade practice conference associations, told Hoover in June that "the reappointment of Commissioner Humphrey would hasten [the] collapse" of the trade practice conference movement "which is now on the verge of liquidation and has already been abandoned by a large if not the larger part of the industries originally participating in it." Undeterred, Hoover had reappointed Humphrey. The Congress of Industries abandoned hope of salvaging the codes through presidential intervention and turned to the new session of Congress for a legislative remedy. This animus against Humphrey was, in fact, misdirected. Though Humphrey had, during mid-1930, pressed for prompt revision, his principles of revision were less strict than those which Ferguson proposed in January 1931 and which, with Humphrey opposed, a majority of the Commission in effect accepted the following March when a second and more stringent revision of the codes began. Humphrey did vote for restoring the original oil code, but it was Charles H. March, not Humphrey, who voted with Commissioners Charles W. Hunt and Ferguson to make possible the emasculation of all the other codes which Ferguson had demanded.[20]

Why did Hoover, as certainly appears likely, intervene in the spring of 1931 to bring about restoration of the oil code? The step implied the end of Justice Department attempts to police the marketing of gasoline, made the execution of a consistent antitrust-enforcement policy impossible, and exposed the Administration to harsh and apparently justifiable charges of favoritism from all the other trade practice conference associations. The step was extraordinary but in keeping with the development of Administration policy toward the oil industry. From the beginning of his tenure, Hoover had moved progressively toward support of more direct methods for controlling petroleum production; by 1931 he found that vigorous enforcement of the antitrust laws against the marketing end of the oil industry was incongruous when efforts were being made to restrict petroleum production. In 1929 Hoover had urged the oil states to adopt uniform unitization laws, a conservation proposal which held out some hope of more restricted production. Apparently earnest and serious in offering it, Hoover ought to have known the proposal was foredoomed.

Hoover has been severely criticized for offering his solution against a background of affronts to the sensibilities of oil men and oil-state politicians. At the very outset of the new Administration, Secretary of the Interior Wilbur had withdrawn all public oil lands from entry in an effort both to conserve oil and to draw attention through a dramatic gesture to the pressing need for a general oil conservation program. This action had angered oil men, especially those in the Rocky Mountain states where the order had a relatively significant impact. Oil-state governors protested angrily and, it can be argued, were put into an uncooperative attitude by the Administration's precipitate action.[21] A second affront, if it can be so characterized, occurred in March when representatives of the API came to Washington to attempt to secure FOCB endorsement for a production-restriction agreement which a substantial part of the industry was prepared to put into effect. The step was bald effrontery, the oil men acknowledging that the FOCB had no power to relax the antitrust laws but stating that, if the Administration, through an FOCB endorsement were to support the agreement, the courts might accept the agreement if it were attacked, and knowing that it had been endorsed by the Administration, the Attorney General would be unlikely to attack it in the first place. When the oil men's delegation, led by C. B. Ames, general counsel of the Texas Company, appeared before the FOCB on April 4, they were met with a blunt rejection put in terms which to Ames meant that the Attorney General was accusing them of seeking an "immunity bath." Ames's blustering denials merely underscored the truth of the Administration's analysis.[22]

But neither of these episodes at the beginning of the Hoover presidency destroyed the likelihood of the oil conservation proposal's winning acceptance. It was the proposal's moderation, the fact that it was addressed primarily to oil conservation rather than to restricted production, that it would be an extremely difficult and lengthy process to apply effectively, which explains the oil industry's lack of interest in it. In the present context, however, the point requiring stress is that Hoover, in making his proposal, had acknowledged that the normal working of the competitive process was not an adequate means of securing good performance in this industry. Once affirmed, the acknowledgement made it difficult wholly to reject other, more drastic departures from the competitive framework, both in this industry and in other "national resource" industries in which the case could be argued that competition led not merely to low profits but to wasted resources as well. The proposal of 1929 set Hoover on a road toward later cooperation in some degree with oil industry production-restriction programs. During 1929 and 1930 most of the oil-producing states strengthened or adopted prorationing schemes in an effort to raise oil prices. Discovery, and wide-open operation, of flush pools in Texas and Oklahoma threatened during 1931 to subvert these programs entirely, but the governors of these states resorted to martial law in the latter part of 1931 to control production, while the legislatures sought to formulate more effective control measures which also could secure support in state and federal courts. More importantly, an interstate agreement executed late in 1931 fixed an overall production limit and apportioned quotas for each of the oil states. These correctives slowed oil output during 1932, raising oil prices considerably above the record lows of 1931.[23]

Hoover participated at certain points in this drama, although he appears to have retained a genuine repugnance for production control as such, despite the extremely low petroleum prices of the depression years. Cooperation with state production-control programs was tolerable, but he continued to shy away as much as possible from oil industry proposals for direct inter-producer production-limitation agreements. "Any convention of oil men," he commented dourly to Secretary Wilbur in 1930, "will result merely in a desire on their part to have legalized some control which is illegal, otherwise they would do it themselves."

During 1930 the Administration took three steps in support of state efforts. The FOCB began publication of periodic reports of actual production and expected demand, complete with exhortations to the producers voluntarily to tailor output accordingly. These reports began in April 1930 and continued until 1933. Begun at the request of the API, the reports were initially prepared by a "Voluntary Committee on Petroleum Economics" and published by the board "merely as an expression of opinion by gentlemen having no official connection with the Board." Beginning in April 1931, however, Commerce Department officials served on the Voluntary Committee, giving the reports a more official character, as the industry recognized. The reports served as a basis for interstate agreements on relative shares of a reasonable total output. In a second step the Administration played the leading role in bringing the flush pool at Kettleman Hills, California, under control. Much of the land involved was still in federal hands, and Wilbur was able to bring about unitary operation. Output was then controlled in accordance with the California regulatory policies. In a third action the Administration, through the FOCB, urged the states to strengthen their production-control agencies and to join together through an interstate compact to apportion state quotas.[24]

The Administration's most dramatic entry into the situation came in 1931. One barrier to producers' cooperation with the attempts of the oil states to control output was the large-scale importation of crude oil by east coast integrated companies. Petroleum extractors in Texas and Oklahoma resented continuing importation of oil while they were attempting to cut domestic production. Oil-state congressmen pushed for an oil tariff in the 1930–31 session. The FOCB responded with a legislative proposal for empowering the FTC to limit imports through prorationing. The question became extremely important in February and March 1931 as output from the flush East Texas field began to flood the market. On March 1, the oil-state governors meeting in Fort Worth wired Hoover to urge a conference of oil-importing companies to achieve the desired cutback. But Secretary Lamont had already initiated the conversations with these companies which led in March to their agreement to reduce imports by twenty-five per cent. Lamont worked with J. F. Lucey of Dallas, a leader of independent petroleum-producers in Texas, who in return for the import reduction of the majors attempted to bring about restriction of the East Texas field through agreement of the operators. Hoover believed that Texas Governor Sterling had little real intention of curbing East Texas production and thus moved directly to mediate between importers and western oil-producers. For a few months the importers maintained their cutback, but their cooperation was not easy to maintain. The "agreement made with the large importers early in the year to curtail imports . . . has been continued on rather an indefinite basis depending upon extent of control of proration in this country," Lamont wrote in July. Lucey's attempt to control East Texas was at one point close to success, but it failed and the import agreement lapsed—although it appears that Lamont secured its renewal during the fall of 1931 and at least part of 1932, after state prorationing became more effective.[25]

During these critical months when state efforts to curb production broke down, Hoover seriously considered a scheme which was as bold in conception as it would have been illegal in execution. Late in June, API representatives approached Lamont with a plan for a five-man committee to draw up a definite method for pro-rata cutbacks for all producing units. Personnel would have to be men of the highest standing, such as, the oil men suggested, Owen D. Young. But Calvin Coolidge they thought indispensable. No other "disinterested private citizen . . . would serve equally to impress the public." Hoover at once commissioned Edward Clark to sound out Coolidge, who apparently flatly declined to participate. As Clark elaborated on the scheme for Coolidge, it would have been an extension of Lamont's efforts, an attempt to forge an agreement between western independents and importers for cutbacks. Clark thought the scheme rather nebulous and legally quite dubious. Hoover, he said, "felt that any combination which would bring the operators together for the time being was worth while even if later it seemed advisable to dissolve it because of possible conflict with the Anti-Trust law." Attorneys in the Justice Department would have agreed with Clark's point about conflict with the law. Earlier, they had noted the illegality of the agreement among importers which Lamont had brought off in March. The Attorney General had promptly informed them they were mistaken.[26]

All these events—the oil code restoration, Lamont's negotiations, the Coolidge scheme—speak to one point: Hoover's determination, during 1931, to assist the stabilization of the oil industry despite antitrust limitations. At one point, in considering the API proposal for a board of prominent men to effectuate control, the President actually seemed prepared to go the limit, to arrange for a nationwide production-restriction agreement, using the board to sway public opinion. Afterward, there is no evidence he again considered going so far. In fact, Administration involvement in the oil situation retreated after the summer of 1931 as state control programs became relatively more effective.

Did this pattern of behavior betoken an impending general relaxation of antitrust policy? In at least one other industry a similar pattern can be perceived. In 1930 Hoover established the Timber Conservation Board, patterned upon the FOCB. The Secretaries of Commerce, the Interior, and Agriculture manned the board, together with several industry leaders, including William Ritter, long a resourceful partisan of antitrust revision. Hoover charged the board with developing a program of "private and public effort, with a view to securing and maintaining an economic balance between production and consumption of forest products." Among its activities was a periodic report, begun early in 1931, of timber production. These bulletins offered calculations of what percentage cut in stocks on hand of the different types of lumber would achieve "balance" between production and consumption and urged every timber producer to reduce his output by the recommended proportion. The bulletins obviously were apt instruments for implementing restrictive agreements among producers, though it is impossible to know whether they did serve that purpose. Certainly, the lumbermen appreciated the potential, at least. As Wilson Compton, secretary of the National Lumber Manufacturers Association and a member of the board, said of the reporting system, "it has become . . . the focal point around which to secure the balancing of production and consumption." [27]

Two other industries benefited from Administration stabilization efforts in which it may be argued that antitrust relaxation was selectively applied. In one case the dispensation was brief, if it was actually given. It occurred in late 1930 when William J. Donovan pleaded with Lamont to call a conference of the cement industry. "SITUATION SERIOUS LEADERS OF INDUSTRY FEEL MUST BE DEALT WITH IMMEDIATELY BUT YOUR ASSISTANCE ESSENTIAL," he wired. "Orderly curtailment program regulation production difficult of fulfillment because of fear federal attack. . . . Unless such orderly program agreed upon drastic price cuts with disorderly curtailment inevitable lower wage scale serious unemployment and danger of receiverships. . . . Your intervention may be able to prevent general demoralization of industry." The conference apparently was held, on December 5, 1930, and was understood, it appears too, by the industry to be a "stabilization" conference. No record of what took place has yet been discovered, but indications are that Lamont was planning to stop a price collapse if he could. The other case of this type was practically coterminous with the Hoover Administration. It consisted of support given to the CTI's efforts to introduce the "55–50" plan of limiting day and night shifts in the industry, and to eliminate women and children from employment on the night shifts. Clearly, Administration policy was to foster the industry's efforts to "stabilize" (i.e., restrict production) by supporting voluntary agreements among the industry's members. But since the institute chose as its method the introduction of reasonable limitations upon hours of labor, a very indirect method for limiting production, it is very doubtful whether the Administration should be charged with another instance of selective antitrust relaxation.[28]

It would be mistaken to magnify these activities and assign them an undue significance. Hoover cooperated with state prorationing programs, eased up on antitrust enforcement in the marketing of petroleum products, sanctioned Lamont's continuing attempts to secure agreement of the majors to import reductions, and for a few months even backed an attempt to control the East Texas field through producers' agreements. However, sponsoring a national production agreement was never more than a proposal entertained at the worst point of overproduction. Generally, Hoover firmly rejected market agreements for the industry. The antitrust relaxation granted the timber industry was minimal. Businessmen who were conscious of the special treatment given the oil industry, notably the members of the Congress of Industries, called it favoritism and did not regard it as a sign of an impending moratorium on antitrust enforcement. The main thrust of antitrust policy in 1930 and 1931 meant, both actually and in the impression businessmen received, that if trade associations attempted to maintain concerted market behavior by using codes, reports, check-ups, and other paraphernalia of cartelistic associationism, the odds were fair they would be prosecuted, or at least have their plans frustrated as happened in the case of the trade practice conference industries. Even more impressive than the FTC code revisions during 1931 were the Justice Department activities of March 1931 dissolving the Bolt Association and initiating the *Sugar Institute* case. Unlike all the other trade associations against which O'Brian brought an action during 1930 and 1931, the Sugar Institute fought back, through the press and in a long court-battle which made the case one of the classics of antitrust history. In its propaganda the institute emphasized that its program had been approved under Donovan and that, through it, all associations were being prosecuted. The government's suit would determine "whether a great industry shall have the right to apply that self-regulation which appears to be the only alternative to unfair and ruinous competition." *The New York Journal of Commerce*, which followed enforcement activities very closely during the spring of 1931, found that the Justice Department was causing a shake-up among associations, and abandonment of practices attacked in the *Bolt* and *Sugar* cases, and saw forming a trend away from the tightly-knit "institutes" which had proliferated during the previous five years. *Manufacturers Record*, the chief business journal of the South, found that "Business at the moment, in search of a clearer course ahead, is disturbed over government anti-trust activities directed against various trade associations." *The New York Times*, responding to Mitchell's public statement that hard times did not justify "winking" at antitrust violations reported that, according to "trade association circles," the Justice Department's failing was that it did not "apply the rule of reason in establishing restraint of trade. If the Department were 'reasonable' a change in the trust laws would be unnecessary." [29] Perhaps this—the rising frequency and intensity of calls for antitrust revision—provided the best indication that the Administration's enforcement efforts were having a significant impact.

What were Hoover's motives in renewing legal restrictions on market agreements, in reversing his predecessor's policies of encouraging the legalization, by degrees, of quasi-cartelistic associationism? Ideological and principled motives aside, the political factor in itself can provide a near-adequate explanation. His championing of legitimate associationism had always rendered Hoover vulnerable to critics who tried to link him with exploitative combinations. Hoover shrank from such charges during the Commerce years; it is only natural that his sensitivity on this score would increase during the presidential period. The NCF's warnings of an impending political attack in early 1929 hastened an evaluation and revision of the previous Administration's antitrust-enforcement policy which would have had to come, for the same political reasons, at some point. Politicians were still, in 1930 and 1931, as in the 'twenties, aware of the potential of "trusts" as an issue. Wright Patman, for example, speaking on the floor of the House in the spring of 1930, condemned the API code which the FTC had recently approved, and accused the Attorney General, by tolerating it, of "encouraging monopolies and trusts and . . . assisting in the destruction of independent business." The Justice Department worked hard to mute critics such as Patman. In this case an investigation and a suit were already underway. But Senator King's outburst in 1931 against the cement industry provides an instructive example. King's charges of price-fixing quickly triggered an investigation of the Cement Institute. There was no court action, but only because a successful outcome was so uncertain. Though suspicious of certain practices and of the fact of uniform prices, investigators found no effective proof of conspiracy. This circumstance, together with the fact that the Cement Institute membership had fallen off drastically during the depression, persuaded the Department's attorneys that the evidence did not warrant a suit. King, informed of all this by O'Brian in a telephone call, was at least partially mollified and contented himself with lecturing the antitrust chief on Hoover's wishes. The senator, he informed O'Brian, had "told the President a few days ago how greatly he was exercised over the conduct of the large trusts and expressed hope that the President would not lend his influence to support their endeavors, and had received assurance that he would not." [30]

NOTES

1. FOCB, *Report to the President, September 1926, Part I*, pp. 14–16, 18, 24. Hoover press statement in Oil file, HHPP. Hoover's 1929 position was framed so as to avoid conflict with the antitrust laws. The FOCB's 1926 position may have implied liberalization but, nevertheless, was based upon the concept of unitary pool operation, not upon production quotas.

2. On Donovan's estrangement see Christian Herter to Hoover, March 6, 1929, Justice Department file, HHPP. Thacher to Hoover, April 17, 1929; Hoover to O'Brian, August 30, 1929; O'Brian to Hoover, September 4, 1929, *ibid.*; Butler to George E. Akerson, April 20, 1929, Antitrust Laws file, *ibid.* Hoover memo, "Reasons Donovan was not taken into Cabinet," Donovan file, *ibid.*

3. Hoover to Mitchell, March 23, 1929, Oil file; to Mitchell, September 18, 1929; Mitchell to Hoover, September 20, 1929, Justice Department file, *ibid.*

4. Hays to Hoover, August 28, 1929, Antitrust Laws file, *ibid.* Hays's pious assurances are of course self-serving. In his conference with Hoover the previous day, Hays had sought support for his plea that the criminal prosecution of the movie producers then in progress be put in abeyance and a civil suit initiated to settle the legal issues involved. Hoover sent Hays to speak to O'Brian, perhaps approving, certainly not rejecting, Hays's plea. The point remains, however, that Hoover chided Hays about the alleged misbehavior of the producers and implied that this sort of criticism of big business caused problems for his Administration.

5. "Industry and the Federal Laws" (an O'Brian speech before the Associated Industries of New York), *The Monitor* (August 1930), 56–57.

6. Bloodgood to Ralph Easley, April 6, 1929 (enclosing a copy of Bloodgood to Lamont, April 6, 1929), April 13, 1929; Lamont to Bloodgood, December 28, 1928, box 66, NCF Papers.

7. Bloodgood to Levy, June 17, 20, 1929; to Lamont, January 20, 27, July 5, 1929; to Easley, June 17, 22, 1929; to Lamb, June 26, 1929; Lamont to Bloodgood, June 20, 1929; Lamb to Bloodgood, July 3, 1929, all in General Correspondence, *ibid.*

8. Donovan to O'Brian, August 9, 1929; memo for Russel Hardy by O'Brian, n.d.; O'Brian to Donovan, September 3, 1929, file 60/10/5, RG 60. See file 60/44/0, *ibid.*, for December 1929, for another example of a refusal to consider association codes; also O'Brian to Benjamin Kirsch, October 22, 1929, file 60/0, *ibid.*

Bloodgood to Lamont, Matthew Woll to Lamont, November 1, 1929, box 66, NCF Papers. Bloodgood to John G. Hervey, November 2, 1929, General Correspondence, *ibid.*

National Electrical Manufacturers Association, Executive Committee, "Minutes," November 15, 1929, NEMA office, New York City.

9. Bloodgood to Lamont, November 11, 1929, General Correspondence, NCF Papers.

10. *New York Journal of Commerce*, February 1, March 18, 1930. O'Brian to Mitchell, January 7, July 7, 1930; Justice Department press release, May 15, 1930; John T. Flynn to Mitchell, June 30, 1930, file 60/0, RG 60.

11. O'Brian to Edward McCulloch, July 9, 1929; memos for O'Brian by James L. Fly, December 16, 1929, January 3, 22, 1930; memo for Attorney General by O'Brian, January 16, 21, 1930, file 60/126/13, RG 60.

12. O'Brian to Garland Ferguson, January 27, 1930; to Attorney General, January 27, February 7, 26, 28, 1930; memos for files by O'Brian, February 6, 20, 1930, file 60/126/13, *ibid.* See Edward T. Clark to Coolidge, May 24, 1929, Clark Papers, for a glimpse of Burke in the White House; also H. G. Warren, *Herbert Hoover and the Great Depression* (New York: Norton, 1959), p. 57.

13. Felix Levy to James L. Fly, March 3, 1930; S. F. D. Meffley to Russel Hardy, March 13, 1930; Burke to O'Brian, May 6, 1930, file 60/126/13, RG 60.

14. File 60/167, *ibid.*, for the investigation. The files of the National Wool Manufacturers Association, Merrimack Valley Textile Museum, have some records of the Wool Institute and of the case. For the comments, see *New York Times*, June 28, July 6, 1930. Another Donovan-approved plan, that of the Industrial Alcohol Manufacturers Association, also was broken up during the summer of 1930, but in this case O'Brian was satisfied with simple abandonment of the illegal practices. See O'Brian to William C. Cannon, June 7, July 7, 1930; memo for O'Brian by James L. Fly, July 25, 1930, file 60/105, RG 60.

15. Donovan to William R. Boyd, December 27, 1928; memo for Donovan by Horace R. Lamb, January 4, 1929, of conference with API representatives, file 60/57/32; memo by Lamb, February 1, 1929, file 60/57/35; John H. Amen to O'Brian, December 27, 1929, file 60/57/35, RG 60.

16. Memos for Attorney General by O'Brian, December 6, 1929, January 20, February 5, 1930; memo for O'Brian by Mitchell, January 21, 1930, file 60/57/35, *ibid.*

17. O'Brian to Ferguson, December 16, 1930; Ferguson to O'Brian, December 20, 1930; memo for Attorney General by O'Brian, January 6, 1931, file 60/57/32, *ibid.* FTC, "Minutes," February 12, 14, 26, March 3, 14, 17, 24, 1930.

Louis E. Flye to Hoover, August 22, September 3, 1930; Lawrence Richey to Flye, September 16, 1930; Myers to Richey, November 19, 1930, Federal Trade Commission file, HHPP.

18. FTC, "Minutes," April 9, May 23, 26, June 3, 16, 23, 30, September 26, October 13, November 14, December 3, 12, 1930; January 30, 1931.

19. Julius Klein to William R. Boyd, March 21, 1931; Boyd to Klein, March 25, 1931, file 82272/1, RG 40. Boyd to FTC, February 5, 1931; memos for Attorney General by O'Brian, March 25, July 21, 1931; memo for O'Brian by Mitchell, July 21, 1931; memo for O'Brian by W. B. Watson Snyder, December 9, 1932; O'Brian to Snyder, December 12, 1932, file 60/57/32, RG 60.

20. Clipping from *National Sphere* (July 1931); Fisher to Hoover, June 17, 1931, Federal Trade Commission file, HHPP. *New York Journal of Commerce*, August 10, 1931; *New York Times*, August 16, October 4, 1931. The record of the September Congress of Industries meeting is available in ATAE, *Proceedings* (1931), pp. 103–53. FTC, "Minutes," February 20, March 10, 17, 19, 30, 31, May 5, 1931. Ferguson's formal proposal was rejected at the February 20 meeting of the Commission, but was accepted in effect during the revision of March and May, with the aid of March's vote.

21. Gerald Nash, *United States Oil Policy: 1890–1964* (Pittsburgh: University of Pittsburgh Press, 1968), pp. 101–105. Mark L. Requa to Lawrence Richey, May 15, June 12, 1929; "Memorandum by M. L. Requa, re: Colorado Springs Petroleum Conference," June 13, 1929; "Memorandum—June 24, 1929" by Requa, Oil file, HHPP.

22. Nash, *Oil Policy*, pp. 102–103. George Otis Smith to Ray Lyman Wilbur, March 18, 1929; Wilbur to Hoover, March 29, 1929; Mitchell to Wilbur, March 29, 1929; to Hoover, March 30, 1929; "Record of Meeting between Federal Oil Conservation Board and Representatives of the American Petroleum Institute," April 4, 1929; all in Oil file, HHPP.

23. Useful accounts appear in Nash, *Oil Policy*, Chapters 5 and 6, and in Donald C. Swain, *Federal Conservation Policy: 1921–1933* (Berkeley: University of California Press, 1963), pp. 62–66. Nash is highly critical of Hoover, mainly on the grounds that he left the oil industry and the oil-producing states to solve the problem of overproduction largely by themselves. The focus here is different as my purpose is to ascertain to what extent the Administration consented to, or arranged for, a weakening of antitrust norms for the industry, and this naturally leads to a stress upon actions of this kind. The difference in focus accounts in part for Nash's conclusion that Hoover's leadership was weak; but I feel, nonetheless, that he has underestimated the Administration's role in the evolution of state and interstate controls before the New Deal.

24. See Hoover to Wilbur, December 5, 1930, Oil file, HHPP, for the Hoover comment. For the work of the Voluntary Committee, see the FOCB materials filed, unaccountably, in box 1979, Records of the Timber Conservation Board, RG 151. Included here is correspondence of E. S. Rochester, the FOCB secretary, on the committee's periodic reports. Also, the correspondence in box 7, Record Group 232, Records of the Federal Oil Conservation Board, National Archives, especially Rochester's letter to Wilbur, April 1, 1932. See Ely Northcutt to Wilbur, October 26, 1931, box 13, Ray Lyman Wilbur Papers, Hoover Institution, Stanford University, for a discussion of the way in which the Voluntary Committee's estimates were serving, by that time, as the basis for the allowable monthly production under the agreement between the major oil states.

Swain, *Conservation Policy*, p. 64, has a succinct account of the Administration's success at Kettleman Hills. Secretary Wilbur's letter of May 11, 1929, to Mark Requa, box 27, Wilbur Papers, explained the purpose of the Administration's efforts: "If we can show in Kettleman [that] field drilling and waste can be controlled [through unitary operation] then [a] compact for such purposes will look more reasonable." Through 1929 the Administration continued to press the states to enact parallel conservation (unitary operation) laws. (See undated "Suggestions With Reference to an Interstate Oil Conservation Compact," mimeographed, *ibid.*) By 1930 it was acquiescing in and seconding the movement toward simple prorationing within and among the states. Two press releases, of March 13 and August 7, 1931, in the Oil file, HHPP, review the main lines of Administration policy during 1930 and 1931.

25. Presidential press statement, March 13, 1931; governors to Hoover, March 1, 1931, both in Oil file, HHPP. Lamont to Richardson Pratt, February 3, 1931; to Lucey, June 24, July 9, 1931; Walter Teagle to Lamont, June 16, 1931; Lucey to Lamont, July 6, 1931, Lamont Papers, RG 40. Lamont to Addison H. Gibson, June 25, 1931; to R. G. Brown, July 23, 1931; file 82231/17; to Robert C. Stewart, March 20, 1931, file 82272/1, *ibid.*

26. William R. Boyd to Lamont, June 25, 1931, *ibid.*; Lamont to Lucey, June 29, 1931, Lamont Papers, *ibid.* Clark to Coolidge, June 25, August 17, 1931, Clark Papers. Israel B. Oseas to O'Brian, March 25, 1931; memo for Oseas by Mitchell, n.d., file 60/01/6, RG 60.

27. See "Third Executive Meeting of the TCB," November 25, 1931, box 1974, General file, RG 151.

28. Blaine C. Smith to Lamont, November 6, 1930, file 82276/21, RG 40. Smith to Donovan, November 15, 1930; Donovan to Lamont, October 20, 21, November 18, 1930; Smith to Lamont, November 24, 29, 1930; Lamont, wires to cement producers, December 1, 1930, Lamont Papers, *ibid.* Galambos, *Competition and Cooperation*, pp. 141–57, 167–69, has an account of the Administration's relationship to the CTI which utilizes the archival sources thoroughly. Galambos emphasizes the latitude of the Administration's policy. One explicit piece of evidence favoring my view is that the Commerce Department lawyers believed the "55–50" plan was not an illegal restraint of trade. See William L. Cooper to Malcolm Kerlin, March 8, 1930, file 87481, RG 40.

29. *The Sugar Institute, Inc.: Its History, Policies and Achievements* was circulated widely by the institute as a rebuttal to the government's charges. *New York Journal of Commerce*, March 31, April 1, 6, 7, 18, 1931. *Manufacturers Record*, 99, No. 16 (April 16, 1931), front-page editorial. *New York Times*, April 16, 19, November 29, 1931.

30. Congressman L. T. McFadden to William Mitchell, May 31, 1930; Mitchell to McFadden, June 7, 1930, file 60/57/0. Memo for O'Brian by George P. Alt, May 20, 1931; memo by O'Brian, June 22, 1931, file 60/12/0, RG 60.

7

The Emergence of Antitrust Revision as a Major Political Question: Leadership, Themes, and Issues, 1930–1932

THE DEPRESSION plus the revival of anti-cartelist government policies stimulated businessmen to raise the antitrust-revision question to the level of an urgent public issue by the fall of 1931. The two major business organizations, however, were notably tardy in assuming leadership of this development, and it was left to others to take the initiative. During 1929 and 1930 the ABA attracted more attention to the issue than did either the NAM or the Chamber of Commerce. Public hearings the Association's Commerce Committee held in New York in April 1930 received some press attention, as did the committee's report, in the fall to the ABA convention, which argued for the wisdom of the administrative amendment proposal the Association had endorsed the year before. Neither of the major business groups had come this far by the end of 1930. At its convention in the fall of 1929, the NAM approved formation of a committee to study the antitrust problem and it was appointed during the following winter. But it had no visible impact, not even at the NAM's October 1930 convention, where reference to the revision issue was minimal. During 1930 the Chamber of Commerce, at its May convention, in its journal, and otherwise, seemed to be studiously ignoring the antitrust question altogether.[1]

The slow response of these major organizations to the new economic and legal setting probably did not greatly lag the rate of increase in the intensity and generality of business interest in revision. Certainly, there was a step-up in the pace of agitation by men and industries already established as revisionist leaders during the year following the market crash and of pronouncements by prominent new additions to their ranks. Bernard Baruch, for example, now openly, in May 1930, denounced as "public lunacy" the Sherman Act's prohibition of regulated production of a business "system which periodically disgorges indigestible masses of unconsumable products" and called for cartelization of industry under the aegis of a "court of business" composed of top-ranked business leaders.[2]

But the NCF's experiences during 1929–30, when it sought to develop support for revision, seem to indicate that, though steadily expanding, the intensity and breadth of that support among businessmen grew at a moderate pace. The Federation's activities illuminate several other aspects and problems of the developing revisionist movement and are significant enough to deserve a recounting.

The Federation's antitrust committee moved revision a step forward during 1929 by torpedoing the Graham Plan and trade association schemes of similar pretensions. The committee faction responsible for this maneuver consisted of Wheeler P. Bloodgood, J. Harvey Williams, and Ralph Easley. Backers of radical Sherman Act revision, this group opposed another committee luminary, Rush Butler, chairman of the ABA's Commerce Committee, who was committed to his group's administrative amendment proposal. In December 1929, the argument between the two viewpoints came to a head when the Federation's Committee on Anti-Trust convened in New York. Butler's appeal for endorsement of the administrative approach was overwhelmed, rhetorically at least, by Bloodgood's argument for amending the norms, not merely the procedures, of the Sherman Act. The current economic decline, he argued, together with the Justice Department's new, tougher stance on antitrust violations, would generate the necessary support. Ellis Searles, a UMW official and, with Matthew Woll, organized labor's representative on the committee, seconded Bloodgood. There was a widespread feeling that "the Sherman Law has outlived its usefullness, that it is archaic and . . . as Mr. Bloodgood said, [this feeling] is more pronounced now than it was a few months ago. If ever there was a time when a frontal attack should be made on that law, it seems that now is the time to do it and make this as strong as possible." Not at this meeting but within a few months, the majority of the committee accepted the thesis that prevailing conditions were compressing history and had brought within reach a change previously relegated to the long run, and they endorsed a specific formula for reworking and emasculating Section 9, the heart of the Sherman Act.[3]

Justification for this step was provided by certain ideological convictions which the members of the radical group within the committee shared. J. Harvey Williams, known and respected throughout the business community as an authority on antitrust and a leading protagonist of revision, capsulated this ideology in a letter to Bloodgood in February 1930. "From an economic standpoint it is my deep rooted conviction that the absence of cooperative price fixing to the extent of affording protection for the sellers . . . is mainly responsible for . . . [an] antisocial sequence of events now plainly discernible." Williams, generalizing from the experience of industries with which he was personally connected, perceived a business world consisting of disorganized sellers (e.g., the auto-parts makers) and organized buyers (the auto producers). "Increasing mergers" were resulting from the "inability to pit mass selling against mass purchasing." This merger movement was leading to "loss of independence and initiative of the independent proprietor; loss of his job by the middle aged victim of merger in the interest of so-called efficiency; loss to the local communities through absentee direction and financing; regulated monopoly in industry; a Frankenstein that cannot be unscrambled; and lastly, a country like Germany so 'efficient' that it is better to live somewhere else." That the NAM and the Chamber of Commerce were behindhand in championing revision and would not even consider substantive revision, Williams attributed to the grip in which they were held by the modern "consumer philosophy," which tested economic outcomes solely in terms of efficiency. That other organizations were considering less fundamental proposals for revision was, for Ralph Easley, another member of the committee's radical group, a sign that they lacked frankness and simple courage. Without losing sight of the perspective emphasized by the AFL representatives on the committee—that cartelization would promote a more stable economy—the inner circle which dominated it saw the problem as a moral one above all.

Williams and his like-minded committee colleagues saw themselves, then, as defenders of independent business, of the corporations ranging from small to substantial (as was Williams' own firm) which individually were, in their view, threatened from without by highly concentrated industries exerting leverage as buyers, from within by mergers. As will be seen, leaders of high concentration, giant-firm industries also, depending upon circumstances, would strongly favor legalization of cooperative market control, though their perspective and rationale were different. There were, of course, certain industries which, for reasons arising from their place in the structure of the industrial system, opposed the cartel philosophy. The NCF committee, in fact, harbored an articulate representative of this opposition, William T. Grant, the chain store magnate. Distribution chains were, of course, a rapidly growing sector of the economy during the 'twenties, overriding small distributors by the score—the latter attempting to fight back in many states and localities with drives for anti-chain legislation. The rapid growth and marked success of these chains had made leaders such as Grant content with market enterprise in its current form and very defensive about suggestions for tampering with outcomes a competitive order was producing. To the last, Grant pressed the grossly heretical view upon his colleagues that relative efficiency should determine the economy's structure. "If we were all doctors here," he said at the committee's April 1930 meeting, "and someone came along with a panacea which made all the people well without doctors, we ought to be thrown out of a job and made to work at something useful." Unimpressed, the committee, leaving intact the Sherman Act protections for independent enterprise against monopolistic competitors, adopted an amendment for Section 9 of the Act which would make "restraint of trade" (i.e., interfirm agreements) illegal only when, after "due regard [had been given] to the interests of producers, workers and consumers," it was found to be "to the detriment of the public." [4]

It was agreed to work out a companion bill along the lines of the ABA's measure, but no time was to be lost in pressing forward the formula for substantive revision. Arthur E. Foote, the committee's executive secretary, was assigned the task of mobilizing trade association support for the measure; Matthew Woll was to arrange for publicity support for it through AFL periodicals; and Bloodgood and Woll together were to secure Hoover's and Lamont's endorsement and find a Congressional sponsor for it. In trying to move so far so fast, the committee overreached itself. Foote found it impossible to obtain the cooperation of any of the major business organizations. His request for a place on the program at the forthcoming Chamber-of-Commerce-sponsored conference of trade association leaders was too late to be honored. Turning next to the ATAE, whose president, M. L. Heminway, was a personal friend, Foote initially received an encouraging response, then a cold rebuff when the organization's executive committee decided that the committee's propaganda "should be approached by your organization to each Association interested," not through the ATAE. Without sponsorship of an organization well known to trade association leaders, Foote found his work slow going. It was easy enough to circularize trade associations, but building up contacts and active support proved difficult.[5]

Similarly, though Bloodgood and Woll secured an interview with Hoover in late April, and though Bloodgood thought the meeting "most satisfactory" and believed "the administration will support the legislation recommended by the National Civic Federation," the consequences were nil. Efforts to launch the bill in Congress met with no success. "Although," Easley informed an interested businessman in June 1930, "the situation in Washington seems ripe for just such a proposal as the Committee has in mind, it came to the conclusion, after conferring with political leaders, that no consideration would be given to the Trust question in the present session on account of the excitement over the tariff." The attempt to introduce a bill would be postponed to the next session.

Despite these setbacks, the committee remained optimistic. Bloodgood in July felt that his group's amendments "have gained many adherents who were luke warm, in doubt or actively opposed prior to the break in the stock market and the general depression in business." After a summer lull, the committee enthusiastically turned to preparations for the new session of Congress. A plan to secure endorsement of their bill by leaders of both parties received a boost when John Jacob Raskob, Democratic National Chairman, showed interest in the measure. When the President in his Annual Message of December 1930, recommended a Congressional investigation into the effects of the antitrust laws, the committee's members felt the "current real live agitation of this subject," had "taken fresh impetus" such as to carry revision to a successful culmination.[6]

Hoover's recommendation to Congress in December 1930 almost certainly did advance the cause of revision, but its major effect probably was to raise hopes Hoover had no intention of requiting. Hoover came closer to pushing revision during the fall of 1930 than at any point later in his term. In October, speaking before the AFL on economic disorganization of the bituminous coal and similar industries, Hoover had offered the reduction of "destructive competition" as a method for introducing more stable operations and employment. "It certainly is not the purpose of our competitive system that it should produce a competition which destroys stability in an industry and reduces to poverty all those within it. Its purpose is rather to maintain that degree of competition which induces progress and protects the consumer. If our regulatory laws be at fault they should be revised." Interpreted broadly, the AFL speech implied Administration support for a thorough overhaul of the antitrust laws. But Hoover intended the narrow construction, making this plain in his December message to Congress. The recommendation was for a study of the laws as they affected the natural resource industries only; and it was to "destructive competition" only in such industries that the attention of Congress was directed. Hoover's intention evidently was to conciliate the business leaders and groups which, since he had entered office and especially since the crash, had been pressing him to approve and lend respectability to antitrust revision. Rush Butler had kept Hoover abreast of the ABA's proposals; NCF leaders had, of course, repeatedly presented their ideas; spokesmen for the oil and timber industries had tenaciously urged their case for special consideration; and many others had added their own demands. The Hoover recommendations in October and December may have given an impetus to revisionism for a time, but the President's influence afterward, to the dismay of the movement's leaders, would go mostly toward braking it.[7]

Despite the awakening by early 1931 of the NAM and the Chamber of Commerce to the mounting interest in revision among their members, the NCF still for some months into 1931 could claim leadership toward that goal. Its leaders represented their organization as the only major business-oriented body which was so constituted as to attract public confidence, and they sought support from all sides—from corporate magnates as well as small businessmen—as the only group in a position "to go ahead and accomplish the desired results." Easley, Bloodgood, and Williams attempted to persuade the House Judiciary Committee chairman, George S. Graham, to hold hearings on the antitrust question. Graham, at the NAM's request, had already introduced a resolution authorizing hearings, but by late February had despaired of securing a favorable report from the Rules Committee. The Federation again put off hope of Congressional action to the next session and made plans for a trade association conference which could certify the broad appeal which, it felt, existed for its proposal. From the late spring through the early fall, Foote labored to secure a large attendance for the projected conference. At some intervals discouraged, he nevertheless benefited from what, to the associations most anxiously awaiting the emergence of strong leadership toward revision, appeared still to be the unenergetic evolution of the NAM and the Chamber of Commerce positions. Flint Garrison, for example, director of the Wholesale Dry Goods Institute, a leader of the Congress of Industries and an influential member of the fraternity of trade association executives, agreed to attend Foote's proposed "Congress" because he thought "the recent [May 1931] meeting of the Chamber of Commerce in Atlantic City was so barren of results." By the early fall Foote believed he had succeeded. Commitments to the conference were "so numerous and favorable that I wish to suggest that the time and place" for the meeting should be fixed at once.

The Federation, however, had already played its leadership role to an end. The conference melted away as the Chamber of Commerce, especially, moved rapidly in the fall of 1931 toward formal adoption of a relatively strong proposal for revision. Though the Federation dropped entirely out of sight afterward, its contribution to the development of the revision movement should be judged significant. Between 1928 and 1931, it circularized trade associations several times with reports and questionnaires; and in 1929 and 1930, its antitrust committee provided a common meeting ground for the country's most prominent trade association attorneys. Two of these, Butler and Bloodgood, were committee members, and others—including Gilbert Montague, Benjamin Javits, and Benjamin Kirsch—were often invited to join in the debate over the proper approach to revision. Perhaps the most important contribution was the assist the NCF gave in 1929 to the renewal of an orthodox antitrust policy.[8]

From the standpoint of our understanding of the revision movement, there is still another contribution. The Federation's repeated, large-scale, and apparently random appeals to trade associations for information or support constitute a very crude polling process which provides specific though imperfect evidence concerning what types of industries were most eager to support antitrust relaxation. In a previous chapter the responses to the questionnaire of 1928–29 were used to locate industries of this sort; replies to the invitation to the 1931 conference serve the same function for the later year. An affirmative response to the invitation certainly signified that the replying industry wished to take positive action to advance antitrust amendment, though not necessarily through the substantive NCF proposal. There are many difficulties in using the responses, however. A negative reply to the invitation would not necessarily signify an absence of active support for revision; it could reflect a lack of faith, for example, in the effectiveness of the Federation's plan. Moreover, the Federation's records leave unanswered some questions as to how many associations were sent invitations and whether those thus "polled" were selected entirely at random. The apparent procedure was that Foote and his workers simply used standard lists of national trade associations, such as those provided by the Commerce Department, as the basis for their invitation list, and mailed to a large number (at least 350) in a more or less random fashion. The positive replies to the invitations can, therefore, be used as a crude index to the type of industry most actively supporting legislative revision in 1931.

The businessmen who, in the later 'twenties, initiated the movement for revision, said they represented the industries afflicted by "profitless prosperity," and there were many indications, including the fact that the NCF questionnaire of 1928 tended to elicit more interest from such industries, that this was so. This tendency seems to have extended into the depression years when revisionism quickened; that is, those industries which entered the depression with a history of relatively low profitability in the 'twenties were most likely to lend positive support to proposals for revisionist legislation. I have attempted to test this thesis using the NCF acceptance list. The task is somewhat complex because the tools available are clumsy. It is not difficult in most cases to pinpoint with relatively secure accuracy the industry products each listed association represents. But the chief reference on individual industry profits in the 'twenties, Epstein's *Industrial Profits*, can be used only with great caution in assigning each industry a profit rating. Epstein distinguishes only 73 manufacturing industries, some of which are composites, combining what are really distinct industries if the concept—the only one relevant here—of an industry as a group of firms selling a closely similar product is applied. Epstein's study gives the annual, 1919 through 1928, profits for each of 73 "industries." Two rates are given for each, one for the larger, another for the smaller, firms. The rate for the large firms is regarded as more reliable and significant because it is more representative and is based on the same group of firms for each year. Epstein ranks the industries in terms of the ten-year average (large corporations) profit rate for each. In this ranking, toilet preparations stands at the top with a ten-year average rate of 31.6%; toys with a 15.9% rate marks the bottom of the first quartile; mining machinery with 13.6% is the median; factory machinery with 10.7% marks the bottom of the third quartile, and meat packing with 1.9% brings up the rear. Table II gives several characteristics for each of the NCF positive respondents. The leading product is given for the industry each association represents, unless, as is usually the case, this is clear from the association name itself. Next is given the number of the Epstein industry which most closely corresponds to each association industry. In the last three columns are given, respectively, the following characteristics of each association industry: whether its product is differentiated or not, its degree of market concentration, and its quartile profitability ranking, as determined by the corresponding Epstein "industry." [9]

As Table II shows, the majority of positive respondents to the NCF invitations were industries whose profit record in the 'twenties was relatively poor. Of the 75 entries, 61 correspond to, or form part of, the 37 composite "industries" Epstein ranked below the median for all 73 of his groups. It is important to make clear that this does not mean these 61 industries had a profit history of less than "average" merit, or that they ranked behind some absolute number of corporations in profitability. Epstein's ranking of the 73 "industries," which makes possible the ranking in Table II of the NCF positive respondents, simply shows that there was a hierarchy of profitability in the 1920s and indicates the relative standing in that hierarchy of the various industries.

That businessmen in industries with a relatively poor profit history in the 'twenties would have led in agitating for legalized cartelism after the depression's impact was felt is a plausible hypothesis and is lent credibility by Table II. One could expect that in such industries the ideology of cartelism would have taken a deeper root as its members found they could not hope to attain, even during a period of sustained national economic growth and prosperity, the levels of return enjoyed by the relatively more successful profit-making industries. Such businessmen would have been more likely to respond to the weakening prices and profits of 1930–32 with demands for price protection than would men from more fortunate industries, and less likely to acknowledge the possible drawbacks and risks in antitrust relaxation.

A history of relatively low profitability seems to be the relevant characteristic which nearly all the Table II industries share. They vary considerably in degree of concentration. If they tend to be producers' goods and undifferentiated consumers' goods industries, this is logically a factor which helps account for the weak-profit history. What causes this inter-industry variation in profitability is not a question within this book's scope. But the impression gained from studying Epstein's ranking is that the older industries, most of them producers' goods and undifferentiated consumers' goods, tended in the 'twenties to fall behind the rapidly growing newer industries, whether these were producers' goods or, as was often the case, differentiated consumers' goods industries. Presumably the less profitable industries suffered from excess productive capacity and a market which grew only in proportion to the growth of the whole economy, while the more profitable industries often enjoyed relatively rapid market growth and, if selling differentiated goods, benefited from their ability to minimize price competition by emphasizing supposed

TABLE II
Trade Associations Supporting 1931 NCF Revision Movement

Epstein No.	Trade Association	Industry	Product Type — Prdcrs.	Product Type — Consumers Un	Product Type — Consumers D	Conc. Class I	Conc. Class II	Conc. Class III	Conc. Class IV	Profit Quartile I	Profit Quartile II	Profit Quartile III	Profit Quartile IV
1	Am. Bakers Assn.				√				NRC 250	√			
29 (5)	Am. Brush Mfrs. Assn.		√	√	√			NRC 254				√ S	
45	Am. Ceramic Soc.		√						NRC 250			√	
45	Am. Face Brick Assn.		√						NRC 250			√	
46	Am. Glassware Assn.		√	√	√	TNEC 455				√			
49 / 70	Am. Inst. Steel Const.		√					NRC 250					√
49 / 50 / 51	Am. Iron & Steel Inst.		√			TNEC 462	T N E C 447						√
40 / 101	Am. Petroleum Inst.	extraction & refining	√	√									
41	Am. Pharmaceutical Mfrs. Assn.		√						NRC 250	√			

Association	No.	References
Am. Supply & Machinery Mfrs. Assn.	58 59 65	Conc 212–13 ✓ ✓s
Asbestos Brake Lining Assn.	62	✓ TNEC 452 ✓
Asphalt Inst.	40	✓ TNEC 447 ✓
Associated Cooperage Industries of Am.	29	✓ Conc 202 ✓
Associated Leather Gds. Mfrs. of U.S.	23	✓ ✓ NRC 250 256 ✓
Associated Tile Mfrs.	45	floor tiles ✓ TNEC 453 ✓ ✓
Chemical Fire Extinguishers Assn.	74	NRC 252 ✓ ✓
Common Brick Mfrs. Assn.	45	✓ NRC 250 ✓
Concrete Reinforcing Steel Inst.	49 70	TNEC 465 TNEC 463 ✓ ✓
Copper & Brass Research Inst.	68	✓ ✓
Cordage Inst.	17	✓ Conc 199 ✓
Dairy & Ice Cream Machinery & Supplies Assn.	59	✓ ✓ Conc 89 ✓
Educational Jewelers Assn.	69	✓ ✓ NRC 254 ✓ ✓

TRADE ASSOCIATION	Epstein No.	INDUSTRY	PRODUCT TYPE Prdcrs.	Consumers Un	Consumers D	CONCENTRATION CLASS I	II	III	IV	PROFIT QUARTILE I	II	III	IV
Envelope Mfrs. Assn. of Am.	32			✓				Conc 204					✓
Felt Floor Covering Assn.	54			✓		NRC 252			Conc 213			✓	
Food Service Covering Assn.	59 67		✓						Conc 214			✓	✓
Foundry Supply Mfrs. Assn.	59		✓			TNEC 454							✓
Glass Containers Assn. of Am.	46		✓						Conc 210	✓			
Gray Iron Inst.	49		✓			NRC 252							✓
Gypsum Assn.	102		✓				Conc 211					✓	
Hack Saw Mfrs. Assn.	65		✓									✓	✓
Independent Petroleum Assn. of Am.	101 44	petroleum extraction	✓			TNEC 440			✓				
Industrial Alcohol Inst.	38		✓					TNEC 423				✓ ✓	
Inst. of Margarine Mfrs.	11				✓								

Organization	No.	References / Notes
Machinery Bldrs. Soc.	59	212
Malleable Iron Research Inst.	49	Conc 210; Conc 197
Malt Inst.	9	
Manufacturing Chemists Assn. of U.S.	38, 44	TNEC 442
Millers Natl. Federation	2	NRC 250
Motor & Eqpt. Mfrs. Assn.	62	automotive parts; Conc 216
Natl. Assn. of Farm Eqpt. Mfrs.	70	TNEC 466; NRC 250
Natl. Assn. of Furniture Mfrs.	28	NRC 250
Natl. Assn. of Ice Industries	11	Conc 201
Natl. Assn. of Lace Curtain Mfrs.	21	NRC 256
National Assn. of Leather Glove & Mitten Mfrs.	23	
National Assn. of Ornamental Iron & Bronze Mfrs.	49, 70	TNEC 464
National Assn. of Safe Mfrs.	70	NRC 252
National Assn. of Wool Mfrs.	15	TNEC 433
National Battery Mfrs. Assn.	53	TNEC 467

TRADE ASSOCIATION	Epstein No.	INDUSTRY	PRODUCT TYPE Prdcrs	Con-sumers Un	D	CONC. I	CONC. II	CONC. III	CONC. IV	PROFIT I	PROFIT II	PROFIT III	PROFIT IV
National Building Granite Quarries Assn.	102		✓						✓ TNEC 420			✓	
National Canners Assn.	6			✓	✓		✓				✓		
National Coal Assn.	100		✓	✓					✓				✓
National Crushed Stone Assn.	102		✓				✓					✓	
National Fertilizer Assn.	9		✓					TNEC 444				✓	
National Hardware Assn. of U.S.	64		✓				✓	NRC 250			✓		
National Hosiery & Underwear Mfrs.	20			✓	✓				NRC 250		✓		
National Lime Assn.	48		✓						NRC 256				✓ S
National Luggage & Leather Gds. Mfrs. Assn.	23				✓				NRC 256				✓
National Lumber Mfrs. Assn.	25		✓						TNEC 437				✓
National Petroleum Assn.	40, 101	extraction & refining	✓	✓				TNEC 447	C				✓
National Sand & Gravel Assn.	103		✓						✓		✓		

Organization	No.											
National Slate Assn.	102						√					
National Standard Parts Assn. (automotive parts)	62	√				Conc 216 / NRC 254					√	√ s
National Wood Heel Mfrs.	29	√								√		
North Carolina Pine Assn.	25	√						TNEC 437			√	
Northern Hemlock & Hardwood Assn.	25	√						TNEC 437 / Conc 606			√	√
Oakum Inst.	21	√									√	
Sporting Arms & Ammunition Mfrs.	63		√								√	√
Stearic Acid Assn.	38	√				TNEC 440					√	
Structural Clay Tile Assn.	45	√				TNEC 454 / TNEC 424					√	
Sugar Inst.	11			√		TNEC 444						√
Synthetic Organic Chem. Mfrs. Assn.	38	√									√	
United Wall Paper Crafts of N. A.	33				√		NRC 254				√	√
Window Glass Mfrs. Assn.	46	√			√				√			
Writing Paper Mfrs. Assn.	32	√	√	√			TNEC 439					
Industrial Truck Assn. (hand trucks, etc.)	59	√		√	√			Conc 213			√	
TOTALS	75	53	12	10	12	17	20	26	6	7	31	31

product superiority and so on in the manner Chamberlain first described in *Monopolistic Competition*. The degree of concentration tends to be high in the high-profit industries; indeed, one gains the impression that sheer degree of concentration played the main role in determining the high ranking of many industries (e.g., cement) in the first quartile of Epstein's ranking, though it is evident, from the position of iron and steel, petroleum refining, and numerous others in the ranking, that concentration was not always a sufficient guarantee of relatively high profitability.

What Table II suggests is that the movement for antitrust revision during the depression depended for its cutting edge upon the industries which were relatively "depressed" for a considerable length of time. Almost entirely absent from Table II are the fabled industries which played so great a role in remaking the American economy during the 1920s, the automobile and electrical manufacturing industries. Other booming industries, high in Epstein's ranking but absent from Table II, which enjoyed a new prominence during the 'twenties thanks to the emergence of modern advertising methods and to the availability of higher disposable income were toiletries, patent medicines, newspapers and periodicals, cleansing preparations, packaged foods, toys, tobacco and confectionery. Heavily represented in Table II, on the other hand, the assumedly active prorevisionists, are older, sometimes (but more often not) highly concentrated, but in almost every case undifferentiated, product industries such as lumber, factory machinery, oil refining and extraction, iron and steel, textiles, grain milling, and builders supplies. The NCF data suggest, in other words, that revisionism did not have universal backing; rather, that only one segment of industry, spurred by specific experience and needs, led the way while the other looked on.

The foregoing description of the NCF's attempt to seize control of the widespread but diffuse revisionist sentiment among many businessmen between 1929 and 1931 reveals the same themes or tendencies one discerns in observing the major business organizations as they came to grips with the antitrust question in 1931. As they were for the NCF, the major problems would be how radical the approach to revision should be, and by what arguments cartelism could be made to appear to be in the public interest. An additional question would be the role of the natural resource industries. Lumber, petroleum, and bituminous coal, because of their relative size and importance and their unceasing agitation for relief from anti-cartel restrictions, were potentially major factors in the movement for general antitrust relaxation. But at times they seemed inclined to choose the option in which they would ignore the question of generalized revision and seek relief only for themselves.

In the tenor of this discussion over goals and strategy, there always appears an element of anxiety, a fear that raising the antitrust issue involved serious risks. Clearly implied is a recognition that, no matter how forthrightly or ruthlessly organized business might pursue its traditional negative goals of balanced budgets and the shifting of taxation to consumers, increments to the price and income leverage businessmen already enjoyed could be approached only with the utmost finesse. Such gains might be successfully challenged by counter demands.

Considerations of this kind prolonged to remarkable length the debate over what kind of antitrust amendment to seek and at times led business leaders into waffling on the issue and rhetorical absurdity.

Both the NAM and the Chamber of Commerce gave antitrust relief a new priority rating around the beginning of 1931. After a year of quiet consideration, the NAM's antitrust committee tentatively endorsed the administrative amendment approach in December 1930 and, through James A. Emery, persuaded the House Judiciary Committee's chairman to introduce a resolution mandating hearings on the proposal. In a more decisive step, the NAM called together a sizable number of corporate leaders and business attorneys the following March in what was publicized as an attempt to consolidate businessmen behind a single proposal and to mobilize broad support for it. The conclusions of this conference on goals and strategy governed the NAM's handling of the issue for many months. The Chamber of Commerce initiated its own move toward advocacy of antitrust relief when, in January 1931, Julius Barnes secured from that body's Board of Directors, of which he still was chairman, authorization to set up a Committee on Continuity of Business and Employment. Nearly a year elapsed before the committee's report was completed, submitted in a referendum to the Chamber's members, and adopted, but from the time of its May 1931 meeting, the influence and prestige of the Chamber and its Committee on Continuity grew rapidly among revisionists.[10]

The first question both groups had to resolve was how radical a departure from the traditional legal norms they should propose. James Emery, the NAM's persuasive and even domineering counsel, judging that the limited reforms of the administrative approach to revision were best, had "jammed" (according to a somewhat prejudiced witness, J. Harvey Williams) a recommendation for it through his group's antitrust committee at the end of 1930.[11] The NAM's Anti-Trust Conference held a few months later confirmed this recommendation and left a record of its proceedings, unusually frank because it was never intended for publication, which illuminates the reasons why Emery and the NAM chose for so long a time to sponsor a cautious and limited proposal for antitrust revision.

The NAM leaders had invited to the conference more than seventy-five business leaders who had achieved note in some way as knowledgeable on the subject. Of these, approximately twenty-five appeared for the one-day session, most of them leaders of prominent national corporations or top-ranked trade association lawyers. Emery, in an opening address and throughout the conference, often seconded by others, set forth the case for the administrative approach and against any attempt to tackle the antitrust laws through substantive change. In the first place, administrative amendment was realistic. Discussion in the previous weeks with Representative Graham and with others had made it "very plain to us who were in contact with Congress in discussing this matter that there was among those whom I would call the more thoughtful and conservative members of Congress a strong opposition to any consideration of substantive amendment, but they were willing to consider and discuss administrative amendment. So that was a practical situation to be confronted." An attempt to secure substantive change, Emery said, would arouse fierce opposition. As Silas Strawn, soon-to-be president of the Chamber of Commerce, said in seconding Emery, an attempt to repeal the Sherman Act or to amend it substantively would be "perfectly futile" and might result in "something a great deal worse." Emery's trump was the supposed certainty of government regulation of prices and profits if cartelistic practices were legalized openly through substantive amendment. This threat compelled a public conversion from more than one participant who had come, some of them as a result of contact with J. Harvey Williams, with a strong preference for revision which would more promptly and more certainly allow price-fixing. C. B. Ames of the Texas Company, E. M. Herr of Westinghouse, and others joined Emery in underscoring the dimensions of the danger.[12]

Administrative amendment was not merely the only practical course, Emery argued, but the one likely to secure cartelistic privileges within a reasonable period because it would encourage judicial revision of the Sherman Act. Gilbert Montague seconded Emery on this point. All agitation, all resolutions and assertions that business was being hampered and persecuted by the antitrust laws and its supposed uncertainties were to the good. The proposed tribunal to give advisory opinions and dispense immunity from criminal prosecution would have great "educational value." It would be a rallying point, a "flagstaff" upon which business would hang its grievances. "Public opinion will then begin to work, gentlemen," Montague concluded, and the courts would provide the desired latitude through reinterpretation. As Emery explained, too, the tribunal would be likely to have a sympathetic attitude, to encourage practices which the Supreme Court could not continue for very long to hold unlawful. Clinching the argument with predictions that the Court already was moving toward liberalization, that a well-managed brief would even then secure approval for production-restricting agreements in the natural resource industries, Emery carried the conference almost unanimously despite considerable initial skepticism that the administrative proposal might merely "deaden the nerves of Congress" and "postpone some real constructive action for a longer period of years." [13]

The NAM, chiefly through Emery, expounded the position taken by the March 1931 conference for over a year before beginning to shift to a more radical line. In frequent public appearances in print and in person, Emery stressed in particular the probability of business salvation through the courts. "No pending question," was his repeated message, "is more deserving of judicial answer than whether a rational plan of voluntary cooperation to relate supply to ascertained demand in a chronically overproduced industry, is an illegal restraint of trade or a legitimate promotion of commerce." [14]

For the first half of 1931 appearances were that the Chamber of Commerce would also hew close to the moderate line the NAM adopted. When the Chamber's annual meeting convened in May, the Committee on Continuity had as yet no contribution to offer, and consideration of the depression and of the antitrust laws came out of the usual sessions and resolutions. The solution mentioned most frequently was the administrative amendment proposal. A few voices at some of the round-table discussions were raised in advocacy of more thoroughgoing measures, but the meeting concluded by endorsing a proposal similar to the one the ABA and the NAM were supporting. When, shortly after the meeting, the Chamber's newly elected president, Silas Strawn, chairman of Montgomery Ward, indicated his own commitment to the administrative amendment approach, it seemed that the organization had finalized its position. An additional resolution of the annual meeting, however, authorized study of the various proposals made during the convention, and left the way open for further developments. This resolution and, undoubtedly, pressure from oil, coal, and lumber men persuaded the Chamber's directors to set up a Natural Resources Committee shortly after the convention. The resolution also, no doubt, fortified the Committee on Continuity to broaden the scope of its work beyond consideration of unemployment reserves to the broader question of stabilization through cartelization. [15]

By the fall of 1931, when the committee was preparing its report, the tone and the sheer amount of discussion businessmen and politicians were giving to the antitrust question had greatly enlarged. In September Gerard Swope offered his well-known proposal for trade association planning. Senator La Follette opened hearings on his bill for a National Economic Council in late October, providing a platform for business spokesmen such as Swope. Conferences on antitrust reform suddenly blossomed at major universities. The concentration of so much activity in the fall and early winter reflected the hope building up within the business

TABLE III

Participants in NAM, New York University Conferences
Members of Chamber of Commerce Committee, 1931

PARTICIPANT AND COMPANY	Epstein No.	INDUSTRY	PRODUCT TYPE — Prdcrs.	PRODUCT TYPE — Consumers Un	PRODUCT TYPE — Consumers D	CONCENTRATION CLASS I	II	III	IV	PROFIT QUARTILE I	II	III	IV
C. B. Ames (NAM, NYU) Texas Co.	40 / 101	gasoline, etc.	✓	✓				TNEC 447					✓
C. S. Anderson (NAM) Norton Co.	48	abrasives	✓				Conc 209			✓			
G. J. Anderson (NAM) Consolidated Coal Co.	100	coal	✓						✓				
Robert Ballantine (NAM) Hazel-Atlas Glass Co.	46	glass bottles and jars	✓			TNEC 455				✓			
G. S. Barnum (NAM) Bigelow Co.	17	carpets	✓		✓		NRC 250				✓		
N. D. Becker (NAM) Inter-type Corp.	55	type-casting machines	✓					Conc 213				✓	
J. R. Bell (NAM) Rollway Bearings Co.	65	roller bearings	✓				Conc 214					✓	
J. R. Boyd (NAM) API	40 / 101	gasoline, etc.	✓	✓				TNEC 447					✓
S. P. Bush (NAM) American Rolling Mill Co.	49	steel sheets, etc.	✓					Conc 210					✓

Name	No.	Product									
J. F. Callbreath (NAM) Am. Mining Congress	100 104	mining industries	✓					✓	✓		
C. H. Cashmore (NAM) Patterson Parchment Paper Co.	32	writing paper				TNEC 439	✓	TNEC 437 NRC 250	✓	✓	
W. Compton (NYU) Natl. Lumber Mfrs. Assn.	25	lumber	✓	✓					✓		
S. W. Cramer (C of C) Cramerton Mills	13 14	cotton textiles	✓							✓	
H. S. Dennison (C of C) Dennison Mfg. Co.	34	envelopes, wrapping paper, etc.	✓	✓		Conc 204			✓		
W. H. Eager (NAM) Whitman & Barnes, Detroit	65	drills, reamers, etc.	✓					Conc 212 Conc 213	✓		
P. O. Geier (NAM) Cinci. Milling Mach. Co.	59	factory machinery	✓						✓	✓	
E. L. Greever (NAM, NYU) Natl. Coal Assn.	100	coal	✓				✓		✓		
T. J. Hargreaves (NAM) Kodak	71	cameras	✓	Conc 217					✓		
E. M. Herr (NAM) Westinghouse	53	electrical eqpt., etc.	✓	TNEC 467–70							✓
W. D. Hines (NYU) Cotton Textile Inst.	13 14	cotton textiles	✓		✓			NRC 250	✓		
C. Kelly (NYU) Anaconda Copper	104	copper	✓		✓						
W. J. Kohler (C of C) Kohler Co.	64	plumbing supplies, fixtures	✓			Conc 209 211					✓

PARTICIPANT AND COMPANY	Epstein No.	INDUSTRY	PRODUCT TYPE Prdcrs.	Con-sumers Un	D	CONCENTRATION CLASS I	II	III	IV	PROFIT QUARTILE I	II	III	IV
P. W. Litchfield (C of C) Goodyear	24	rubber tires, etc.			✓	Conc 207							✓
H. C. McCormac (NAM) Va. Woolen Co.	15	wool cloth	✓					TNEC 433					✓
L. F. Sperry (NAM) Amer. Radiator & Standard Sanitary Corp.	52	heating eqpt., plumbing fixtures	✓					Conc 211			✓		
R. E. Tally (C of C) Un. Verde Copper Co.	104	copper	✓			✓							
M. Tibbetts (NAM) Packard Motor Car Corp.	62	automobiles			✓	TNEC 479				✓			
J. H. Williams (NYU) J. H. Williams Co.	65	tools	✓						Conc 212			✓	
J. D. Windsor (NAM) Borden Milk Corp.	5	milk, etc.		✓	✓				Conc 196			✓	
TOTALS	29		20	3	6	6	6	7	10	4	4	8	13

community that the time had come when Congress, about to meet for the long session of the Seventy-Second Congress, might seriously undertake review of antitrust matters.[16]

For the Chamber's committee, more radical solutions than before thought realistic now assumed political plausibility. The core of the committee's report recommended legalization of "agreements increasing the possibilities of keeping production related to consumption." Here definitely was frank advocacy of substantive amendment. Under direction of a supervising government body, perhaps the FTC, businessmen would enter contracts among themselves limiting an industry's production. The only power of the supervising agency would be to refuse to approve a contract. Open and direct, this proposal after a time aroused in its sponsors the same doubts and fears which still persuaded the NAM not to advocate substantive change. The Chamber was plainspoken in explaining and advocating the Committee on Continuity's proposal during the fall of 1931. But within a few months it began to retreat. By June 1932, H. I. Harriman, now president of the Chamber, was explaining that "it is not desirable that either the Sherman Act or the Clayton act be repealed or radically modified," that it was a question of the laws' lacking clarity, that a special tribunal was needed to advise businessmen in advance of execution of contracts and give them immunity from criminal prosecution. This retreat from the stand of the previous year was short-lived, but it did underscore organized business' grave reluctance, as late as the summer of 1932, to risk having Congress openly undertake revision of the substance of the antitrust laws. Still other major leaders betrayed the same reluctance. Gerard Swope's frequent presentations before Congressional committees and other public bodies during the fall of 1931 of his plan for stabilization crayfished awkwardly as to whether his program involved substantive legal change. If he acknowledged that his scheme required definite production-planning agreements, he implied that they actually were already legal in the eyes of the Supreme Court and suggested that something on the order of the ABA's proposal was all the situation required.[17]

A further and even more striking element of the restrained spirit in which business approached the revision issue during 1931 and much of 1932 was the frequent assertion that only voluntary agreements were contemplated. Harriman, speaking for the Chamber, stressed the point repeatedly and unequivocally. There was "no thought," he told the La Follette committee, that all companies "in a given trade should be forced into" contracts limiting production. "It is not thought wise for a moment that everybody in a given trade should be forced into the combination. That is to be left to the free will." The voluntary nature of agreements would "still leave the competitive factor a very important factor in determining the price level," Harriman explained, so that government regulation

TABLE IV

Trade Associations of the Manufacturing and Mining Industries Supporting the Nye Bills at the Hearings Early in 1932

TRADE ASSOCIATION	Epstein No.	INDUSTRY	PRODUCT TYPE			CONCENTRATION CLASS				PROFIT QUARTILE			
			Prdcrs.	Un	D	I	II	III	IV	I	II	III	IV
Asbestos Brake Lining Assoc.	62					TNEC 452						✓	S
Association of Mfrs. of Woodworking Eqpt.	59		✓					Conc 213				✓	
American Institute of Steel Const.	49 70		✓					NRC 250					✓
Chemical Fire Extinguisher Assoc.	74		✓			NRC 252					✓		
Common Brick Mfrs. Assoc.	45		✓						NRC 250			✓	
Associated Knit Underwear Mfrs. of Am.	19				✓				Conc 199	✓			
Amer. Assoc. of Creamery Butter Mfrs.	5			✓					Conc 196			✓	
Educational Jewelers Assoc.	69			✓	✓			NRC 254				✓	
Face Brick Assoc.	45		✓						NRC 250			✓	
Fan Belt Assn.	62		✓				Conc 216					✓	S

Association	No.	Industry	25	17	4	2	5	7	11	2	4	14	5
Feldspar Grinders Inst.	102								Conc 209			✓	
Independent Petroleum Assoc. of Am.	101	petroleum extraction	✓	✓								✓	✓
Jute Twine Inst.	17		✓								✓		
Millers National Federation	2		✓	✓	✓							✓	
Natl. Assoc. of Furniture Mfrs.	28		✓		✓			Conc 199 / NRC 250	NRC 250			✓	S
Natl. Crushed Stone Assoc.	102		✓	✓			✓	✓				✓	✓
Natl. Assoc. of Lace Curtain Mfrs.	21		✓	✓					Conc 201			✓	S
Natl. Battery Mfrs. Assoc.	53		✓	✓			TNEC 467			✓			
Natl. Fertilizer Assoc.	9		✓	✓				TNEC 444				✓	
Natl. Lime Assoc.	48		✓	✓				NRC 256					S
Natl. Paper Box Mfrs. Assoc.	31		✓	✓					Conc 204		✓		
Natl. Standard Parts Assoc.	62	automotive parts	✓	✓			Conc 216					✓	S
Ornamental Iron, Bronze & Wire Mfrs.	49			✓					NRC 250				✓
	70												
Steel Office Furniture Inst.	70			✓	✓	✓	TNEC 436 / NRC 254						✓
Natl. Wood Heel Mfrs. Assoc.	29		✓								✓		
TOTALS			25	17	4	2	5	7	11	2	4	14	5

would be unnecessary. Voluntary cartelism was easier to defend too in constitutional terms. "Involuntary restraint," as Emery piously asserted in October 1931, was "clearly oppressive and intolerable." The argument that involuntary adherence to agreements was desirable and necessary did enter the antitrust discussion during the winter of 1931/32 but only in an attenuated form. In December 1931 Senator Gerald Nye introduced a series of bills designed to revise and strengthen the FTC trade practice conferences which had been discredited during the previous year. Hearings during February and March 1932 revealed the Congress of Industries and its member associations as the inspiration for Nye's move. Though the Nye bills masqueraded merely as a means for resuscitation of fair trade practice codes, their actual effect would have been to expand the concept of "fair practice" until it included legitimate competitive practices. Selling below cost originally was prohibited by one of the bills, though Nye dropped the provision when its implications were exposed in the hearings. But other, such open-ended provisions remained; the bills, moreover, would have given immunity from Justice Department challenges to FTC-approved codes and would, finally, have made a code binding upon every member of the affected industry. Since the contemplated codes would ostensibly not have included price or production agreements, the universally binding aspect of the proposed codes seemed a mild form of coercion. Except in this apparently innocuous form, there were very few public defenders of third-party coercion in the debate over cartelism until much later. Charles R. Stevenson, one of the most successful trade association consultants and managers, acknowledged early in 1931 to Arthur Foote of the NCF that his notion that seventy-five per cent of an industry ought to have the right to impose controls on the "unintelligent minority" was "a very advanced step and that we probably could not hope to take any such step at this time." A year later and even months after that, Foote would have agreed that the proposal did "seem to be somewhat radical." Involuntary adherence to cartel agreements was rarely seriously advanced in public until very late in the debate.[18]

What justification to use in urging antitrust relief caused no dissension, though there were differences in emphasis. The Chamber of Commerce stressed the thesis that recovery and economic stability required a new program of social responsibility from business. The Chamber's production planning proposal in the fall of 1931 was only one element, albeit the central one, in the Committee on Continuity's report, which called upon industry to sponsor a national economic council to forecast future problems and recommend solutions to them and to adopt industry-wide insurance schemes, including unemployment insurance. Production planning itself was justified in terms, not of business' need for profits, but of its responsibility for maintaining employment. The original publicity

about the Committee on Continuity had mentioned only its responsibility for studying "employment stabilization." Julius Barnes, however,
had hinted to potential members as he recruited them that a show of
interest in unemployment would open the door to cartelism. "If a prac-
ticable plan of general assurances of continuity of employment, perhaps
underwritten by national trade associations, could be devised," as Barnes
told Roy Chapin, head of the Hudson Motor Car Company, in April
1931, "it seems quite likely that public sentiment would be more favorable towards uniform trade practices in various industries that would
eliminate much destructive competition, and provide a healthier basis
for industry." From this beginning the committee, encouraged by proposals made at the May 1931 convention and by suggestions from Chamber members during the summer of 1931, went on to devise the report
which proposed a new era of stability through planning and insurance,
all to be exclusively under business control. This "business commonwealth" viewpoint was not, of course, simply and only an ideological tool
for prying the public away from reliance upon the Sherman Act, though
it certainly was that. Gerard Swope echoed Julius Barnes when he discussed with his fellow electrical manufacturers the plan he had unveiled
for the first time in a radio speech two days earlier. Swope urged that
for business to plan for employee insurance and stabilization of employment would open the way to acceptance of planned production. "I
was hoping in my own mind that by taking those two major issues we
could tie to that a modification [of the law] which would give us more
latitude in doing what I think should be done." But the new eagerness
to assume the role of guarantor of employment and welfare which the
Chamber of Commerce and leaders such as Swope demonstrated resulted,
too, from the fear that Congress might begin to move toward putting the
national government into that role. Swope spoke of these fears when he,
in company with Chamber and NAM representatives, put on the record
of Senator Wagner's unemployment insurance hearings in the fall of 1931
his objections to government insurance schemes. "I think that industry
ought to take care of its difficulties and its problems. You see, the
moment government begins to help there is no economic restraint. You
vote money." But the connection between the business community's
antipathy for taxes (upon business), government doles, and social insurance, and its sudden (oral) willingness to accept responsibility for
planning a system of private social insurance, at precisely the time when
discussion of governmental action in the field was mounting, is obviously
more than coincidental.[19]

Every group agitating for revision employed the "business commonwealth" viewpoint, at least in the sense that it was affirmed that the
control of production and prices would guarantee stable employment
and wages. But no other group stressed the concept or extended its im-

TABLE V

Supporters of the Truce Plan, 1932

COMPANY	Epstein No.	INDUSTRY	PRODUCT TYPE Prdcrs.	Con-sumers Un	Con-sumers D	CONCENTRATION CLASS I	II	III	IV	PROFIT QUARTILE I	II	III	IV
J. Harvey Williams Co., N.Y.C.	65	tools	✓						Conc 212			✓	
C. K. Eagle & Co., N.Y.C.	16	silk cloth		✓			TNEC 432					✓	
Corticelli Silk Co., N.Y.C.	16	silk cloth		✓	✓		TNEC 432					✓	
Malcolm D. Whitman & Sons, N.Y.C.	65	tools	✓						Conc 212			✓	
The Elco Co., Bayonne, N.J.	57	boats	✓					NRC 250				✓	
Dowst Mfg. Co., Chgo.	72	novelties and toys			✓				NRC 256	✓			
Florence Pipe & Foundry, Florence, N.J.	49	cast-iron pipe	✓						Conc 210				
Louis F. Hall & Co., N.Y.C.	13	cotton	✓						NRC 250				✓
The Belden Brick Co., Canton, Ohio	14	textiles	✓					NRC 250				✓	
Red Lion Cabinet Co., Red Lion, Pa.	45	furniture ra-	✓						NRC 250			✓	
	28	dio cabinets			✓							S	

Company	No.	Product		Reference	
Winton Engine Corp., Cleveland	53	elec. engs. generators	✓	Conc 214	
Munsingwear Corp. Minneapolis	19 20	knit goods, swim suits, etc.	✓	NRC 250	✓
Magnolia Metal Co., N.Y.C.	68	bronze bearings, etc.	✓	TNEC 465	✓
Carry Ice Cream Co., Beatrice Creamery Co., Wash., D.C.	11-8 5	ice cream, butter	✓	NRC 254 256	✓
Poland Laundry Machine Co., Boston	59		✓	Conc 214	✓
Barbar & Ross, Inc., Wash., D.C.	49 70	structural steel fabrication	✓	NRC 250	✓
Albemarle Paper Co., Inc., Richmond	33	blotting paper, kraft paper	✓	TNEC 438 439	✓
John Lucas & Co., Phil.	39	paint and varnish	✓	NRC 250	✓
Duquesne Slag Products Co., Pitts., Pa.	70	blast furnace operations	✓	NRC 252	✓
National Bridge Works, Long Island City, N.Y.	49 70	structural steel fabric.	✓	NRC 250	✓
Montgomery Iron & Steel Co., Phil.	49 70	structural steel fabric.	✓	NRC 250	✓

COMPANY	Epstein No.	INDUSTRY	PRODUCT TYPE — Prdcrs.	Consumers Un	Consumers D	CONCENTRATION CLASS I	II	III	IV	PROFIT QUARTILE I	II	III	IV
Hercules Powder Co., Wilmington, Del.	44	explosives, gunpowder	✓			NRC 252							✓
Comet Rice Co., N.Y.C.	2	rice milling & pkg.			✓			NRC 254				✓	
Hamilton Sangamo Corp. N.Y.C.	74	clocks	✓					NRC 254		✓			
Chapman Slate Co., Bethlehem, Pa.	102		✓				TNEC 456					✓	
Botany Worsted Mills, Passaic, N.J.	13	cotton textiles	✓						NRC 250			✓	
Fayette R. Plumb Co., Phil.	14	axes, hammers, etc.		✓					Conc 212			✓	
Hardware & Supply Co., Akron	65	gears, pulleys, etc.	✓						Conc 212			✓	
William Bal Co., Newark	59	trunks		✓					NRC 256				✓
W. M. Ritter Lbr. Co., Wash., D.C.	23		✓						TNEC 437				✓
J. B. Lyons Co., Albany	25	book publ.			✓				Conc 204		✓		

Company	No.	Product								
Crane Co., Chgo.	45	valves, plumbing fixtures	✓			Conc 209 211			✓	✓
Acme Evans Co., Indianapolis	64	flour & corn meal	✓	✓		NRC 250 Conc 211			✓	✓
Lukenheimer Co., Cincinnati	64	corn meal / valves	✓							
Warner Co., Phil.	102	lime, sand-stone	✓			✓			✓	✓
Candy Brands Inc. Brooklyn	3	candy bars etc.	✓	Conc 65 197			✓			
E. L. Bruce Co., Memphis	25	hardwood flooring	✓				Conc 202			✓
Klamer Furniture Corp. Evansville, Ind.	28						NRC 250	✓ / S		
Home Furniture Co., York, Pa.	28		✓				NRC 250	✓ / S		
Skinner & Eddy Corp. Seattle	6	canned goods	✓		TNEC 420				✓	
N. Y. Knitting Mills N.Y.C.	18	men's clothing, etc.	✓	NRC 252			NRC 250			✓
Proctor & Gamble, Cincinnati	43	soap	✓							
Rome Oil Mills, Atlanta, Ga.	2	cottonseed crushing	✓		Conc 206				✓	
S. S. White Dental Co., Phil.	71	dental supplies	✓	Conc 216						✓

			PRODUCT TYPE			CONCENTRATION CLASS				PROFIT QUARTILE			
COMPANY	Epstein No.	INDUSTRY	Prdcrs.	Con-sumers Un	Con-sumers D	I	II	III	IV	I	II	III	IV
New South Cotton Oil Co., Helena, Ark.	2	cottonseed crushing	✓					Conc 206					
Hodgson Oil & Refining Co., Athens, Ga.	2	cottonseed crushing	✓					Conc 206				✓	
Bloomington Limestone Co., Bloomington, Ind.	102	limestone	✓				✓					✓	
Morris Nagel & Co., N.Y.C.	74	clocks			✓			✓ NRC 254			✓		
Schneidereith & Sons, Baltimore	36	printing	✓						Conc 204		✓		
Morris & Eckles, Baltimore	67	pumps, hy-draulic dredges	✓					Conc 212–13				✓	
Rickert Rice Mills, Inc., New Orleans	2	rice milling		✓				NRC 254				✓	
Dennings Point Brick Works, Beacon, N.Y.	45	plywood shooks	✓					NRC 250				✓	
Datz Mfg. Co., Phil.	25	alarms,	✓						Conc 202				✓
E. J. Trum Co., Brooklyn	71	mo-tion picture mchny.	✓				Conc 96 217			✓			

Company	Product	No.			Reference
Apex Hosiery, Phil.	silk & rayon women's hosiery	16	✓		Conc 199
Robert Gair Co., N.Y.C.	paper boxes	31	✓	✓	Conc 204
Schiavrone Bonomo Corp. N.Y.C.	iron & steel scrap	70	✓	✓	✓ NRC 250
Brand & Oppenheim, N.Y.C.	cotton converting	14	✓	✓	
Ludowici-Celadon, Chgo.	shale roofing tiles	48	✓	✓	Conc 209 · NRC 250
B. Mifflin Hood Co., Atlanta, Ga.	brick	45	✓	✓	NRC 250
Am. Cone & Pretzel Co., Phil.	ice cream cones, pretzels	1	✓	✓	Conc 197
Lehigh Struct. Steel Co., N.Y.C.	structural steel fabricating	49	✓	✓	NRC 250
Joseph Elias & Co., Long Island City, N.Y.		70			
	mirrors, glass prods.	46	✓	✓	Conc 208
McCormick & Co., Baltimore	manufacturing chemist spices, extracts, etc.	4	✓	✓	Conc 197
Kohler-Brambach Piano Corp. N.Y.C.	pianos	73	✓	✓	TNEC 479
Waverly Musical Products Co., Inc, Long Island City, N.Y.	musical instruments	73	✓	✓	Conc 217

COMPANY	Epstein No.	INDUSTRY	PRODUCT TYPE Prdcrs.	Consumers Un	Consumers D	CONCENTRATION CLASS I	II	III	IV	PROFIT QUARTILE I	II	III	IV
McCymount Marble Co., Milwaukee	102	cut marble products	√				TNEC 456					√	
Minneapolis Honeywell Heat Regulator	52		√				TNEC 461				√		
Cleveland Steel Band Co.	65	saw bands, etc.	√				Conc 211						√
Draper Mfg. Co., Cleveland	50	steel barrels	√					Conc 212					
Samuel H. French & Co., Phil.	39	paints & varnishes	√					NRC 250			√		
Astoria Importing & Mfg., L.I. City, N.Y.	28	furniture			√				NRC 250			√ S	
Charles P. Vaughn, Phila.	23	pocketbooks Leather, etc.			√				Conc 208				√
McGraw-Hill Publishing Co., N.Y.C.	34	periodicals			√			Conc 204			√		
	35	books			√								
Geyers Publications, N.Y.C.	34	periodicals			√			Conc 204			√		
	35	books			√								
J. William Stair, Machinery, York, Pa.	59	mixers & sifters	√						Conc 212				√
Drybak Corp., Binghamton, N.Y.	18	men's clothing			√				NRC 250			√	
77			48	8	21	2	12	23	30	9	16	34	18

plications in the way the Chamber did. The NAM tended still to rely upon arguments from legal and constitutional rights, the approach it had used so successfully over its many years as champion of anti-union and anti–social-welfare agitation. "Government is the servant not the master of the American people," Emery declaimed. "Rights are to be asserted, and the vindication of the just limits of cooperation, with courage and intelligence, is the performance of a public duty." The NAM, and the Chamber too, often adopted the position, even in arguing with knowledgeable individuals, that the purpose of antitrust revision was to save small business. "We should try . . . to preserve the smaller business units," Julius Barnes wrote to Hoover. "At present they are forced progressively into destructive price competition in which the smaller and weaker and, oftentimes most worthy units, are eliminated first." The Congress of Industries especially pushed this thesis during the Nye hearings, attempting to capitalize upon the still-large reservoir of sympathy congressmen felt for "small" and "independent" businessmen. Inasmuch as many of the associations actively supporting the Nye bills were formed preponderately of genuinely small firms in the distribution field—retail grocers, for example —or of small and middling-sized manufacturing corporations, the argument here had some plausibility. The most interesting instance of the use of the pro–small-business argument was by a large group of businessmen which styled itself as "Independent Industrial Units . . . for the Trial of a Two Years' Truce in Destructive Competition," who organized early in 1932 and met with Hoover in an attempt to persuade him to arrange for suspension of the antitrust laws. Though leaders of the largest class of corporations were excluded, many of the firms represented were quite substantial. But the "small business" role was played out with emotion-laden imagery. They were, they said, "representative of the masses of independent industrial units," from which "the future increase of the capital concentration movement . . . will necessarily come" if "destructive competition," which prevented "the unit of average efficiency from normally realizing cost plus a fair profit in return for the service rendered to the consuming public," was not checked.[20]

One additional aspect of the ideology and tactics of the revision movement should be noted: the anomalous position of the natural resource industries. Whether these industries, whose need for relief was widely accepted, would assist the general movement for antitrust relaxation or seek special legislation for themselves remained unclear. At the NAM conference of March 1931, natural resource industries were seen as the entering wedge which would secure favorable consideration for all industry by both Congress and the courts. J. F. Callbreath of the American Mining Congress, addressing the fear another participant had mentioned —that any attempt to change the law might stir the "progressives" in

Congress to counteraction—argued that a shrewd presentation "would easily bring a number at least of the progressives to believe that [revision] is a conservation measure and is carrying out and building up their old pet." The case for revision should be made initially in terms of these industries. As for manufacturing: "Wouldn't it be rather wise to keep that in the background until you have what you want and then tie it on?" Emery agreed: "We always anticipated that. It was our intention to put that right forward as the very first form of discussion." Emery and the conferees failed to note that this supposedly superior claim to relief of natural resource industries might be used by those groups in their own behalf alone.

Leading representatives from oil and lumber certainly took a principal part in the numerous business conferences of 1931 at which the antitrust question was agitated, and they generated more newspaper headlines by advocating legislation than did the representatives of other industries. Though the Chamber set up a special Natural Resources Committee in the spring of 1931, that body's report—issued for a referendum vote the same day as the report of the Committee on Continuity—offered a proposal which was parallel to, and could easily have been absorbed by, the more general recommendations of the latter committee. The signs of readiness to cooperate as a part of the general movement were somewhat contradicted by other actions. The most significant of these occurred when Senator Steiwer of Oregon persuaded Senator Nye to amend one of his trade conference bills with a provision permitting natural resource industries to make production agreements. The National Lumber Manufacturers Association supported the amendment wholeheartedly, though the position of the oil and coal industries was less certain. The failure of the Nye bills to emerge on the floor of the Senate postponed the question whether a fracture of the revision movement might occur.[21]

The conferences, committees, petitions, and hearings of 1931 and the earlier part of 1932—the period when definite proposals and strategies for revision were formed—provide another opportunity for analyzing the leading sources of support for revisionism. Table III lists, with appropriate identification as to industry, and with each industry classified as in Table II, the industrialists who responded to an invitation to the March 1931 NAM conference, together with the ten members of the Chamber of Commerce's Committee on Continuity who represented the manufacturing and mining industries (leaving aside the remaining seven from finance and distribution) and, finally, the businessmen who participated in the New York University antitrust conference in the fall of 1931. Table IV lists associations (industries) recorded as actively backing the Nye bills. Table V identifies and classifies the companies which joined in the Truce Plan petitioning in February 1932.[22]

The argument that these lists show which industries tended actively to support revision seems evident for Table IV. Tables III and V list individuals, and the assumption is that the opinions of an individual in such matters as the revision question tend to be similar to those of the other members of his industry. But does inclusion among the members of the NAM conference, the Chamber's committee, and the proceedings at New York University, necessarily indicate a pro-revision stance for each individual concerned? Not quite; but the purposes of those who formed each of these groups, and other circumstances, indicate that most of those listed would be committed to revision. The purpose of the NAM in calling its conference, and of the Chamber in appointing its Committee on Continuity, was to formulate a proposal, not to start a debate over whether revision was needed at all! Similarly, it is clear from the record of the NYU antitrust conference that business representatives received invitations precisely to present the case for revision from their industry's point of view. If this considerable body of industrialists known to be active proponents of revision tends to be drawn from certain industries and types of industries, it is reasonable to conclude these are the industries most likely to produce revisionists.

Tables III, IV, and V reveal the same pattern of support discerned in the NCF data. The natural resource industries are heavily represented, as are textiles, factory machinery, and many of the other industries which were seen as predominant in the NCF list. The earlier impression that industries with low-profit histories predominated in the revisionist movement finds support. Again, the industries vary greatly in terms of degree of concentration, of the extent to which large corporations are typical of the industry, and of the type of goods produced.

These, then, were the issues and themes in the business debate over antitrust liberalization during 1931. Few raised a voice against it. All participants shared a dread of seeming too radical and thereby inviting government regulation. Much opinion, exemplified by the NAM and the ABA, therefore advocated relaxation of the content of the Sherman Act through indirect means, by administrative amendment. The Chamber of Commerce took a more straightforward stand and then retreated from it as though shocked by its own audacity. Responsible opinion agreed that voluntary cartelism was the limit of the possible and the desirable, whether it was achieved by direct or indirect means. Several justifications for liberalization were used, the most impressive being the thesis that cartelism bred economic stability and recovery. Natural resource industries were among the leaders of the revision movement, but there was a possibility they might abandon the general movement if that seemed politic. Finally, a certain, definable segment of American industry was in the vanguard of the movement to remake the Sherman

Act—the segment which was, on the whole, older, more static, had been less profitable, and had begun to work toward revision before the depression.

NOTES

1. *Report of the . . . Meeting of the American Bar Association* (1929), pp. 104–105, 310–12; (1930), pp. 321–27. NAM, Executive Committee, "Minutes," February 14, 1930. The 1930 NAM proceedings are contained in abbreviated form in *American Industries* (October 1930), apparently a special issue as the journal seems to have ceased publication for a time.

2. *New York Times*, May 2, 1930.

3. "Transcript of Luncheon Conference, Committee on Study of Anti-Trust Legislation . . . ," December 10, 1929, box 65, NCF Papers. Searles was editor of the UMW *Journal*.

4. Williams to Bloodgood, February 28, 1930, box 66, NCF Papers. Williams' eminence as a spokesman for revisionists was attested to by his appointment to the NAM's antitrust committee early in 1930. Easley to William D. Baldwin, June 17, 1930. "Proceedings, Luncheon Conference, Committee on Study of Anti-Trust Legislation, . . . April 11, 1930. . . ." More information on the April 11 meeting is available in "Meeting of Committee on Plan and Scope of the Commission on Industrial Inquiry, December 15, 1930." Boxes 65 and 66 and, for Easley letter, General Correspondence, *ibid.*

5. Bloodgood to Foote, April 22, 1930; Foote to Bloodgood, April 23, 1930; Foote to Warner S. Hayes, April 28, 1930; Hayes to Foote, May 13, 1930; Foote to Bloodgood, September 24, 1930, box 66, *ibid.* ATAE, Executive Council, "Minutes," May 1, 1930.

6. Bloodgood to Felix Levy, May 2, 1930; to Easley, July 15, 1930; to Woll, November 28, 1930; to Foote, May 31, 1930. Easley to William Baldwin, June 17, 1930, box 66 and General Correspondence, NCF Papers.

7. *New York Times*, October 7, 12, 26, November 23, December 3, 7, 1930. *The State Papers and Other Public Writings of Herbert Hoover*, ed. William S. Myers, 2 vols. (New York: Doubleday, 1934), I 437–38. Hoover to Butler, November 7, 1930; Lawrence Richey to Walter Newton, November 24, 1930, Antitrust file; Isaac Mann to Hoover, October 29, 1930, Coal file; Manny Strauss to George E. Akerson, July 9, August 8, 1929; Benjamin Javits to Akerson, July 25, 1929, Unemployment file; Javits to Hoover, November 29, 1929, Business file, HHPP.

8. Rudolph Spreckels to Easley, January 20, 1931; Francis B. Loomis to Easley, January 26, 1931; Easley to Samuel Insull, March 3, 1931; to Javits, February 20, 1931; to C. B. Ames, February 25, March 7, 1931; Williams to Foote, February 7, 1931; to Butler, April 4, 1931; Foote to E. W. McCullough, March 20, 1931; to Williams, April 16, 24, 1931; to Roscoe Edlund, January 9, 23, February 9, 1931; Edlund to Foote, January 21, 26, May 11, 1931; Foote to Charles F. Abbott, May 14, 1931; to Easley, October 9, 1931; Garrison to James W. Gerard, June 24, 1931. "Memorandum in Re Mailing of Judge Gerard's Letter," October 1931; boxes 65, 66, and General Correspondence, NCF Papers.

9. The trade associations listed in Table II are those given in two memoranda in box 66 and in General Correspondence, NCF Papers: "Memorandum in Re

Mailing Judge Gerard's Letter" and "Trade Associations which have Indicated their Interest in Mr. Woll's Proposal . . . ," October 19, 1931.

Epstein's Table 23, on pp. 122–23 of his *Industrial Profits*, is the basis for the quartile assignments for each of the association industries. Epstein's descriptions for each of his industries are given on pp. 246, 252, 262, 270, 283, 287–88, 295. The procedure for determining with which Epstein "industry" each of the association industries best corresponds was simply to inspect Epstein's descriptions and to pair the leading product of the association industry with the appropriate group. The fundamental pitfalls involved in this matching, arising from the broad character of Epstein's "industries," are touched upon in the text. In a few cases, it should be noted, the profit rate Epstein gives for the "Large Corporation" sample was put aside in favor of the rate he gives for the "Small Corporation" segment of his industry (the ten-year averages being calculated by the present author) in assigning a profit rate to an association industry. This was done in three types of instances. (1) When it was clear from the Epstein "industry" description that two distinct producing groups were included; that one of these would necessarily be covered by the "Large Corporation" data, the other by the "Small Corporation" data; and that the association industry clearly represented smaller firms of the industry, it was given the "Small Corporation" profit rate. The main cases of this first type were the automotive parts associations, in which it was evident that the "Large Corporation" figures, concerned mainly with the integrated automobile manufacturers, could not apply. (2) The second instance occurred whenever an association industry was composed of numerous firms, many or most of which could not have been represented by the "Large Corporation" data of the Epstein "industry." An example of this type of case is the National Furniture Manufacturers Association; while the "Large Corporation" profit rate is high, the rate for the numerous small firms of the furniture industry is low. (3) The third instance arose when the Epstein "industry" embraced more than one industry in the market sense, and it was clear from the concentration data concerning a relevant association industry that the largest firms of that industry could not be among the firms in the Epstein "Large Corporation" profit data. An example is the National Lime Association. According to the concentration data, the largest companies in this association could not have been in the "Large Corporation" sample for Epstein's "industry" number 48, "Misc. Clay and Stone." All cases in which the "Small Corporation" profit rate was used are noted in Table II itself by the letter S following the mark indicating the quartile class for the association industry.

The several extractive industries among the association industries were assigned a quartile ranking, according to the profit rates given in Epstein, on pages 330 and 333, even though these industries were not included in the Epstein ranking of manufacturing industries in his Table 23. The numbers involved are few.

Three sources were used to assign concentration ratios: Willard L. Thorp and Walter F. Crowder, *The Structure of Industry*, Temporary National Economic Committee (Washington, D.C.: Government Printing Office, 1941), especially Part 5, Appendix B; Gardiner C. Means, *The Structure of the American Economy: A Report Prepared by the Industrial Section of the National Resources Committee* (Washington, D.C.: Government Printing Office, 1939), Table 2, pp. 248–57; and Senate, Committee on the Judiciary, *Concentration in American Industry*, 85th Cong., 1st sess., 1957, especially Table 38, pp. 63–98, and Table 42, pp. 198–219. The first two sources give concentration data for the mid-1930s; the third, data mainly for 1947 and later. On the assumption that most industry concentration ratios had not radically changed between the 'thirties and the 'forties, this last source, by far the most thorough, was used when the first two failed to provide adequate information. Users of concentration data are aware of the difficulties and pitfalls in assigning a concentration ratio to a given industry such as those listed in Table II. The census industries for which concentration data are given sometimes match the real life industries for which information is needed, sometimes are more or less inclusive.

In the majority of cases the former pattern prevailed, and the National Resources Committee table provided a satisfactory concentration rating for the association industry. In cases in which the association industry was more inclusive than any one NRC industry, two or more of the latter were combined and a rough calculation made to arrive at an average concentration ratio for leading products within the resulting compound. When an association industry was less inclusive than an NRC industry, or was more inclusive than any one NRC industry but no suitable compound could be made of two or more NRC industries to cover the situation, it was necessary to use the "product class" concentration data of the TNEC and *Concentration* tables. The procedure simply was to use the concentration ratios of the most important products of the association industry to arrive at a rough calculation of the typical concentration ratio for products within that industry.

Appropriately abbreviated, the source(s) used, with relevant page numbers, for each concentration class assignment, is given in Table II itself. The definition of each concentration class is as follows: I (high concentration), largest four producers sell 75% or more of industry output; II (moderate concentration), first four, 74%–50%; III (low concentration), first four, 49%–25%; IV (unconcentrated), first four, less than 25%.

In the few cases in which the sources left uncertainty as to profit and concentration class or product type, this uncertainty is indicated in the Table by a check mark in the two most convincing classifications. In the totaling of the columns, these instances were paired and divided equally within the totals.

10. Memo by Walter Newton, December 24, 1930, with memo by Emery attached, Antitrust file, HHPP. Chamber of Commerce, Board of Directors, *Minutes*, January 23, 1931.

11. Williams to John C. Gall, January 3, 1931; to Arthur E. Foote, January 3, April 7, 1931, box 66, NCF Papers.

12. NAM, "Anti-Trust Conference . . . Proceedings . . . March 24, 1931." This document of 143 typescript pages is in the NAM papers. See pp. 11–13, 31–34, 43–55, 65–67, 71, 120–21.

13. *Ibid.*, pp. 9, 35–37, 49–55, 88–110, 136–37.

14. NAM, Board of Directors, "Minutes," March 25, 1931. Emery, "Business Recovery and the Anti-Trust Laws," *Manufacturers Record*, 100, No. 3 (July 16, 1931), 18–20; *idem, The Legislative Development of the 'Anti-Trust' Laws: Address of James A. Emery . . . to National Conference on the Relation of Law and Business, October 26, 1931*, pp. 32–36. *New York Times*, June 27, 1931.

15. Chamber of Commerce, Executive Committee, *Minutes*, March 21, 1931, for resolutions submitted for coming annual meeting; *New York Times*, April 30, May 1, 1931, for discussion at the convention; "Business Goes on Record," *Nation's Business*, 19, No. 6 (June 1931), 29–30, for resolutions passed at meeting; Strawn, "Are Our Antitrust Laws out of Date?" *ibid.*, No. 5 (May 1931), 32–34, 152.

16. Some interesting information on the details of the committee's work is in Julius Barnes to Hoover, September 4, October 5, 1931, Chamber of Commerce file, HHPP.

17. Chamber of Commerce, *Referendum No. 58: On the Report of the Special Committee on Continuity of Business and Employment. October 30, 1931.* "Planning Business Stability," *Nation's Business*, 19, No. 11 (November 1931), 56.

See *New York Times*, June 25, 1932, for Harriman's announcement of program approved by Board of Directors; and *Proceedings of the Thirty-Ninth Annual Convention of the New York State Bankers' Association* (1932), pp. 227–33, for another Harriman statement of June 1932. Senate, Committee on Manufactures, *Establishment of National Economic Council: Hearings . . . on S. R. 6215*, 72d Cong., 1st sess., 1932, 2 vols., I 300–317, for Swope's explanation of his plan. Swope before Senate, Select Committee on Unemployment Insurance, *Hearings . . . on S. R. 483*, 72d Cong., 1st sess., 1932, p. 4245. Also, Swope, "Stabilization of Industry," Academy of Political Science, *Proceedings*, 14 (1930–32), 561–70.

18. Senate, *Establishment of National Economic Council*, I 167–69. Emery, *Legislative Development of 'Anti-Trust' Laws*, pp. 32–36. Senate, Committee on the Judiciary, *Amendment of Federal Trade Commission Act and Establishment of a Federal Trade Court: Hearings . . . on S. 2626, S. 2627, and S. 2628*, 72d Cong., 1 sess., 1932, pp. 1–5, 62. Stevenson to Foote, March 11, 1931; Foote to Stevenson, March 17, 1931, box 66, NCF Papers. The coercion of those who, within a relatively brief space of time, would be branded "recalcitrants" and treated roughly still seemed a foreign concept to publicists. Two editorials in the *New York Journal of Commerce*, a newspaper deeply and militantly committed to thoroughgoing antitrust revision, of May 2 and September 18, 1931, critical of proposals for enforced cooperation, illustrate how foreign and even shocking the concept of involuntary cartelism seemed to many commentators during 1931. The May 2 editorial has it that, if such authority were given to industry majorities, "this country would soon be given over to a form of despotic domination that would be much worse than any conceivable degree of government interference with private institutions."

19. Chamber of Commerce, Executive Committee, *Minutes*, March 21, 1931; *New York Times*, April 2, 1931; Barnes to Chapin, April 20, 1931, Roy Chapin Papers, University of Michigan; NEMA, "Policies Division Meeting," September 1931 (typescript proceedings of meeting, at NEMA offices, New York City). Senate, *Unemployment Insurance*, pp. 23–51, 293–308, 486–521. Ellis Hawley has popularized the "business commonwealth" term in his *The New Deal and the Problem of Monopoly* (Princeton: Princeton University Press, 1966). See pp. 36–43.

It is true of course that leaders such as Swope had been advancing and putting into practice welfare capitalist proposals for some time. But the rapid broadening of interest in such proposals during 1931 does appear as a defensive reaction to increasing pressures for governmental welfarism.

20. Emery, "Business Recovery," 18–20; Barnes to Hoover, September 17, 1931, Chamber of Commerce file, HHPP. Senate, *Amendment of Federal Trade Commission Act*, pp. 8–9, 58–60, 134–51. A copy of "A Plea From Representatives of Independent Industrial Units and of Labor for the Trial of a Two Years' Truce in Destructive Competition," is in Business file, HHPP.

21. NAM, "Anti-Trust Conference," 69–72. *New York Times*, January 1, March 8, June 8, August 17, September 13, 25, October 27, 28, November 1, 1931; January 31, March 31, April 1, 1932. *New York Journal of Commerce*, March 23, 1931, April 1, 1932. Chamber of Commerce, *Referendum No. 59: On the Report of the Departmental Committee on Natural Resource Industries* (1931). Senate, *Amendment of Federal Trade Commission Act*, pp. 219–54.

22. Table III is compiled from NAM, "Anti-Trust Conference," Chamber of Commerce, *Referendum No. 58,* and for participants in the New York University conference on business and the antitrust laws, the *New York Times* for August 17, October 27, 28, 1931.

Table IV is compiled from Senate, *Amendment of Federal Trade Commission*

Act. Table v consists of all the manufacturers listed in a document, "Group who will call on the President," prepared for the White House by the leaders of the Truce Plan. The list is in the Business file, HHPP. The *Thomas Register of American Manufacturers* was used when necessary to ascertain the industry to which the company for each individual listed in Tables III and v belonged. The proportion of higher-profit industries is somewhat greater for Table v than for the other tables, because, I would argue, the Industrial Group, formed in early 1932, is indicative of sentiment at a late stage of the revision movement, after the impact of the depression had broadened the base of revisionist support.

8

Hoover, the Revisionists, and Congress, 1931–1932

THE FIRST BIG PUSH for antitrust revision came during the long session of the Seventy-Second Congress, one of the most memorable sessions in recent history. A Democratic majority now sat in the House, the outcome of the 1930 elections. Still, during the session's early months, Hoover secured solid support for a new anti-depression program; its main feature, the Reconstruction Finance Corporation. The latter half of the session, however—the months between March and July—was marked by a bitter contest between the Democrats and the Administration over relief and taxation legislation. Among the congressmen of both parties were numbers eager to sponsor innovations also in national policy toward business and the competitive system. With Congress seemingly more receptive to new remedies than before, many businessmen felt antitrust relaxation might be within reach.

The same forces propelled businessmen, during the long session of 1931–32, to move the antitrust question into the swirl of politics which had stimulated them to debate the issue during the preceding two years. The depression was worsening during the winter of 1931/32, and the Hoover Administration still withheld relaxation of antitrust enforcement and refused to use governmental agencies to promote collective market controls. The Antitrust Division initiated, it is true, few new anti-cartel cases after mid-1931. Of the two cases started during 1932, one—against the Corn Derivatives Institute—ended promptly in a consent decree. But the other case, brought against the Appalachian Coals sales agency in June 1932, was of crucial importance. Like the *Sugar Institute* case, also argued during 1932, *Appalachian Coals* was a test of the Sherman Act to determine whether the Supreme Court intended it to be upheld regardless of economic conditions.

Appalachian Coals was planned as a test case, but not as one in which the government would try to tilt the scales of justice by framing evidence and issues to encourage reinterpretation of the Sherman Act. Hoover had urged Congressional study of antitrust modification in favor of the natural resource industries as early as October 1930 and repeated the recommendation in his Annual Message of December 1930. The Justice

Department itself was not unfriendly to revision, especially, as O'Brian told a representative of the mineral industries in 1930, "in industries like bituminous coal mining where the experience of years has demonstrated that there is a wastefulness in competition which apparently cannot be corrected under existing laws." There was a difficulty, however, which all revisionist proposals seemed to confront, "how to protect adequately the public interest," and none of the proposals O'Brian had seen passed this test. Mitchell stated this viewpoint publicly in May 1931 and several times afterward. This consideration—that simply relaxing competitive norms without introducing effective regulation was bad policy—was coupled with the conviction that the Department's constitutional obligation was to uphold the law as it had been interpreted by the Supreme Court. As O'Brian said, in assuaging the bitterness of an association whose stabilization plan contained "distinct elements of illegality," it was not the "aim of the Department to improperly obstruct the efforts of business men to remedy existing evils." But the Department was obliged to enforce the law. Moreover, O'Brian doubted wholeheartedly that the Supreme Court would reinterpret and relax antitrust standards as so many trade association lawyers predicted. He felt the classic doctrines of *Maple Flooring* and *Trenton Potteries* would be maintained.[1]

Such considerations and what was apparently Hoover's reluctance to assume any responsibility for judicial or Congressional antitrust revision, even for the natural resource industries, compelled the Justice Department to initiate suit in good faith against the coal producers of West Virginia and adjacent areas (the Appalachian field) when they made plans to form a common sales agency. The plan was in response to the National Coal Association's overall strategy for limiting competition in the industry. In a published report of 1931, the Association called for formation of regional sales agencies in each of the twelve major producing fields, thus eliminating competition among the numerous producers in each field. The Appalachian producers met early in December 1931 to draft a definite agreement, their adviser, William J. Donovan, assuring the Department of Justice that the scheme was not illegal since some operators in the field would not join the cartel and that, even after formation of all twelve regional sales agencies, there would still be competition between the Appalachian and other fields. Donovan and his legal associates apparently hoped at first that the government might accept this opinion and desist from prosecution, but O'Brian told them in January 1932 that, although the Department had "full appreciation of the distressing conditions of the industry," those who were "promoting this plan ought to proceed on the understanding that they must either obtain legislation permitting it or face litigation to test this plan."

The coal attorneys also tried to secure the Department's cooperation on certain matters of crucial importance for the formation of the plan and the success of the appeal to the Supreme Court which was planned. Would the Department withhold action until the sales agency had been perfected? Otherwise too many producers might withdraw, and the plan might never go into operation. On this point O'Brian was equivocal. The Department saw no reason to start its suit immediately, but intended action in time to prevent the plan "from being put into actual operation before its legality has been judicially examined." A second request, this one for agreement to try the case on the basis of stipulated facts, was also rejected as the Department insisted upon making an independent investigation of the methods used in the actual formation of the agency.

O'Brian and Mitchell did agree to cooperate with the industry's wish to bring the case as soon as possible before the Supreme Court. O'Brian vigorously denied, however, in opening his argument on August 1, 1932, before the District Court for the Western District of Virginia, that this was a "test case" except in the sense any case was. "This is a straight out, bona fide litigation for which no issues have been framed for this court," he asserted, "and in which both parties are acting in utmost good faith. Counsel for the Government are in deadly earnest in opposing the legal contentions of defendants." The prosecution's case contained in the many volumes of testimony and argument before the district court seems to bear O'Brian out. His closing argument was a clear and forceful rebuttal, on both economic and legal grounds, of the defense contention that depressed business conditions justified the Appalachian coal producers' market agreement. The district court sustained the government's argument as did the circuit court before which, a few weeks later, the coal attorneys argued their appeal. Lawyers who had built reputations upon the presumption that the courts would uphold the cartelistic arrangements of hard-pressed natural resource industries appeared to be headed for eclipse.[2]

The industry's appeal from the circuit court decision went immediately to the Supreme Court, which considered the case during the winter of 1932/33. But by the time the Court handed down the *Appalachian Coals* decision, in mid-March 1933, accepting the coal industry's argument, the action was anticlimactic. The drive for Congressional revision had gathered too much momentum by then to be slowed by a decision, however favorable to the bituminous sales agency, which was based on the circumstances of a given industry and amounted to far less than a general dispensation from the antitrust laws.

The magnitude of the importance of the *Appalachian Coals* case compensated somewhat for the dearth of new cases started during 1932. The *Sugar Institute* case, argued before the District Court for the Southern District of New York in several installments (because of the great mass of testimony offered) during the course of 1932, was also of major importance. Mitchell admitted, near the end of the Hoover Administration, that maintaining antitrust standards had been difficult because of the great pressure for laxity in enforcement. He acknowledged that "we have sometimes procrastinated or postponed action for limited periods, so that no unnecessary injury be done to business enterprises." But throughout his tenure, despite such lapses, the Department did move with vigor and usually with prompt success against the more egregious trade association violations of the *Maple Flooring* guidelines.[3]

Meanwhile another department, Commerce, attempted through positive steps to preserve trade association acceptance of the traditional concepts about industrial cooperation and its proper limits. Orthodox trade association doctrine of the 1920s had condemned cartelism but praised the market stability which trade associations could supposedly produce by encouraging informed decision-making among their members. The Commerce Department had spurred the development of practices consonant with these ideas, and toward the close of the 'twenties began to emphasize a new service for associations: market studies—in particular, studies designed to reduce the "costs of distribution." Domestic Commerce Division officials, of the Bureau of Foreign and Domestic Commerce, described to Robert P. Lamont with heady enthusiasm the importance of the work and the demand trade associations were making for it when he moved into the Secretaryship in March 1929. "There are many evidences that this work promises to be epoch making. . . . It has the possibility of doing for distribution what Frederic [*sic*] Taylor did for manufacturing." Trade association interest in programs of this kind, tailored to fit the pattern of orthodox ideas, was sustained for some time, but Bureau officials found on occasion that it was not easy to work with associations within the traditional guidelines. One outgrowth of the emphasis upon marketing and distribution research was the discovery by the Bureau's high command of the benefits of encouraging "verticalism," the linkage of associations of manufacturers, wholesalers, and retailers to develop more rational distribution practices. Asked, in 1931, to implement "verticalism," a troubled Chicago-based Bureau official commented upon certain risks. He had thought of calling together the furniture associations but, knowing they were at every level desperate for some withdrawal of the "shadow" of the Justice Department, wondered "what will happen to us if we are able to get these three or four associations into the same room for [a] perfectly legitimate conference on economic affairs relating to their business and they 'take the bit' into their teeth and do things which they should not do and then say they were called by the Department of Commerce and were under the Department's protection?" [4]

Perhaps to combat the increasingly widespread dissatisfaction with orthodox cooperationism which incidents like this, as well as the growing demand for antitrust relaxation, indicated, Hoover brought Frederick M. Feiker to Washington in July 1931 to head the Bureau of Foreign and

Domestic Commerce. Feiker had been a Hoover aide in the Commerce Department during the struggle to vindicate orthodox associationism during the early 'twenties; more recently he had been managing director of the Associated Business Papers, the trade association representing trade journals, and therefore had the contacts necessary for a try at renewing interest and faith in the traditional trade association practices. Whether appointed specifically for this purpose or not, Feiker immediately set out to rekindle faith in the serviceability of such practices and in the ability of the Commerce Department to foster them effectively. Even before his tenure began, Feiker appointed an Economic Planning Committee to reconsider the Bureau's relationship with industry in domestic concerns. During August the Domestic Commerce Division reported on trade association programs which might offer hope of improvement to hard-pressed industries. Meeting with his division chiefs in mid-September, Feiker asked for "discussion of the relations of trade associations to stabilization plans." Could "some of the objectives sought by Mr. Swope's plan . . . be reached without adopting the plan as a whole?" they wondered. Could a way be found, short of "greater Federal participation in the control of industry than the present," to "control capital investment . . . in boom periods so that the ogre of overproduction . . . may not be a part of the next depression?" At least a few of the Bureau division heads had concluded by now that the old voluntaristic practices no longer could help achieve stability. "I do not believe production can be controlled as long as there are so many small mills (wild-cat mills) operating," thought Leighton Peebles, Lumber Division chief, as he recommended the elimination of such troublemakers.[5]

Feiker's mission, however, was to refurbish orthodox ideas, not to experiment with new ones. In his lexicon, "economic planning" still meant individual production and price making based upon the data and informed advice the trade association could provide. Though dressed in up-to-date terminology, this idea was not much different from the associationist aims as the Department had visualized them at the opening of the 1920s. Feiker fixed upon the fall meeting, at Asheville, North Carolina, of the ATAE as the opportunity to begin the reinspiration he planned and to deflate the rapidly multiplying economic proposals of such writers as Stuart Chase and Charles Beard. His intention, apparently carried out, of conferring directly with the President before the convention, implies that Feiker felt he was executing a mandate of Administration-wide importance and interest.

Feiker wanted some sign of acquiescence in his viewpoint by the assembled trade association executives and prepared carefully to secure it. On September 11, he met with Roscoe Edlund, ATAE secretary, and Earl Whitehorne of McGraw–Hill in New York. Whitehorne, whose firm was by far the single largest publisher of trade journals, agreed to present a resolution endorsing Feiker's presentation and calling for formation of a business advisory committee to broaden the Commerce Department's contacts with trade associations. Feiker's speech itself on September 24 was in effect merely a re-presentation of all the old trade association ideas and practices. Several other speakers seconded Feiker during the convention, one asserting that the movement for antitrust revision was representative of only a minority viewpoint among businessmen. The resolution Feiker had planned for was readily accepted. But Feiker, after the convention, confessed to Lamont that the ATAE's public stand had masked much contrary sentiment. "There were distinctly two camps of thought at the meeting; one believing that the present anti-trust laws should be adjusted, and the other—which I believe, however, to be in the minority —thinking that the removal of the restraints of the anti-trust laws was not necessarily the solution of the control of production or of prices." The reticence of the majority (if Feiker was right) was explained perhaps by Wilson Compton, secretary of the National Lumber Manufacturers Association, who had sponsored a resolution proposing an emergency suspension of the antitrust laws at the convention. It had not received serious consideration, he felt, because "as Trade Association Executives we are a little too self-conscious, and in such circumstances as these we refrain from consideration on its merits of a proposition of this kind." [6]

Feiker made continuing efforts to devise a way to return the Bureau of Foreign and Domestic Commerce to the leadership role it had held. At conferences with his aides, he tried to arouse enthusiasm by drawing the parallel between the days of the early 'twenties when Daugherty's policies had threatened associations and the present when depression threatened to render them outmoded, suggesting "that we now have the same opportunity for crystalizing our thought regarding organized business activity" which Hoover had so successfully confronted in the early 'twenties. These efforts were somewhat pathetic. At every turn they ran up against the great barrier to new formulations: that, as they reminded themselves, "all plans should be within the limitations imposed by present laws." This, at a time when, as Jay Junkin, chief of the Commercial Laws Division said, the main question from industry was, "Is this permissible?"

In the spring of 1932 Feiker again tried to spark a rebirth of orthodox associationism. Three times—on March 2, April 11, and May 9—he met in New York with groups of trade journal editors to discuss "the trade association movement, with particular reference to a program of action involving relation[s] between the trade association and the development of business at the present time." There was, Feiker argued, "an opportunity for business paper editors in association with the American Trade Association Executives to set up four or five objectives for immediate action by trade associations." The meetings had another purpose, too: to defend the Department of Commerce against the criticism of erstwhile friends, notably the Chamber of Commerce, which had charged it with extravagance at a time when Congress was searching for ways to curtail the budget. Why were business groups standing aside and not opposing (or actually backing) proposed budget cuts for the Bureau? *The New York Times* speculated that the Department's failure to support trade association thought and practice as these moved beyond orthodox precedents was the reason. Associations, the newspaper commented, had been "led to believe" in times past that the Department "along with the Federal Trade Commission was behind them in certain aspects of organized business work." They had "suddenly found themselves 'holding the bag' when critics arose in Congress, the Department of Justice and other quarters." [7]

Feiker had loyally upheld the Hoover ideological tradition. But by the fall of 1932 he too had weakened. The nation was "entering into a period of the control of production and of price," he confided to Roscoe Edlund, "not on the basis of some of the old slogans or old philosophies," but on the basis of the control of capital expansion through the RFC and the control of production itself through labor agreements. After all, he noted, "the garment industry in New York, by coordination with the labor unions, is enabled to set up contracts which really control output. Perhaps coordination with unions in other associations would permit legal control of supply and demand." [8]

Though disciples might eventually apostasize, Hoover steadfastly opposed cartelistic associationism except, with qualifications, for the natural resource industries. As pressure built up during the fall of 1931 for Congressional action on antitrust policy at the First Session of the Seventy-Second Congress, Hoover remained aloof. The Swope Plan of September, the Chamber's committee report of October, the frequent proposals from lesser groups and individuals, kept the issue under continuous public review. No concerted, firmly executed, push for revision emerged, however. Instead, there was fragmentation of businessmen behind competing proposals.

The default of leadership by the Chamber of Commerce was the obvious reason for this fragmentation. As the largest and most representative business organization by far, the Chamber had potentially the strength to unite businessmen behind a common proposal and to lobby effectively to get Congressional action. But after nearly a year's preparation—after Silas Strawn had announced, shortly before the Congressional session began, the intention of introducing a bill embodying the principles of the Committee on Continuity's referendum resolutions which were then being voted upon favorably—the Chamber failed to act.

Possibly this was partly because the Chamber's officers and directors found it difficult to turn the referendum principles into a concrete measure. The Chamber's gyrations later in 1932, when the Committee on Continuity's proposals were interpreted as requiring only administrative amendment, have already been noted. The major reason for the Chamber's timorousness, however, was likely Hoover's rejection of its plea for support. If Chamber leaders felt Hoover owed them this backing and genuinely expected to obtain it, their hope would be readily understandable. Cordial relations had obtained between the Chamber and the White House from the outset of the President's term. Hoover had symbolized his appreciation of these relations at the beginning of his presidency when he entertained a large selection of business leaders during the Chamber's May 1929 convention.

Most of the tangible benefits, however, had flowed in the President's direction. In November 1929, Hoover turned to Julius Barnes and asked him to make the Chamber a virtual instrument of Administration policy. On December 5, Barnes responded when the National Business Survey Conference met to speed, as Hoover said in his address before it, the adoption by "industry as a whole the measures which have been taken by some of our leading industries to counteract the effect of the recent panic in the stock market." The Business Survey, actually an appendage of the Chamber of Commerce, functioned mainly through periodic reports which reiterated Hoover's policies—the maintaining of wages, employment, and spending—and reported news items showing their broad acceptance by business. As economic statistics transmitted a picture less and less capable of optimistic interpretation, the Survey's work became more difficult and finally impossible. But, for over a year, the Chamber had tried to coordinate the machinery of organized business precisely with Hoover's policies. The Business Survey was the Chamber's main service for Hoover, but there are some indications that Barnes wished to, and perhaps did, use the Chamber's influence to enlarge Hoover's support within Congress.

There were times of criticism, of course, sometimes harsh, notably of farm policy. While the 1930 convention of the Chamber warmly praised Hoover's leadership since the crash and voted to continue the Survey program, it also approved a resolution sharply criticizing the Federal Farm Board. The Chamber Directors acted immediately after the convention to soften even this relatively minor blow, adopting a statement explaining the true "purport" of the FFB resolution. It had been directed against any "permanent policy of the government" in performing functions "in competition with established agencies," and was not necessarily a call for immediate dissolution of the Farm Board.[9]

Possibly Barnes hoped that the credits the Chamber had stored up could be cashed in as he approached Hoover, seemingly confident, in the fall of 1931 to secure his backing for the proposals of the Committee on Continuity. To this time the Administration had given no indication it would support or even tolerate radical antitrust revision. Hoover's recommendation in his 1930 Annual Message for a Congressional investigation had heartened the revisionists, but it had actually been quite limited in scope. Hoover's lieutenants had, moreover, during 1930 and 1931, consistently thrown cold water on revisionist proposals, claiming these were simply not within the boundaries of practical politics. Lamont's response to William Ritter's request early in 1930 for an appraisal of his latest proposal was typical. "My own judgement is that such a proposal can never pass Congress in the present state of public opinion." "Clarification" might be forthcoming but "my opinion is it will be a long time before [the antitrust laws] will be practically neutralized or repealed." Lamont felt much the same in October 1931. As he told Henry Doherty, "There is no possible chance of a repeal of the Anti-Trust Law—though, I think, there is a possibility of an amendment that would allow cooperation—under certain restrictions—among members having to do with natural resource industries."

In October, as Barnes's campaign to secure Hoover's support gathered steam, another business leader, George H. Bailey, counsel for the American Mining Congress, was explaining at length to Lamont why the Administration could not possibly support the Chamber's antitrust-revision proposals. "Can anyone imagine any Democrat in Congress voting for this measure," a measure placing in a government agency appointed by the President the power to approve market agreements? "Any Democrat will say, it will place in the hands of the present Administration the power to obtain unlimited millions of dollars to *control* the *next* as well as *future elections*. . . . Many Congressmen will believe this proposed amendment was an Administration scheme to control business and obtain campaign funds which they must defeat." Lamont seemed to agree. To attempt modification of the Sherman Act along the lines the Chamber proposed "would be unwise. At the first opportunity, I will discuss it with the President of the Chamber." [10]

Bailey was almost certainly correct in thinking that an Administration move to present so controversial an issue before a Congress the opposition would control would have been ill-considered. None of this deterred Barnes, however. Early in September he began to send a steady stream of letters informing Hoover of the progress of the Committee on Continuity's work and of the importance of the antitrust question. He was "moved . . . out of long friendship and a desire to strengthen your own public leadership" to show Hoover that "this subject is the largest question in business today." Barnes pressed the thesis repeatedly that "small business" was faced with obliteration through mergers, though this was not at all the argument of the Committee on Continuity's report, which stressed market and employment stabilization as the reason for revision. A second tack was that if there was "one note which could be emphasized by you with more promise of direct result in stimulating confidence, it would be the subject of our Anti-Trust laws."

To the last of Barnes's requests Hoover had given a reply: "I have your letter of November 30th. I am hoping to be able to handle the matter to your satisfaction." But Hoover's reference to revision in his Annual Message a week later was perfunctory. He referred to the "wide conviction" that there should be change "especially in the procedure of these [antitrust] laws," denounced the suggestion that they be repealed, and ended by alluding again to the special justification for change in relation to natural resource industries.[11]

This was the limit for Hoover in advocating revision. He proved far more resourceful in resisting it. In September he had with what appears to have been a partisan and almost malicious gusto attacked the Swope Plan. The plan, he told one lieutenant, would be "launched under important Democratic auspices during the next week," and, he advised another, would be "given tremendous publicity," and supported by "a large organization." To Solicitor General Thacher, Hoover assigned the task of deciding whether the plan was constitutional, though Hoover had no doubts on that score, informing Thacher that "It appears to my amateur legal mind that aside from wiping out the Sherman and Clayton Acts, this plan is thoroughly unconstitutional." To Senator Felix Hebert of Rhode Island, Hoover supplied the comments needed for a newspaper attack which Hebert placed in the Providence papers on September 18. The broadside employed the usual figures of Hooverian demonology. The Swope Plan contemplated "price-fixing," it said, and this would "bring into existence such a union of forces in the industrial world as has never been dreamed of before. It would lead to the creation of a series of monopolies, . . . raise obselete [sic] plants . . . to the level of the most efficient, and the pubic would be called upon to bear the burden." Hebert's blast fell a little flat, however, when the national press disappointed Hoover's expectations, failing to pick the statement up and give it "the nationwide distribution it deserved." [12]

Revisionists who had the temerity to request Hoover's aid (Swope did not) met with the same suspicion and hostility. Hoover's aides treated the September request of Alison Reppy, director of the New York University Conference on Law and Business, one of the symposia on the antitrust question held that fall, for a "general letter" from the President, "approving the holding of such conferences under educational auspices," as though it were an attempt to entrap Hoover into a seeming endorsement of revision. Hoover also eyed the Truce Plan proposal suspiciously when the Industrial Group headed by, among others, Gordon C. Corbaley, J. Harvey Williams, and Malcolm Whitman, handed it to him during a meeting on February 11, 1932. Hoover misinterpreted, perhaps willfully, the plain meaning of the document, "A Plea . . . for . . . a

Two Years' Truce in Destructive Competition," so as to make it seem that the group had asked him to suspend the antitrust laws through some sort of highhanded executive action. "It would occur to me," he wrote, officiously, "that any action of this kind must be preceded by legislation. It would be a gross violation of the obligations of the President to make any suggestion undertaking any organization in the country which would in effect nullify the law." The "Plea" in fact clearly asked Hoover to seek bipartisan support for Congressional action suspending the antitrust laws, plainly not for a unilateral presidential suspension of antitrust enforcement.[13]

When, in December 1931, Hoover chose not to support revisionism, except through his tepid suggestion of a Congressional study, and the Chamber of Commerce decided to withdraw temporarily from leadership in the revisionist cause, lesser groups pressed competing and somewhat conflicting proposals through Congressional sponsors. The NAM remained in the background, though it probably was behind the resolution which Hatton Sumners of Texas, the new, Democratic chairman of the House Judiciary Committee, introduced authorizing hearings on the antitrust question. Sumners was quoted during February 1932 as hopeful that the House Rules Committee would vote out the resolution, which his own committee already had approved, but this never occurred. The most encouraging development for revisionists was the hearings Senator Nye held during February and March on his bills to strengthen the FTC's trade practice conferences. Backed at the hearings by the member associations of the Congress of Industries, the Nye bills failed to attract the interest of industries which felt that unequivocal legalization of market agreements was the only goal worth seeking. In late March, however, the hearings caused a flurry of excitement when Senator Steiwer of Oregon persuaded Nye to accept an amendment definitively granting the natural resource industries liberty to make cartel agreements under FTC supervision. When Secretary Wilbur appeared before the committee to endorse Steiwer's amendment, the Nye bills became for a time a focus of interest for leaders of the natural resource industries.[14]

Only Nye's bills progressed to the stage of hearings. Senator David I. Walsh of Massachusetts submitted a bill in January which offered complete fulfillment of the wishes of substantive revisionists, but no identifiable organizations stood behind him. Walsh ascribed the inspiration for the bill, which allowed price-fixing as long as the price was "fair and reasonable," to Pope Pius xi's encyclical on reconstructing the capitalist order. To judge from the interest the measure aroused in the New England press, Massachusetts and Rhode Island textile manufacturers were, however, a more direct influence than the pope. The bill, too, may have responded to "the demand long made in the Hearst newspapers for rationalization of our anti-trust laws" which the *Boston American* recalled in describing Walsh's proposal. Walsh also belatedly introduced, in June 1932, a bill providing for the two-year suspension of the antitrust laws which the Industrial Group had sought in February and March. Walsh presumably acted at the request of certain of the leaders of the movement. The group itself was never more than an *ad hoc* body and apparently no longer functioned after the spring of 1932.[15]

Consideration of the antitrust problem during the 1931–32 session prefigured the handling of the issue during the session of the Hundred Days in the spring of 1933. The solution ultimately settled upon, the National Industrial Recovery Act, employed the concept of strengthening trade practice codes which the Nye bills had popularized, though the later measure also made room for the price-fixing and production agreements called for in the Steiwer amendment and the Walsh bill. The notion of a two-year suspension of the antitrust laws which the Truce Plan advocates invented in 1932, realizing that, as J. Harvey Williams explained, "rightly or wrongly . . . no bill conferring permanent relief . . . could receive approval by Congress this year," also helped pattern the N.I.R.A. Even the labor provisions of the New Deal recovery act appeared during the long session of the Seventy-Second Congress, in a bill sponsored by the UMW and certain unionized mine-owners, which the mass of coal men and the major business organizations stoutly opposed. This Davis–Kelly bill to create a Bituminous Coal Commission provided for price stability through market agreements under the commission's approval. The right of labor to organize and bargain was stated in terms remarkably like those of Section 7 (a) of the N.I.R.A. Aside from these labor provisions, which NAM and Chamber representatives, of course, opposed at the lengthy hearings on the bill during March and April 1932, the leading cause for criticism was the bill's provision for the licensing of coal corporations by the commission. The Chamber's Natural Resource Committee spoke at the hearings of its fear "of a measure which places the destiny of an industry of such magnitude . . . so completely in the hands of a Government agency." All the planning for antitrust revision of 1931, all the business-sponsored proposals which entered the Congressional hopper during this session of 1931–32 agreed upon one point: that concessions on the antitrust laws were not to be purchased by accepting a significant increase in effective government influence over industry's behavior. Both the Nye and Walsh bills used the "fair competition" concept, simply expanding the meaning of the term until, in Walsh's case, it meant price-fixing, but leaving the FTC with merely the old, negative regulatory powers. The Truce Plan advocates designated a panel of businessmen to approve the market agreements made during the antitrust suspension. This preoccupation with avoiding effective regulation also carried over into the New Deal session.[16]

There were striking differences between the two sessions, of course.

In 1932 only the Nye proposal contemplated coercion of industry members who rejected agreements, and since the Nye bills envisioned only a slight advance beyond the traditional FTC codes, this was not a radical departure. Both the Walsh and Truce Plan proposals were as innocent of third-party coercion as the Chamber of Commerce's recommendation of the previous fall. Another difference was the quiescence of the Chamber and the NAM. Most important was the President's opposition to full-scale revision, his reluctance to take a lead even for natural-resource-industry relief. The Truce Plan's leaders recognized what the Chamber of Commerce had seen in December 1931: that it was "useless for us to proceed except through [the President's] leadership in a non-partisan manner"; that "no substantial progress can be made unless the President is convinced of the wisdom of the plan, and is ready to give it his support." Toward the end of the session, the Chamber's new president, H. I. Harriman, after a lapse of many months in contact with Hoover on this subject, once again tested Hoover's attitude. Could the President do anything to stir the House Rules Committee into approving the Sumners Resolution authorizing hearings on the economic effects of the antitrust laws? Hoover's laconic reply insulted Harriman's intelligence. "I wish to thank you for your letter of June 13th. I have requested Congress to investigate the matter referred to and hope this will be done." Hoover's request had, of course, been in his Annual Message a half year earlier! [17]

Without Administration support, without the leadership of the major business organizations and their lobbying expertise, antitrust revision was impossible. The issue might not be as controversial as in the days of Theodore Roosevelt, as one newspaper commentator said, but "it may incite political complications." Strong opposition, another writer predicted, could be counted on "from certain quarters which will always spring to fight anything that savors of assisting big business." All this was true, but William Kiplinger's assertion, in April 1932, that "the truth is that there is more interest in Congress in preventing price-fixing than there is in liberalizing the antitrust laws," was almost certainly misleading.[18] In the absence of any test votes in either house, it is difficult to judge how greatly Kiplinger exaggerated, but if the number of bills introduced in the Senate favorable or hostile to liberalization is any guide, sentiment in that body at least was running toward the revisionists. During the session, four senators, in addition to Nye and Walsh, introduced bills providing for antitrust relaxation, though in some cases they also included features objectionable from the business point of view. Senator Davis' coal bill was in the latter category, as was Millard Tyding's bill which Gerard Swope might have recognized as an unpleasant caricature of his plan. The bill allowed trade associations to control markets, but also charged them with giving work to all the unemployed through work-sharing. Senator Daniel Hastings' bill was free of obligations, but its exemptions from certain aspects of the Sherman Act applied only to smaller firms. Royal S. Copeland's bill would have, somewhat in the fashion of Nye's, expanded the usefulness of FTC codes. To counterbalance these, Senators King and McKellar introduced resolutions calling for investigatory hearings on antitrust, but these hearings were to be aimed at strengthening not weakening the law. Huey Long went further, calling in his bill submitted in April for abolition of the rule of reason and a stricter interpretation of the meaning of restraint of trade.[19] A ream of similar resolutions and bills, many of them companions to these, appeared in the House. The business argument that competition generated instability, that falling prices and profits meant wage-cutting and unemployment, had become common currency. It is fair to say that, by the close of the 1931–32 session of the Seventy-Second Congress, passage of antitrust revision was no longer visionary. It had been translated into the domain of practical politics. It was a problem in tactics.

NOTES

1. Memo for Attorney General by O'Brian, November 12, 1930, file 60/187/67; V. G. Iden to Mitchell, November 5, 1931; O'Brian to Iden, November 13, 1931, file 60/138/37, RG 60. Memo, "Some Causes of Failures of Trade Associations" for Frederick M. Feiker by C. J. Judkins, August 1932, box 17, Feiker Papers, RG 151. Attorney General, *Annual Report* (1931), pp. 4–5. *New York Times*, April 16, May 17, November 29, 1931. The Judkins memo relates a conversation with O'Brian on O'Brian's expectations concerning the courts.

2. Donovan to O'Brian, December 10, 1931; memos for O'Brian by James L. Fly, December 4, 22, 1931; file memo by O'Brian, January 7, March 10, 1932; memo for Attorney General by O'Brian, January 27, 1932; O'Brian to firm of Donovan and Raichle, January 26, February 9, 1932; O'Brian to Williamson (of Donovan and Raichle), January 27, 1932; "Transcript of Proceedings, U.S. v. Appalachian Coals," 10 vols. (August 1932), all in file 60/187/67, RG 60.

3. *New York Times*, February 9, 10, October 4, December 8, 1932; January 28, 1933 (Mitchell's statement). *New York Journal of Commerce*, February 10, 11, August 11, October 4, 1932.

4. Memo for Lamont by Frank Surface, March 15, 1930; memo for Lamont by William L. Cooper, July 31, 1930, Lamont Papers, RG 40. W. G. Jamison to Surface, November 2, 1931, file 711 General, RG 151.

5. Feiker to Ray Fling, June 20, 1931; Feiker to Dewey, August 15, 1931; Marketing Service Division memo for Feiker, September 9, 1931; "Notes for Use in Asheville Speech, dictated after Division Chiefs Meeting," September 19, 1931; Peebles to Feiker, July 22, 1931, boxes 2, 4, 7, Feiker Papers, *ibid.* Feiker to John M. Carmody, box 19, Personal Correspondence, John M. Carmody Papers, Franklin D. Roosevelt Library.

6. Feiker to Julius Klein, September 16, 1931, Business file, HHPP. "Notes on a Meeting in the Engineer's Club . . . September 11th Concerning Relationship of the Department in the Trade Association Movement and the Asheville Convention of the A.T.A.E."; Compton to Leslie C. Smith, October 6, 1931, all in box 4, Feiker Papers, RG 151. Feiker to Lamont, September 14, 18, 1931, Lamont Papers, RG 40. ATAE, *Proceedings* (1931), pp. 144–56.

7. "Notes on the Second Saturday Morning Conference," October 10, 1931; "Minutes of Division Chiefs Meeting," February 13, 1932; Arthur D. Anderson to Feiker, March 22, 1932; Feiker to E. W. Davidson, May 4, 1932; memo, "Business Paper Editor Meetings, 1932," boxes 2, 17, 19, Feiker Papers, RG 151. *New York Times,* May 1, 1932.

8. Feiker to Edlund, September 22, 1932, box 17, Feiker Papers, RG 151.

9. *New York Journal of Commerce,* November 5, 1932. Barnes to Lawrence Richey, April 20, May 3, July 13, 1929; *Business Conditions and Outlook* (booklet summarizing National Business Survey Conference of December 7, 1929); Barnes to Hoover, January 25, 1930; Julius Klein to Hoover, February 19, 1930; NBSC, *The Business Situation,* March 25, 1930; William Butterworth to Hoover, May 7, 1930, all in Chamber of Commerce file, HHPP. Barnes to Hoover, November 20, 1930, Business file, *ibid.,* concerning what was evidently a plan for creating bipartisan support for solution of several major issues.

10. Julius Klein to Charles F. Abbott, April 1, 1930, file 85872, RG 40; Lamont to Ritter, May 5, 1930; to Doherty, October 19, 1931, Lamont Papers, *ibid.* Bailey to Lamont, October 12, 1931; Lamont to Bailey, October 12, 1931, file 82248/48, *ibid.*

11. Barnes to Hoover, September 4, 17, October 5, 10, November 30, 1931; Hoover to Barnes, December 3, 1931; Lawrence Richey to Barnes, September 24, 1931; Barnes to Richey, September 26, 1931, all in Chamber of Commerce file, HHPP. Myers, *State Papers . . . of Herbert Hoover,* II 51–52.

12. Hoover to Thacher, September 12, 14, 1931; to Hebert, September 11, 16, 22, 1931; Hebert to Hoover, September 15, 18, 1931, Business file, HHPP.

13. Reppy to Hoover, September 25, October 20, 26, 1931; memo by Lawrence Richey, October 22, 1931; G. A. Hastings to Reppy, October 22, 26, 1931; unsigned memo of October 28, 1931, Antitrust Laws file; "A Plea . . . for . . . a Two Years' Truce in Destructive Competition"; Hoover to Malcolm D. Whitman, February 11, 1932, Business file, HHPP.

14. *New York Journal of Commerce,* February 3, 15, 23, 1932. Senate, *Amendment of Federal Trade Commission Act,* pp. 219–45, 250–54.

15. *Boston Financial News,* February 2, 1932; *Boston American,* February 25, 1932; *Fall River Herald News,* February (?), 1932; *Boston Globe,* April 28, 1932; *Boston Post,* July 23, October 1, 1932; all clippings from Walsh scrapbooks, David I. Walsh Papers, College of the Holy Cross.

16. Williams to John Lord O'Brian, file 60/03/3, RG 60. Senate, Committee on Mines and Mining, *To Create a Bituminous Coal Commission: Hearings . . . on S. 2935,* 72d Cong., 1st sess., 1932, pp. 1–2, 1010–16.

17. Malcolm D. Whitman to George W. Wickersham, March 16, 1932; Wickersham to Whitman, March 17, 1932; Whitman to Lawrence Richey, March 17, 1932, Business file; Harriman to Hoover, June 13, 1932; Hoover to Harriman, June 15, 1932, Antitrust Laws file, HHPP.

18. *New York Journal of Commerce,* February 3, 1932. News feature in Sunday *New York Times,* October 4, 1932. Kiplinger, "What's Likely in Washington," *Nation's Business,* 20, No. 4 (April 1932), 21–24.

19. The Nye, Walsh, and Davis bills have already been discussed. All the other bills mentioned were introduced in the First Session of the Seventy-Second Congress and were numbered as follows; S. 5480 (Tydings); S. 4963 (Hastings); S. 4030 (Copeland); S. 46 (McKellar); S. R. 75 (King); S. 4331 (Long).

9

The Paradox of Hoover's Last Recovery Effort: Preparing the Revisionists' Way

THERE WERE TWO DEVELOPMENTS in the last stages of the Hoover period which had a significant influence upon the context in which the business community finally did achieve antitrust relaxation when the National Industrial Recovery Act was drafted by the Administration and accepted by Congress during the Hundred Days of the New Deal. One of these developments was the popularization and widespread acceptance, through actions both of the Hoover Administration and of business groups, of what might be termed "start-up" plans, bootstrap formulas promising immediate industrial upturn. These plans should be distinguished sharply from the proposals of the antitrust revisionists. The latter had, it is true, vaguely claimed that recovery would result from market controls; but they had tended to stress stabilization, protection of values, and the possibility of social insurance, rather than recovery, as the benefits of cartelization. The revisionists had spent very little rhetorical energy, in fact, upon demonstrating whether and how market controls would initiate an upturn. Thus, while both categories of proposals had to do with recovery in a general way, the start-up planners aimed directly and explicitly at the prompt resumption of pre-depression prosperity. The revisionists were interested in restoring prosperity, but they were equally concerned with securing the collective market-power needed to shore up the political and economic security and ascendancy of businessmen in the national economic order. Neither the start-up planners nor the business-market-control planners should be confused with the publicists and economists who were contemporaneously advocating "national economic planning," the coordination of output and prices through a national planning agency.

The other leading development of the period was the concerted attempt by revisionists which began in about mid-October to resolve the unanswered questions of the previous winter, above all whether the major business organizations would and could assume firm leadership and unify the broad, but organizationally and programmatically divided, support for revision into a single, effective movement. Until the beginning of this attempt to concert the efforts of the different groups and viewpoints in the fall of 1932, the energies of revisionists seemed somewhat dormant after Congress adjourned in July. Antitrust revision figures in the politics of 1932, of course. Both the NAM and the Chamber of Commerce issued policy statements shortly before the party conventions. The NAM drew up its traditional pre-convention "Platform of American Industry" in June, calling for an "Emergency Industries Preservation Act," reviving the Truce Plan proposal of the previous winter. Another NAM plank denounced the dole and asserted industry's ability to stabilize employment through self-regulation. The Chamber of Commerce Board of Directors met late in June to draft a statement similar in substance and intention.

The revisionists' clamor on the eve of the conventions seemed so influential to many of the nation's academic economists that they felt compelled to counter the claims of a movement which was "seeking to break down the Sherman Act." Ninety-seven leading economists signed a statement pointing to monopoly rather than competition as the cause of the depression. Signers of the statement, which was sent to the resolutions committee of both parties, included such luminaries of the profession as Paul Douglas, John R. Commons, Frank Fetter, Willard Thorp, and Arthur B. Adams. The Democratic Platform Committee actually did, in the skeleton platform presented to and accepted by the convention, tuck in a pledge, customarily ambiguous, concerning the antitrust laws, promising help through them for "the small producer and distributor." On its face, the plank (Section Nine) read as a pledge for strict enforcement against the powerful to aid the weak, though it was barely possible to read it as a promise of revision along the lines of the Nye bills. Nor was the antitrust issue missing altogether from the campaign. Roosevelt, in the Commonwealth Club (September 23) and Roosevelt Business and Professional League (October 6) speeches, seemed to give a tentative endorsement to business ideas about market control.[1]

Hoover, of course, made no promise of revision. On the contrary. He portrayed himself in his *Memoirs* as courageously withstanding business lobbying focused through H. I. Harriman, who threatened him with the loss of business support unless he agreed to accept the Chamber of Commerce's antitrust-revision plan. Hoover, according to his own account, firmly resisted Harriman's threat and paid for it with the loss of big business support, which went to Roosevelt. Hoover's description of this alleged event and its supposed aftermath have been accepted by several writers, one of whom sees Hoover's refusal to knuckle under as his "finest hour." Presumably the event—the confrontation with Harriman which Hoover described—did occur, though it is interesting that no confirmation of it independent of the published works Hoover or his associates prepared has yet turned up. Contemporary gossip reported bad feeling between Hoover and Harriman from the time the latter became president of the Chamber in May 1932, its causes only surmised. The truth of this is uncertain, but it is clear, from the Hoover papers, that contact between the Chamber and the President was minimal during the summer and fall of 1932, with little of the overt aid to Hoover's policies and implied help for his political success which was so much in evidence during 1930 and 1931.[2]

This hardly means, however, that the business community, or even the leaders, except for Harriman, of the Chamber of Commerce turned against Hoover during the campaign. Hoover chose to fight the election and to finish his Administration without accepting the business community's view that economic recovery and future stability depended upon cartelization. Instead he attempted to start the upward spiral, upon which his political fate depended, using much the same methods which had failed for three years to stem the downturn. In this effort Hoover had the active cooperation of many leading businessmen and even, in a low-keyed manner, of the Chamber of Commerce.

By the time Congress had adjourned, the belief was current that the depression had finally bottomed out. Many economic indices did turn up very timidly during July, August, and September, which gave currency to the notion that the correct plan for a start-up of the economy would rapidly restore prosperity. Hoover and his supporters linked this suggestion of incipient recovery to the RFC and to the other measures taken during the previous winter to stem the collapse of, and restore confidence in, the nation's banking and financial structure. Whatever the truth of this contention, as soon as the financial crisis had been arrested, businessmen began to show an increasing capacity for believing the plausibility of recovery plans based upon bootstrap methods.

Hoover was urged especially to promote one of the several versions of the employment-expansion plan, a concept which proved a very durable one, surviving even into the next year to help form the context of ideas which influenced the actual legislation the antitrust revisionists finally achieved. Julius Barnes, as early as February 1932, thought he detected "the natural change in tides" betokening better times, and urged Hoover to support the re-employment campaign the American Legion and the AFL were trying to launch. Most architects of re-employment schemes laid great emphasis upon precisely-timed and coordinated moves by employers and put great store by the favorable psychological impact the dramatic unveiling of such moves would have. "The only way I can see to start the ball rolling again," a Seattle real estate broker told Hoover, "is for all the large corporations, in every line of industry, to increase their payrolls by a *certain per centage* . . . *ON THE SAME DATE.*" This would amount to "a resolution on the part of the whole country to call off and forget about the depression." [3]

Related in method, though much more moderate, was another plan, the spreading of work, which was rapidly gaining a following both among businessmen and with the general public. Though in its immediate effect it was a relief measure, advocates of work-sharing usually thought of it as a recovery plan since it would supposedly obviate the threat of the dole and thereby improve investor confidence, and spread purchasing power more widely, if more thinly, and thereby increase spending. By June a campaign for spreading work seemed so likely to achieve great results that even Bernard Baruch and his cronies from WIB days were seriously toying with the idea of leading the crusade themselves, if the AFL would assist.

A corollary to the widespread airing of bootstrap recovery and relief plans was the proliferation of proposals for economic-planning boards to devise and implement them. Most of these proposals, though called to life as a response to the cautious optimism of the late spring and summer of 1932, were patently inspired by the urgent wish of businessmen to downgrade Congressional control over the formation of economic policy and to enhance their own as much as possible.

Such an aim sometimes brought together odd bedfellows, as when Ogden Mills, Hoover's trusted Secretary of the Treasury, discussed with Baruch and Owen Young, both conservative Democratic nabobs, a plan for an "Economic Planning Board," to be headed, Young hoped, by Calvin Coolidge. Mills withdrew from the discussions after only a brief exchange, but the episode was symptomatic of the business community's harried search for plausible recovery ideas during the spring and summer of 1932. Perhaps the most pretentious proposal was the one for reconstitution of the Council of National Defense which Howard Coffin, an influential wartime member of that body, presented, accompanied by a troop of businessmen, at the White House on June 10 after several weeks of preparation by way of press publicity and conferences with political leaders. The claim was made that the legal basis for the CND was still in effect. It could be revived as an economic planning council simply through presidential appointments and directives. The council would be, according to Coffin's statement, a force for "directing and unifying public opinion on the great problems which confront us." These problems "are largely economic, and not political, and some of them should be taken out of the realm of national politics."

Hoover might have chosen a spectacular device such as one of these, and attempted to restart the economy through a re-employment scheme as he turned during July to "see if we can get some unity of action in all branches of industry toward betterment of the situation," believing that "the cumulative effect of unity of action even on small lines might be very effective at the present time." According to what he told Roy Chapin, president of the Hudson Motor Car Company, at just about this time, in order to lure him into accepting the post Robert Lamont was abandoning to head the American Iron and Steel Institute, Hoover intended to be "aggressive all this Fall and Winter—and be this whether he is reelected or not." He planned "to marshall all the forces that have been put at his disposal for a combined assault forward." [4]

To execute this "forward assault," Hoover relied upon a rather commonplace agency, the Banking and Industrial Committees of the twelve Federal Reserve districts. The first of these committees, composed of six each of prominent bankers and industrialists, had formed in the New York district early the previous spring—its goal: to encourage banks and businessmen to take advantage of the credit opportunities which the Administration's recovery program supposedly had created. On May 19 Hoover had publicly urged formation of similar committees in the other districts. Now, in July, Hoover decided to call these committees together and launch a coordinated recovery drive. The Conference of Banking and Industrial Committees of August 26–27 accepted the Administration plan for creation of six national committees, each headed by a prominent businessman. Each national committee would, through the regional Banking and Industrial Committees, promote a specified recovery policy. The activities of these six committees were familiar, relating mostly to stimulating the offering and the use of credit. Pedestrian and hackneyed as the proposed activities might be, however, the apparatus established by the B and I Conference managed to capture some of the glamour which attached to the proposals of recent months for a new agency of planning and recovery. At least one of the conference's national committees, moreover, the one entrusted with launching a national "Share-the-Work" movement, capitalized on the widespread attention given in the immediately preceding months to re-employment and work-spreading schemes.[5]

The cooperation businessmen gave Hoover in launching this recovery program seems to contradict the impression Hoover created, in the story he told about his confrontation with Harriman: that there was widespread desertion of him by big businessmen during the 1932 campaign. It would stretch credulity to the breaking point to believe that Hoover and the cooperating businessmen had no thought of political implications in holding the B and I Conference and in carrying out its plans. A. W. Robertson, who headed the committee on rehabilitation of industrial equipment established by the B and I Conference, denied political motivation a little too self-consciously when he explained his plans to a preliminary meeting of leaders the day before the conference. "His Committee's approach would be wholly economic," he said, "avoiding political propaganda and appealing to the self-interest of the companies concerned." Walter Teagle revealed another ulterior purpose in a "confidential memo" for the members of his national Share-The-Work Committee when he urged that "enlightened self-interest if not patriotism," should dictate employers' cooperation with the committee. The coming months, he wrote, would witness high unemployment, exhaustion of savings, drying up of the sources of charity relief, "and the probability of consequent suffering and with it greater social unrest."

Business cooperation with the campaign was substantial. The business press, especially the McGraw–Hill magazines such as *Business Week* and *Electrical World*, by pre-arrangement with the President, greeted the recovery program enthusiastically and tried for several weeks to maintain belief in its efficacy and existence, while general newspapers gave at least the conference itself the status of a top news story for several days. During September both the Chamber of Commerce and the NAM announced their support for work-sharing and their intention of persuading their members to adopt the practice. The Chamber also acted behind the scenes, in at least one instance, to further the conference's policies, when Harriman and Strawn visited the heads of major railroads to urge them to "avail themselves of the money which the Reconstruction Finance Corporation is willing to loan for the repair of cars, engines, etc." [6]

There are other signs that the desertion of big business, with which Harriman threatened Hoover, was not extensive or serious during the campaign. If Harriman threatened Hoover, Silas Strawn, the Chamber's past president and chairman of the committee charged with drafting and lobbying for a bill which would implement the goals of the 1931 referendum on antitrust policy, called publicly for his re-election. Another revisionist leader, Charles F. Abbott of the American Institute of Steel Construction, worked devotedly to mobilize business support for Hoover, addressing groups throughout the East and distributing stocks of his speech "Crossing the Delaware," which drew a parallel between the loyalty of Washington's troops and loyalty to Hoover in adversity. Thomas W. Lamont, president of the J. P. Morgan Company, experienced little difficulty in calling together representatives from the leading New York financial houses and the largest industrial corporations late in the campaign to plan how to communicate quickly to friendly businessmen the Republican need for an additional $500,000 to finance the President's radio addresses and to pay for a get-out-the-vote drive on election day.

Impressionistic evidence such as this fails to provide a definitive solution to the problem of whether Roosevelt's seemingly more favorable attitude to antitrust liberalization may have moved significant business support away from Hoover during the 1932 campaign. There are some indications that in the case of certain industries there may have been a definite pledge of relaxation from the Roosevelt side and possibly an equally definite reciprocal gesture from the business side. But it appears that such understandings, if they existed at all, were limited; that there was no large-scale defection from Hoover because of his stand on the antitrust issue. [7]

The B and I Conference of late August was Hoover's major contribution to the popularization and legitimization of the bootstrap recovery concept, but the Administration had a continuing role through the fall and early winter in this regard. Walter Teagle's Share-The-Work Committee remained active and energetic long after the other national committees of the B and I Conference had lapsed into inactivity. With offices in the Federal Reserve Bank building in New York and with the facilities of the field offices of the Department of Commerce to assist him, Teagle maintained publication of *Jobs: Progress Bulletin of the Share-The-Work Movement* and kept up a barrage of propaganda, even though this soon fell far below the standard he had originally set, of a drive "organized along the lines of war-time Liberty Loan campaigns."

In late November Teagle secured statements from both Roosevelt and Hoover endorsing the movement, publicized these at a Share-The-Work dinner in New York, and then persuaded the Administration to include them in letters mailed, at Commerce Department expense, by Chapin and Secretary of Labor Doak to 335,000 employers on December 17. Even at this late date Teagle (supported by Chapin, for Hoover's enthusiasm for all such efforts at economic recovery had dimmed by this time) hoped to put new life into Share-The-Work. A questionnaire was included with each letter with plans for having replies showing the progress of work-sharing totaled by the Bureau of Labor Statistics and publicized by Teagle's committee.

Teagle, by early December, believed he had accomplished a great deal, primarily, the "public acceptance of the soundness of work-sharing as an emergency measure to relieve unemployment." Reflecting this acceptance was the "general abandonment of the practice of laying off employees as they could be spared." But in securing large-scale "dividing up time, to make possible the hiring of many more" of the already unemployed, there had been much less success. In half the Federal Reserve districts, the B and I Committees had responded poorly to Teagle's appeals; in most of the districts, the banker-members of the committees had shown "little disposition" to apply work-sharing to their own businesses, a poor example for other white-collar employers; in a number of industries, such as textiles and chain stores, wages were so low that to cut hours of work to introduce work-sharing would drive pay below the subsistence level. Teagle was beginning to reorganize his campaign along industry and trade association, rather than regional, lines of contact; already, good results had been obtained in the steel and petroleum industries, but the process of reorganization was slow. His campaign had not, he admitted, made much progress in re-employment, even if it had, as he thought, stemmed "the growth of unemployment." The basic problem remained, Teagle thought. "Even the good business man has become defensively self-centered," and could not see that "until employment is more general; until those in jobs feel free to spend, and some of those out of jobs are put back to work again, business is not going forward." [8]

After September 1932, Roy Chapin was perhaps the only member of the Administration left who retained any hope that a start-up recovery plan might be found and applied successfully in the last months of Hoover's presidency. He not only helped keep the Share-The-Work movement afloat but strongly encouraged James H. Rand of Remington Rand during the fall of 1932 as he perfected what became one of the best-known of the plans for re-employment and instant industrial recovery. Rand was a staunch Hoover supporter. In April 1932, he had offered to help counter attacks on Hoover's budget policy which "DuPont, an ally of Rascob's [sic]," was circulating among businessmen. During August, he had proposed a mobilization of businessmen to win the election in a much more explicit and flamboyant manner than Hoover had chosen through the B and I Conference. "Business activity is not increasing with sufficient rapidity to materially reduce unemployment prior to November," Rand told Hoover, making clear the partisan implications of his plan. Surely there were "five thousand manufacturing concerns" which would respond to "an old-fashioned campaign with the Liberty Loan spirit back of it," and "place actual orders for six months ahead in a concerted move during the month of September" to diminish unemployment rapidly. "Frankly," he told Hoover, "it will take a cleverly executed, long forward pass to win the game." Hoover unmoved by this proposal, Rand went on a week later to advertise (with the expert help of Bruce Barton), at a cost of $15,000, his own firm's decision to place large orders on the strength of a supposed confidence in the coming return of better times. By late September, advertising costs of this one-company recovery campaign had reached $50,000.

The most extravagant campaign-ploy a businessman suggested to Hoover came from John R. Oishei, a Buffalo manufacturer closely associated with Rand's endeavors. Oishei reached Chapin late in the campaign to urge a maneuver which represented his concept of Rand's "long forward pass." Industrial employers would be organized immediately by the Republicans and radios installed in the plants. Workers would assemble at 11:50 A.M. on four different days to hear a presidential address, delivered by Hoover over a national hook-up or read for him by a local business leader. Chapin, himself a political neophyte, thought this an inspired political stroke and seriously urged Hoover to use it. "You had a great idea," Chapin wrote Oishei a few days before the election. He had hoped "we might have time for at least a record of a speech by the President addressed to the workers of the country;" but "when it came to a show-down, [Hoover] said . . . he [could not] take the time to work up the necessary speech." [9]

What became known as the Rand Plan surfaced early in November when Oishei sent copies of it to Henry M. Robinson, chairman of the central committee of the B and I Conference, and to Administration figures. Some Treasury officials thought it "the bunk," but others, especially Chapin and his Commerce Department associates, believed it could initiate the recovery which had proven so elusive. Rand was indefatigable in behalf of his brain child, a simple plan which called for employers to pledge to add a specified number of the unemployed to their payrolls for a ninety-day period. The plan would be announced when the number of pledges reached three million re-employments. Assistance in maintaining these payrolls, if necessary, would come through a half billion dollars in loans from the RFC. By early December Rand had actually persuaded Walter Teagle to back the plan if both Hoover and Roosevelt endorsed it and if Hoover agreed to give it a semi-official status. "SINCE TEAGLE CONFERENCE," Rand wired Chapin on December 2, "I HAVE SECURED ASSURANCES FROM ONE OF ROOSEVELT'S CLOSEST ADVISORS THAT ROOSE-VELT WILL ENDORSE ESPECIALLY SINCE HE HAS RECENTLY ASKED FOR SOME PLAN OF INJECTING PURCHASING POWER AT THE BOTTOM OF THE INDUSTRIAL STRATA WHERE IT WILL MAKE A QUICK IMPRESSION ON BUSI-NESS." Rand had already reserved an hour of national broadcast time for January 1, 1933, for the announcement of the plan. Chapin pressed Hoover to assume leadership, but the President had already decided not to. "The primary difficulty is that we are between two administrations," he told another advocate of the plan. "It would require a national set-up of a very large character, which means a tremendous application on my part, with the uncertainty of its continuance." Perhaps the B and I Committees would take it up, but he would not.

Rand continued his efforts, nonetheless. On December 7, he published a booklet describing the plan in detail, which he sent to a small group of men who represented many of the nation's largest corporations; Rand evidently hoped that, if he secured their backing, he would be able to reopen the proposal with Hoover. Chapin assisted with this tactic but was disappointed. "My aim," he told Rand in mid-December, "has been to secure judgment on it from a number of men whose backing would be most important were it to go through. . . . So far, I regret to say, it has not received the enthusiastic support of any of these men." By early January, Rand had abandoned hope in the Hoover Administration and had formed the Committee for the Nation to Rehabilitate Purchasing Power and Prosperity to influence the incoming Administration. The Committee for the Nation put greatest stress upon monetary proposals, and John Oishei now came forward during the winter of 1932/33 as the chief protagonist of the scheme.[10]

Rand's plan was predicated upon the belief that rapid increases in employment would create "purchasing power" which somehow would re-create itself and expand. It had many parallels, such as Fred I. Kent's proposal for, as it was explained to Thomas W. Lamont, "guaranteeing manufacturers against loss in the production of goods for which there is not now a demand, in the hope that the manufacture of such goods would start the wheels of industry to a degree which would create the demand for the goods." These re-employment plans—intended, as Kent informed Lamont, "to get the government out of what it is already in, and at the same time prevent it from getting into dole payments from which it would never get out"—had a substantial following among businessmen.

The Hoover Administration, first by sponsoring the B and I Conference in August and then by supporting the Share-The-Work movement and giving the Rand Plan the dignity of careful consideration, had helped to popularize and dignify the re-employment concept. Other industrial start-up plans had gained a wide hearing without, of course, any backing whatsoever by the Administration. The two most widely accepted proposals for stimulating purchasing power, output, and employment, other than re-employment plans of the Rand or Kent type, were proposals for limiting work hours through federal regulation and for pump-priming expenditures. Senator Hugo Black's Thirty-Hour Bill, hotly debated in Senate hearings during the interregnum session of Congress was by far the best-known hours-limitation scheme. Pump-priming public works or relief expenditures had many Congressional partisans, most notably Senators Wagner, La Follette, and Costigan.[11]

With the endeavors of antitrust-revision leaders to combine forces, the Administration had, by contrast, relatively slight association. Chapin during January worked diligently to bring together all the groups and individuals "who have been working hard to revive business." The relevant units for him were the Chamber, Robert Lund of the NAM, Walter Teagle and Matthew Sloan of the B and I group, Rand and his committee (which was trying to establish a working arrangement with the National Industrial Conference Board), and one or two individuals with notable recovery plans. Chapin was trying to achieve business unity on budget and recovery plan proposals, however, and the gathering he arranged for these groups apparently had little bearing on the development of the antitrust coalition which the Chamber of Commerce attempted to form in mid-October 1932.[12]

The Chamber's bid for leadership opened with a conference on October 10 to which Harriman and Silas Strawn invited a number of men "who have been prominently connected with developments in recent years respecting antitrust legislation." The attendance list is of considerable interest as it indicates the men and organizations which, in the Chamber's well-informed estimation, carried the most weight and had the greatest interest in the revision movement. C. B. Ames, the most articulate spokesman for the petroleum industry, was present, together with James D. Francis and C. E. Bockus for bituminous coal. J. Harvey Williams, the Truce Plan advocate, attended as a representative of the factory supplies and machinery industries. Organization leaders included James Emery of the NAM, North Storms of the Congress of Industries, Rush Butler of the ABA's Commerce Committee, and Gilbert Montague and Goldthwaite Dorr, listed as representing New York commercial and legal organizations, respectively. Strawn proceeded cautiously, evidently wishing to weld the organizations and industries represented into a firm coalition. Strawn made it clear that the Chamber now felt substantive revision was definitely required, and he tentatively broached a moderate proposal: liberalizing the standard for judging the legality of cooperative agreements and establishing an agency to give prior approval to them. The safeguard of the public interest was simply that the Justice Department could bring civil suit against agreements if it wished, but under conditions which would tend to lead the courts to accept the prior findings and decision of the approving agency. Obviously, the Chamber still hoped to escape genuine regulation of cartelized business and still was far from broaching the concept of governmental or industrial coercion of firms refusing to accept cartel regulations voluntarily. In mid-November, when Strawn reported upon this conference to his Board of Directors, general agreement had not been reached on this proposal, but Strawn evidently hoped it would soon be achieved.[13]

The frailty of these hopes for the easy formation of an inclusive coalition was demonstrated two weeks after Strawn's report when a conference of natural resource industries, called together by the National Coal Association, apparently pessimistic at this point about the success of the *Appalachian Coals* appeal, met in New York on December 1. Each industry was represented by one of its most experienced and prestigious leaders in antitrust affairs, with C. B. Ames appearing for petroleum. Reporters learned, though the meeting proceeded in closed session, that a central issue at the conference was whether the natural resource industries should push for legislation reflecting "all basic industries" or should seek a remedy only for themselves. At a second meeting on December 16, agreement was reached to take the separatist path. The plan was to draw an analogy between natural-resource-industry problems and those of agriculture and to seek exemption from the Sherman Act through legislation resembling the Capper–Volstead Act of 1922, which had released agricultural marketing-cooperatives from the confines of the antitrust laws. This plan immediately became snagged, however, when the petroleum industry representative on the drafting committee established at the general meeting of the 16th insisted that the proposal cover marketing as well as basic production controls, a demand out of step with the plan of modeling the proposed bill on the agricultural legislation of the previous decade. A third general meeting on January 16 failed to resolve the issue, and the group adjourned amid reports that it was not so sanguine now of obtaining action in the current short session of the Seventy-Second Congress.[14]

For several weeks this natural resource group was inactive. The member industries, for the most part represented by the same men who had taken part in the group's conferences, participated in still another attempt, this one led apparently by the NAM, to forge a general coalition of all revisionist forces. Silas Strawn had not secured general adherence to his October proposal and at this point evidently was not actively attempting to maintain the central leadership role. James A. Emery of the NAM during January persuaded Hatton Sumners, House Judiciary Committee Chairman, to convene his committee for a one-day session to listen to the arguments of revisionists from key industries and organizations. The informal hearing was held on February 8, 1933, with the businessmen and their attorneys holding a preliminary meeting the previous day. Except for Emery himself, Rush Butler, and Matthew Woll, all the participants represented separate major industries. These were drawn from precisely the areas of the economy one would have predicted on the basis of earlier patterns of support for revision. Of the sixteen participants, eight represented the major associations of the natural resource industries. Included were most of the veteran crusaders for revision from such industries, including Wilson Compton and William Ritter (lumber), C. B. Ames (petroleum), and C. E. Bockus (bituminous coal). The other industries represented were iron and steel (by Robert P. Lamont and Charles R. Hook), cotton textiles (by Walker D. Hines and Howard Coffin), and factory supplies and machinery (by J. Harvey Williams). It was stated to the Judiciary Committee that Strawn was cooperating with the group, but no representative from the Chamber actually appeared.

Even at this late date, on the very eve of the new Roosevelt Administration, the group was far from a consensus on a definite legislative remedy. The previous concern with avoiding as much as possible the appearance of substantive revision and of side-stepping detailed government regulation of market agreements still was much in evidence. Prior to the hearing on February 8, no agreement on a definite proposal was reached. Witnesses at the morning session—principally Emery, Bockus, Compton, and Coffin—tried the committee's patience with long recitations of the severity of the depression in their industries. Instructed to make a definite proposal, the delegates decided at the luncheon break to fall back on what amounted to the Williams Truce Plan. Walker Hines presented the case for an emergency antitrust-law suspension in the afternoon session, but the committee seems to have been singularly unimpressed. Hines and others were unable to explain convincingly how the suspension of competition would restore general prosperity and apparently had not given much thought to justifying themselves in this respect. Hines's suggestion, according to a Commerce Department onlooker, "that resulting price stabilization might stimulate demand was made only as an afterthought." Chairman Sumners closed the hearing on a discouraging note, stating "his opinion that as a practical proposition no plan could be adopted which did not at least hold out the promise of increasing buying power," and suggesting that "agriculture held the key." [15]

The parties to the meetings of February 7–8 "seemed to [take] for granted that the various industries present should take an active part in securing emergency legislation," and asked Walker Hines, counsel and former president of the Cotton Textile Institute, to work out a more specific recommendation for emergency antitrust suspension. Goldthwaite Dorr, for many years counsel of the CTI and currently sharing this responsibility with Hines, took on this task, aided by Walter G. Merritt and Rush Butler. Within a few days this subcommittee had drafted an extremely radical proposal for an emergency board empowered to approve market agreements and even to force uncooperative elements in an industry to adhere to them. When the would-be coalition representatives convened again on March 8 to consider Dorr's bill, some criticized it severely for its extreme character, which made it supposedly an invitation for full-scale government regulation of industry; others, because it provided for only emergency, rather than permanent, relief. By this time, too, the natural resource industries were again splitting off, already making individual appeals for special treatment to Roosevelt. At the beginning of the New Deal, the organizations and industries which had taken the lead toward revision in the previous two years were still far from a consensus on what specifically should be done, and from an effective pooling of political strength or a convincing justification of their demands.[16]

NOTES

1. *New York Journal of Commerce*, May 16, June 14, July 7, September 24, October 7, 1932. *New York Times*, May 16, June 25, 30, August 14, 1932.
2. Hoover, *Memoirs*, 3 vols. (New York: Macmillan, 1952), III 334–35. William S. Myers and Walter H. Newton, *The Hoover Administration* (New York: Scribner, 1936), pp. 245–46. Murray N. Rothbard, "Herbert Hoover and the Myth of Laissez-Faire," *A New History of Leviathan: Essays on the Rise of the American Corporate State*, edd. Ronald Radosh and Murray N. Rothbard (New York: Dutton Paperbacks, 1972), p. 145. Warren, *Hoover*, p. 266, also accepted Hoover's account of the interview but not necessarily his estimate of the consequences. The source for the gossip referred to is a letter, the signature indecipherable, to Ted Joslin, written during the summer of 1932, in Chamber of Commerce file, HHPP.

3. Albert U. Romasco, *The Poverty of Abundance: Hoover, the Nation, the Depression* (New York: Oxford University Press, 1965), pp. 187–201. Wilbur and Hyde, *Hoover Policies*, pp. 524–27. Myers and Newton, *Hoover Administration*, pp. 242–44. Hoover, *Memoirs*, III 167–68. Barnes to Hoover, February 25, 1932, Barnes file; Wesley Jones to Hoover, June 16, 1932, enclosing letter for Hoover by A. O. Soreng, June 9, 1932, Business file; Albert H. Lyber to Rudolf Forster, March 10, 1932; Ted Joslin to Lyber, March 12, 1932, Unemployment file, HHPP.

4. Howard P. Ingels to Baruch, June 14, 1932, Bernard M. Baruch Papers, Princeton University. Herbert B. Swope to Mills, April 16, 1932, Ogden L. Mills Papers, Library of Congress. *New York Times*, May 23, June 11 (for the quote in the text), June 25, 1932. Hoover to J. Frederic Byers, July 25, 1932, Business file, HHPP. Chapin to Coffin, August 19, 1932, Chapin Papers.

5. Romasco, *Poverty of Abundance*, pp. 198–210, for a general description of the Banking and Industrial Committees Conference. In box 59, Mills Papers, there is a typescript "Confidential History" of the conference, which provides a good deal of information but nothing of enough significance to warrant the title. The material in the Banking and Industrial Committees file, HHPP, is informative, but also rather limited.

6. An excellent source is the "Minutes of meeting of Chairmen of B and I Committees and members of the Administration," August 25, 1932, Banking and Industrial Committees file, Record Group 56, General Records of the Department of the Treasury, National Archives. Teagle to Julius Klein, September 16, 1932, file 81560/8, RG 40. Paul Wooton to Ted [Joslin?], early September 1932, Business file; Harriman to Hoover, September 24, 1932, Railroad file, HHPP. Chamber of Commerce, Executive Committee, *Minutes*, August 12, 1932; Board of Directors, *Minutes*, September 23, 1932. *New York Times*, September 24, October 3, 1932.

7. *Ibid.*, October 7, 19, 1932. Abbott to Lawrence Richey, September 7, 30, November 1, 1932, Abbott file, HHPP. Lamont to John Markle, October 26, 1932; memo, October 26, 1932, and text of telephone messages sent for Lamont, file 123–17, Thomas W. Lamont Papers, Baker Library, Harvard University Graduate School of Business.

8. A copy of the November 21 issue of *Jobs* is in box 19, Carmody Papers. *New York Times*, August 28, 1932. Teagle to Julius Klein, November 19, 1932; Klein to Ted Joslin, November 21, 1932; Chapin to Hoover, December 14, 1932, all in Share-The-Work movement file, HHPP. Chapin to William Steuart, November 10, 1932; Chapin to Teagle, November 10, 1932; letter samples by Chapin and Doak, and by Teagle; and memo for Chapin by Steuart, December 12, 1932; Teagle to Chapin, December 5, 1932, all in file 81560/8, RG 40.

9. Rand to Lawrence Richey, April 23, August 24 (telephone message), 1932; to Hoover, April 26, June 30, August 19, September 21, 27, 1932, Rand file, HHPP. Oishei to Chapin, October 21, 1932; Chapin to Oishei, October 31, 1932, Chapin Papers.

10. Oishei to Robinson, November 2, 1932; Everett Case to Robinson, November 3, 1932; Robinson to Lawrence Richey, November 5, 1932; Edward H. Butler to Hoover, December 1, 1932; Hoover to Butler, December 3, 1932, Chamber of Commerce (Share-The-Work folder) file, HHPP. Chapin to Hoover, December 2, 1932; to Julius Klein, December 3, 1932; Rand to Chapin, n.d.; Chapin to Oishei, December 12, 1932; to Rand, December 15, 1932, Lamont Papers, RG 40. Copy of Rand's booklet and cross-reference summary of Robinson's letter of January 17, 1933, Rand file, HHPP.

11. The Rand Plan is given in Senate, Committee on Finance, *Investigation of Economic Problems: Hearings . . . on S. R. 315*, 72d Cong., 2d sess., 1933,

pp. 652–56. For the Kent–Lamont exchange, Kent's letters of January 10, 20, 1933; "Memorandum for Mr. Lamont," by A. M. A., January 16, 1933, file 101–11, Thomas W. Lamont Papers. Senate, Committee on Education and Labor, *Thirty-Hour Week: Hearings . . . on S. 5267*, 72d Cong., 2d sess., 1933. The House also held hearings: House of Representatives, Committee on Labor, *Six-Hour Day, Five-Day Week: Hearings . . . on H. R. 14105*, 72d Cong., 2d sess., 1933.

12. Chapin to Robert L. Lund, December 2, 10, 1932; Lund to Chapin, December 2, 1932; Chapin to Teagle, January 25, 1933; to Alfred P. Sloan, Jr., January 28, 1933, Chapin Papers. There is a reference to this attempt during January to bring the major business groups together for coordination of recovery policies in NAM, Executive Committee, "Minutes," and Board of Directors, "Minutes," for January 5, 1933.

13. Montague to Winthrop W. Aldrich, October 17, 1932, box 114, Winthrop W. Aldrich Papers, Baker Library, Harvard University Graduate School of Business, for a description of the October 10 conference. Though Chapin apparently had little influence upon antitrust developments, he was closely in touch with them. See T. R. Taylor to Chapin, October 6, 1932; Chapin to Butler, October 8, 1932, file 82248/48, RG 40. A copy of Strawn's November report to the Chamber's Board of Directors and his proposed bill is also in this file.

14. *New York Times,* November 29, December 2, 17, 1932, January 17, 1933; *New York Journal of Commerce,* December 20, 1932.

15. *Ibid.,* January 4, February 9, 1933. Memos for Board of Directors of CTI by George A. Sloan, February 8, 18, 1933, Donald Comer Papers, Baker Library, Harvard University Graduate School of Business. The fullest source on the hearing of February 8 is the memo to Chapin by C. J. Junkin, February 9, 1933, file 82248/48, RG 40.

16. Sloan to CTI Directors, February 18, 1933, Comer Papers. For information on the bill drawn up by Dorr and on the meeting of March 8, I have relied upon Galambos, *Competition and Cooperation,* pp. 188–91. Galambos enjoyed access to the papers of Goldthwaite Dorr in researching his book on the CTI, an access I have not been able to secure. The Dorr papers appear to be especially helpful on this point.

10

The Triumph of the Revisionists: The N.I.R.A.

THROUGH THE National Industrial Recovery Act of June 1933, the business community achieved much of what it had sought during the depression years in its crusade for antitrust liberalization. The text of the Act did not quite make this outcome certain. Advocates of other policies, including national planners and those who wanted simply to strengthen fair competition and improve wage-and-hour standards, tried, in fact, to interpret the Act in their favor. The history of the NRA became, after the initial victory of business during the summer and fall of 1933 when most of the important codes regulating industry conduct were written, a three-sided contest for supremacy between these two viewpoints and that of the businessmen. The text, however, did give business a very strong position which enabled it to gain the initial advantage as the codes were drafted, an advantage which was never lost. The codes did improve labor standards as the Administration exacted its price for approving the cartelistic arrangements they contained. But these arrangements were the most important result of the Act.

How did it come about that the N.I.R.A. which, with the Agricultural Adjustment Act, formed the basis of the New Deal's hopes for recovery during 1933 and 1934, conformed so closely to the business ideal? Was the Act created principally as a response and concession to business pressure for antitrust liberalization? This, in a direct, immediate sense, is not the case. The N.I.R.A. was the result of an interplay between advocates of different recovery proposals during the Hundred Days. Roosevelt and most of the members of his Administration were searching for an effective recovery proposal and had little interest simply in satisfying the antitrust revisionists. That the plan adopted, the N.I.R.A., was so favorable in substance and in effect to the revisionists was not so much willed by the President and his lieutenants as it was thrust upon them by circumstances. This is the thesis of this chapter. The argument which sustains it differs from previous treatments of the birth of the NRA in that the focus is upon the sequence of the President's decisions leading to the drafting of the Act and upon a detailed tracing of the efforts to influence him made by the protagonists of each of the major types of recovery proposals which contended for the dominance the business viewpoint ultimately achieved.[1]

The identities and the ideas of these groups are for the most part well described, though not treated fully, in Arthur Schlesinger, Jr.'s *The Coming of the New Deal*. He designates business advocates of recovery through trade association control of markets as one source; partisans of labor-standards legislation as a second; those who wished to make a beginning at national economic planning as a third; and supporters of public works spending as a fourth group which influenced the decision to create the NRA. To these four there should be one addition, a result of the distinction, developed in the preceding chapter of this study, between business spokesmen who were pressing primarily pro-cartelist views upon the politicians and those whose primary aim was recovery, the start-up of the economy, and who framed their proposals accordingly. This distinction commonly is blurred and goes unrecognized because the two groups overlapped with respect to personnel and certain elements of their proposals. But it was nonetheless genuine and significant, as I think can be maintained, and it is important for understanding the background of the N.I.R.A.[2]

It is widely held that at the beginning of the Hundred Days there was no plan for a measure such as the N.I.R.A. and that a serious intention to develop a legislative proposal embodying some or all of its goals came only after passage by the Senate of the Black Thirty-Hour bill on April 6, 1933. The statement needs qualification, as I hope to show, but it is nonetheless true that the date constituted a turning point. It is therefore logical to divide the investigation. The period before April 6—the months of Roosevelt's campaign for the nomination and the presidency, the interregnum and the early part of the Hundred Days—makes up the first. The aim here is to see to what extent the various groups and viewpoints which influenced the creation of the N.I.R.A. reached Roosevelt's ear and how well, relatively, each succeeded in making some impression. The time between April 6 and the final passage of the N.I.R.A., June 16, constitutes the second focus, though the center of interest is the period ending May 17 when the President submitted the bill to Congress. Here the purpose is to see how, in a very rapidly developing situation, each of the concerned groups influenced the outcome: the drafting of the N.I.R.A.

THE NATIONAL PLANNING CONCEPT

The least significant of these influences probably was the proposal for industrial planning. Rexford Tugwell alone among Roosevelt's advisers advocated genuine planning in the sense of coordination of the various industries through a central planning mechanism. It is true that the three main Brain Trust members, Raymond Moley, Adolph Berle, and Tugwell, all accepted the thesis of inevitably increasing concentration of industry and disparaged traditional antitrust methods for meeting the concomitant problems. All three also accepted the institutionalist concept of the need for achieving "balance" within the economy, but Moley and Berle drew from such concepts conclusions which resembled those of the business planning position.[3]

Tugwell was the only ascertainable source of advocacy for industrial planning which directly reached Roosevelt's ear during the year before drafting got underway for the N.I.R.A. In *The Brains Trust*, his lengthy recollection of his conversations with Roosevelt before the election, Tugwell represents himself as consistently pressing the case for central planning. The candidate, he tells us, resisted his insistent arguments for introducing "collectivist" solutions into the campaign and continued to feel such solutions were impractical in political terms even though, he claims, Roosevelt felt they might be correct. Tugwell in other writings has downgraded the importance of Roosevelt's Commonwealth Club speech of September 23, 1932, in San Francisco. Because it adverts to the theme of industrial maturity and of adjusting production to fit consumption, the speech has been read as a brief for national economic planning. But the address, Tugwell says, did not represent Roosevelt's own views. It was written by Berle in New York with Tugwell's assistance, and wired to the campaigners in the West. Roosevelt had little time to review or revise it. In any case, the speech read carefully is not an argument for central planning. It cleaves much more closely to the business community's concepts of industrial planning. The well-known passages on economic maturity are, in fact, reminiscent of the argument in the 1931 report of the Chamber of Commerce's Committee on Continuity. Tugwell attributes chief responsibility for the speech to Berle, asserting that his own collectivist views in 1932 were expansionist. This assertion has been challenged, but, in any case, it is easy to accept the speech as Berle's handiwork since it corresponds so well to the approach he took during the whole period before the inauguration, as will be seen shortly. Tugwell claims that he continued his argument with Roosevelt during the interregnum period and that the result was the same as during the campaign months. Aside from Tugwell's statements, evidence is lacking to show that active discussion of these fundamental issues continued into the interregnum period, let alone into the Hundred Days.[4]

THE BUSINESS PLANNERS

If Roosevelt and most of the members of his circle never considered industrial planning in this broad sense a serious policy choice, what of the more limited "business planning" concept which envisioned trade association control of markets in the interest of stable profits and, depending upon the expositor's level of sophistication, other benefits ranging from more stable employment to social insurance for workers? Considering the frequency and intensity of business lobbying for the concept during the depression years, Roosevelt could not have remained innocent of it even had no definite efforts been made to interest him in it.

Advocates left nothing to chance, however. Within the Brain Trust, Berle seems to have been the most determined protagonist of the business planning viewpoint. The first concrete evidence of this is a lengthy memorandum penned by Berle, one of those written for the so-called "Memorandum of May 19," a collection of position papers prepared for Roosevelt by the Brain Trust and taken to him by Sam Rosenman in May 1932 at Warm Springs. The point of departure of Berle's piece is that concentration in business had progressed so far, and business interrelationships had thereby become so complex, that any economic dislocation had broad ramifications and dictated overall controls. The actual program recommended, however—looking to encouragement of further concentration, minimal regulation of concentrated industries, and a requirement from them of social insurance—was not far removed from the business planning concepts of the Chamber of Commerce, Gerard Swope, and the like. That it shared their fundamental social purposes, too, seems indicated by the memorandum's preoccupation with social disorder. There was perhaps "one chance in five" that total collapse might come the next winter. "For the first time," Berle thought, "the United States has come within hailing distance of revolution along continental European lines." Berle's plan included social insurance as "a charge on the earnings of industry," to which policy, he thought, "was largely due the stability of German industry from 1880 to the fall of the Empire."

Other evidence of Berle's continuous efforts to bring Roosevelt to a commitment to the business planning position appear at intervals during the following months. The Commonwealth Club speech, which Berle more or less thrust upon Roosevelt, was a brief for the thesis that production had to be regulated to fit stable market conditions and was perfectly consistent with the business planners' concepts. Shortly after the election Berle drew up a memo for Moley, listing his recommendations for legislation at the Special Session of Congress he expected in the spring. Second among these, next to the implementation of domestic allotment was "Industrial stabilization—limited permission to individuals to get together under suitable supervision on stability plans, *provided* they afford reasonable probability of greater employment . . . and are kept under control." This, of course, as Moley has pointed out in his *The First New Deal*, remarkably prefigures the N.I.R.A. At about this same time Berle established (or, perhaps, strengthened) contact with several leaders of the antitrust movement, including J. Harvey Williams and Gilbert Montague. At the end of January 1933, reviewing for Roosevelt the legislative problems he had been working on, Berle reminded the President-elect that "a strong drive to revise" the antitrust laws could be expected soon and that he had been "trying to block out a line for the last two months."

But Berle was becoming preoccupied with drafting the railway reorganization bill and other legislation of pressing concern, and with his private affairs, and his efforts for antitrust revision seem to have slackened after this. During February he consulted with, encouraged, and evidently conveyed to Roosevelt the revision plans of, the men who were drafting a bill for the coalition which had formed under NAM leadership. And, during the first days of the New Deal, he tried to obtain access to the President for members of that group. But Berle's role would be minimal during the spring of 1933. It seems clear, however, that he especially among Roosevelt's intimate advisers attempted to get sympathetic consideration for what was essentially the business community's concept of industrial reformation.[5]

The Chamber of Commerce, through its president, H. I. Harriman, approached the President-elect through M. L. Wilson, the Montana State agricultural economist who was greatly influential in fostering acceptance of the domestic allotment plan by the farm organizations and in securing its eventual adoption as the policy of the incoming Administration. Wilson's letters to Tugwell during the summer and fall of 1932 portray Harriman as "anti-Hoover" and "very friendly to the whole Roosevelt campaign," a "liberal" who was supporting the domestic allotment scheme despite severe criticism from processors' groups, and whose plan for trade association planning was forward-looking. Harriman prompted Wilson to urge that Tugwell arrange a meeting between the Chamber president and the Brain Trust after the election, hoping "that following this meeting the Governor will send for him and have a conference with him regarding his program and the attitude of the National Chamber of Commerce."

Harriman evidently entertained hopes of assuming the role of intimate and influential adviser. Like many others, he seems to have regarded Roosevelt as pliant and susceptible of domination. Wilson, in one of his letters to Tugwell, recorded a scene during July 1932 in which Harriman, arguing the relative merits of the candidates with a Minneapolis grain trader who felt he could not vote for Roosevelt because he was "not a big man," countered that he was "through with big men" like Hoover who "would not take advice." Roosevelt, Harriman thought, was the type who would "surround himself with advisors of good judgement and follow their advice."[6]

Though Harriman had some very limited contact with Tugwell and possibly with Moley after the election, it was many weeks before he reached the President-elect in a personal meeting. The two met on about January 12. On the 14th, Tugwell journeyed to Washington at Roosevelt's request to discuss farm and business policies with Harriman at greater length. At this meeting and at another a month later, with Moley also in attendance, the possibility of applying the production control principle of the farm program to industry was discussed, Harriman half convincing a skeptical Tugwell with his assurances that businessmen were ready to accept a good deal of central direction to escape intermittent depression.

The document, "An Economic Program," which Harriman delivered to Moley for the President-elect during his stay in New York during January, however, belied these assurances. The "Program" advocated antitrust revision to give the majority of an industry the right to determine fair wages and hours, prices and production levels, with governmental enforcement. It was an advanced proposal, going well beyond the moderate one which Silas Strawn had drawn up for the Chamber some weeks earlier, and one which, apparently, was presented as Harriman's own recommendation. But no substantial role for government in guiding industrial planning was allowed.

Harriman's sensibilities thus received every consideration from Roosevelt and his circle. The President-elect even favored Harriman with a letter from Warm Springs in January expressing a wish to meet with him again, "for you and I," Roosevelt wrote, "have the same broad philosophy and I want to talk with you about a number of things." But prior to the inauguration, Harriman did not make any progress in turning Roosevelt toward serious consideration of antitrust revision as an issue deserving place on the New Deal agenda. Neither did the business coalition which, as recounted already, relayed its proposals of February 1933 to Roosevelt through Berle. Berle's long effort to prompt his chief's attention to revision had also proven futile, for there is no indication that, as Roosevelt came into the presidency on March 4, 1933, he regarded the question as requiring or deserving early attention.[7]

The evidence for this is nearly conclusive. Early in the new year, Moley had drawn up a memorandum for Roosevelt listing projected legislation for the new Administration and noting who was at work on each of the several items. Antitrust was ignored. Roosevelt himself, shortly before the inauguration, jotted down in his own hand the steps he planned. "Mobilize the Governors—like Jefferson," he wrote first, thinking of the Governors Conference he had called for March 6. Federal utility regulation and tightening of the income tax with Felix Frankfurter's aid, making the RFC "aggressive," and a number of additional steps were also listed, but the revisionists' hopes entirely neglected.[8] This neglect continued—it appears to be almost studied during the early weeks of the New Deal—although preoccupation with the banking crisis, and with the relief and agricultural questions, perhaps account adequately for it. The revisionists were kept firmly at a distance, the most insistent group at this point being the coalition the NAM had formed the previous February. The members of this group met again on March 8 to consider the proposal Goldthwaite Dorr and others had drawn up and discussed with Berle. The proposed bill was a revised version of the Truce Plan of 1932, calling for emergency suspension of the antitrust laws, business agreements, and governmental coercion of non-cooperators. The framework for the draft bill was the standard business view that overproduction, and lowered prices and profits, were the cause of the depression. The elements of the coalition could not agree. Several apparently were not yet ready to ask for coercion of third parties, and the Chamber representative objected to the temporary character of the antitrust relaxation proposal. J. Harvey Williams was now commissioned by the group to work out a bill which all could accept, and Walker Hines delegated to speak with Roosevelt. The group after this became less inclusive. The coal and oil industries were already pursuing antitrust relief independently, and their cooperation with the group seems to have ceased after March 8. Harriman called the members together for March 27, but again no agreement was reached and, after this, the Chamber's representatives functioned entirely on their own. The coalition consisted after March 8, in practice, only of the NAM leaders Hines, Williams, and their associates. Each of these approached the White House separately, but each argued for the same proposal and employed the same rationale, and even similar language.

The substance of the proposal had not altered from what had been presented to Sumners' committee early in February. It still held to the Truce Plan concept, but experience had shown the expediency of stressing the program's implications for recovery rather than its aspect as relief from competitive pressures. Accordingly, the "spiralling downwards" of the economy "toward progressively lower levels" and the supposed result, "under wages and diminished purchasing power," which "threatens to become worse," were stressed. The remedy, "cooperative action within and among industries," was presented as having only the public good as an end. Robert Lund, NAM president, gave the argument one additional twist with the insistence that the reference in the 1932 Democratic platform ("our Party Platform," Lund called it) to "better protection of labor and the small producer and distributor" had been a pledge for antitrust relaxation.[9]

None of these attempts during March to secure a personal interview with the President succeeded. Adolph Berle ensured that Hines's and Williams' bids reached Roosevelt and gave them an enthusiastic second. The antitrust question, he wired Marvin McIntyre, the President's secretary, was "getting red hot," and "Williams is a good man to talk to about it." All were put off, as was Harriman, whose request of March 22 for "an appointment to talk over several matters pertaining to banking and ruinous cutting of wages—proposed legislation that will correct," as McIntyre's memo recorded it, was "Postponed Indefinitely." [10]

While Roosevelt during the first month of the New Deal kept the revisionist leaders representing the general business community strictly at bay, he was receptive to the oil industry spokesman's plea for curtailment and set Secretary of the Interior Ickes at work on the question only two weeks after the inauguration. The coal industry, too, received early attention. There are signs that these steps were by previous arrangement. Berle, urging attention to the coal operators early in March, recalled that "during the campaign a pledge was made that the Administration would try to work out a plan for the Bituminous Coal Industry" and that the "heads of several companies" had been "on my neck since that time."

On March 27 Roosevelt did ask Secretaries Perkins and Ickes to consider "legislation to cure some of the outstanding evils of the coal industry." But pressure from the UMW was the only visible cause for this. There is substantial evidence of the union's lobbying during this period for Administration consideration of the Kelly–Davis bill and the like, but little indication that the operators were also thus engaged. Ickes, who made contact with different groups from the bituminous operators during April, found them sharply divided over the advisability of seeking stabilization legislation, some fearing gains for the union. The *Appalachian Coals* decision had been handed down only on March 16, 1933, unexpectedly upholding the joint sales agency scheme which the industry had organized in 1932 and which had been condemned in the lower courts in the summer and fall of 1932. Opinion was, no doubt, divided on whether to take up the opening which the Court had provided or to seek a more comprehensive cartelization program through legislation.[11]

The coal operators were thus not immediately assertive in demanding legislation early in the New Deal, but there is little reason to believe that the promise during the campaign which Berle described was not actually made. Definitely no such pledge was made to the leaders of the general business organizations. Their whole line of behavior after the election makes it clear that they had no notion of prior commitments which they now could claim. But the oil men may have received a pledge such as Berle asserted the coal men had received. The special treatment Roosevelt gave them certainly hints at this. At a time, in the first weeks of the New Deal, when the heads of the NAM and the Chamber could not secure appointments with the President at all, James A. Moffett, Vice President of Standard Oil of New Jersey, who was acting as representative of the API, readily secured a meeting, through W. Forbes Morgan, secretary to the Democratic National Finance Committee. Moffett, "a very large contributor" to the Democratic cause and "a personal friend of the President" according to Morgan, carried the API proposals for production cutbacks to Roosevelt on March 14. The same afternoon, at the Cabinet meeting, Roosevelt asked Ickes to call an oil-states governors conference. By March 27, this conference had convened, and Ickes was meeting simultaneously with a group of oil industry representatives. By March 31, he was laying the latter's proposals before the Cabinet. The proposed oil legislation which resulted was eventually set aside, and the industry simply brought within the NRA; thus, neither coal nor oil actually secured legislative relief prior to general industry. Nonetheless, the President's eagerness to consider antitrust relaxation for these industries, while it may signify nothing more than that he accepted, as had Hoover, that these natural resource industries required differential treatment, does point to the sort of prior arrangement Berle described.[12]

By early April, however, Roosevelt had demonstrated by his actions that antitrust liberalization was a low-priority item in his calculations. It was not clear whether he was well-disposed at all toward revision for industry generally. Perhaps John S. Lawrence, a Harvard classmate and friend of Roosevelt's and a leader of a regional business group, the New England Council, was right, when he urged the new President to ask Congress to "suspend the Sherman Anti-Trust law" and to give the Executive "power to enforce curtailment in any industry," and the incongruity of the request struck him. "I laugh," Lawrence wrote late in March 1933, "when I think of writing you about relief of the workings of free competition which we both believe in."

Roosevelt, in any case, when the revisionists finally did secure an audience, firmly rejected any thought that he would propose antitrust liberalization in the current Congress. The rejection, as Walker Hines, who met with the President on April 11, reported it to James A. Emery, was put in terms of pragmatic calculation. "The President [said] that the matter was so controversial that he could not see his way to deal with it in the present session." [13]

PUBLIC WORKS SPENDING

As late as April 11, then, Roosevelt was still rejecting the revisionists' demands, giving every indication of a firm intention to avoid conceding to them. Neither, by this date, had the advocates of the third recovery proposal which figured in the background of the N.I.R.A. made much progress with the President. The memoirs of the New Dealers and most of the secondary treatments of the Hundred Days mention Roosevelt's resistance, both during his fight for the presidency and during the early New Deal, to proposals for large-scale public works spending, but the tenacity and depth of that resistance and the significance of his duel with the spenders has not, I think, been fully appreciated. During the pre-convention period and the campaign, Roosevelt had never proposed public works spending as a recovery measure and had, of course, sought to present himself as sounder on the balanced budget issue than Hoover. On March 21, 1933, Roosevelt did, in his relief message to Congress (which asked for creation of the Civilian Conservation Corps and replenishment of funds for grants to states for work relief), make a noncommittal reference to public works spending as a recovery measure. The reference, which merely stated his intention of making recommendations on public works after further study, was included only at the insistence of a Cabinet group which included Perkins, Wallace, Ickes, and Dern, and of a number of senatorial public works partisans including Wagner, La Follette, and Costigan. During the following weeks both the Cabinet and senatorial groups continued their pressure, but by mid-April Roosevelt, pressured also by Administration fiscal conservatives, especially Lewis Douglas, Director of the Bureau of the Budget, was, as his remarks in the April 14 press conference show, still delaying a decision.[14]

These three proposals then—central planning, cartelization, large-scale public works—Roosevelt had respectively ignored, explicitly rejected, and stalled up to the point in early April at which, it is usually thought, the series of events which led to the N.I.R.A. began. The other two types of proposal which figured in those events, however—wage-and-hour regulation and industrial start-up plans—had received much more favorable attention during the preceding months and the first weeks of the Hundred Days.

WAGES, HOURS, AND PURCHASING POWER

Assisted by Frances Perkins as his Industrial Commissioner, Roosevelt had worked for state wage-and-hour legislation during his years as governor of New York. Perkins, who continued for a time as Industrial Commissioner under Roosevelt's successor, Herbert Lehman, helped the new governor press for wage-and-hour legislation during the winter of 1932/33. Perkins believed wage-and-hour controls were urgently needed, not only to shore up workers' standards but to arrest the downward spiral of the depression and to create jobs. At least during the prevailing period of massive unemployment, she felt, radical restriction of the work week was necessary. In December 1932, Perkins advised Lehman, who would become governor on January 1, 1933, to demand from the legislature the thirty-five-hour week together with the pegging of minimum wages. She was eager also to promote federal initiatives toward wage-and-hour regulation and did everything she could, in the weeks before and after March 4, when she became Roosevelt's Secretary of Labor, to push toward such action. Seemingly, the surest step the President could take to secure constitutionally acceptable regulation would be to persuade the

states to formulate parallel legislation. In the weeks before the inauguration, Perkins, with Felix Frankfurter's aid, persuaded Roosevelt to add
state regulation of hours and wages to the agenda of the Governors Conference which was to convene on March 6. In mid-March, Sam Rosenman became an ally in Perkins' cause, sending the new President a copy
of Lehman's message on wages and hours recently transmitted to the
New York State Legislature and urging him to make a "statement . . .
to the Governors requesting action in all of the states, not only as to
minimum wage legislation but, what is more important, as to a five-day
week."

The result of further discussion between Roosevelt and Perkins was,
first, on April 3, a message from Perkins to Governor Cross of Con-
necticut and, on April 11, after passage of minimum wage legislation in
New York, messages from the President to the governors of the other
leading industrial states, urging immediate action to regulate wages and
hours. Perkins' plan, as she expained it in a letter to a New York manufacturer at just this time, was to induce at least the great industrial states
of the East to enact wage-and-hour legislation and then stimulate cooperation among them on establishing comparable standards. Federal
regulation was not likely to hold up, she feared, without a constitutional
amendment.[15]

Perkins, however, preferred federal action and, despite these doubts
of constitutionality, was, from the beginning of the new Administration,
seriously and determinedly searching for a form of regulation which
could overcome political opposition and satisfy the Supreme Court's
scruples. According to her memoirs, she had made Roosevelt's pledge of
support, in principle, for federal wage-and-hour legislation a condition
of her accepting the Labor Department post. From the outset of the Hundred Days, Perkins was searching for a way of redeeming that pledge
promptly. In a "Suggested Statement" submitted to Roosevelt for Herbert Lehman to make at the Governors Conference on March 6, Perkins
proposed a direct federal role in backing up state wage-and-hour regulation. Violations, she proposed, could be treated as unfair competition,
subject to the jurisdiction of the FTC. By mid-March, however, Perkins
had decided to explore the extent of support for direct federal regulation. Labor leaders and labor experts were called to Washington for a
March 31 conference on unemployment and labor standards. The principle purpose, as she explained to Donald Richberg, one of those invited,
would be to discuss methods of securing shorter hours and higher wages
as a means of reducing unemployment. The conference was well attended, with many of the AFL unions represented. The "Recommendations" produced at the one-day meeting reflected the consensus which
readily developed favoring public works spending and similar palliatives
of unemployment and, above all, limitation of hours through the Black

Thirty-Hour bill which the AFL had vigorously supported in the previous two sessions of Congress and which now neared a vote in the Senate. Perkins introduced the question of minimum wage regulation, proposing establishment of "industrial boards" for each major industry. She was committed to drastic reduction of the work week, but argued that wage increases and regulation must accompany hours reduction. The AFL had always shied away from minimum wage laws, but the conferees nonetheless gave qualified endorsement to Perkins' idea, stressing the proviso that the right of collective bargaining "be recognized as basic to the work of the industrial boards, if established." [16]

Roosevelt evidently agreed with Perkins' objectives. He had, as she prompted, urged the governors, both at the Governors Conference of March 6 and in special communications a month later, to seek immediate state regulation of wages and hours. Evidently he shared Perkins' insistence, which Lehman and Rosenman too had put in the foreground, that wage-and-hour regulation was an effective means of restoring purchasing power, decreasing unemployment, and reviving the economy. Roosevelt had also agreed to Perkins' calling of the labor conference of March 31, which she intended should result in an appeal for federal measures. That Roosevelt meant from the outset of his Administration to seek federal wage-and-hour legislation is evidenced by his memo of early March (which has already been described), which projected the setting up of a group to formulate substance and strategy in obtaining regulation. The eighth point of the memo reads (with undecipherable words omitted): "Sidney Hillman—Head of Amalgamated Clothing Workers —Wages—Hours—Appoint . . . *now* to work out ways and means to . . . into effect. People: FF [Felix Frankfurter] and any good names." [17]

THE START-UP PLANNERS

During the winter of 1932/33 and the opening weeks of the Hundred Days, Roosevelt was attracted to, though not, apparently, entirely captivated by, the fifth type of proposal which influenced the creation of the N.I.R.A. Trusted advisers had mapped out versions of re-employment and start-up plans for the candidate during the spring and summer of 1932. Berle's memo for the "Memorandum of May 19" mapped out a quick-recovery plan to be used as a prelude to the more fundamental changes in business–government relations he was proposing. Perkins, for another, at Rosenman's suggestion, drafted a re-employment plan providing for ten per cent personnel increases by all firms, the resulting losses, if any, to be made good by a six per cent levy upon the wages of all workers. Roosevelt gave no sign in his campaign speeches of interest in such plans, but after the election several of the leading architects of these creations approached the President-elect through Tugwell and Moley with remarkably substantial results. Malcolm Rorty, a consulting economist, made his contact in mid-November through Oswald Knauth, president of Macy's. This was the family firm of Jesse I. Strauss, head, during the campaign, of the Roosevelt Business and Professional League. Jesse's son, Robert, was a second-rank member of the Brain Trust, serving at least part of the time as Moley's aide, and had evinced an eager interest in Rorty's plan during the preceding months. In the previous spring he had discussed the plan with Moley and, at some point, apparently during the campaign, shown Rorty a speech draft for Roosevelt endorsing the former's plan. Though the speech was, of course, never delivered, Rorty was encouraged to think his plan might be taken up and asked Strauss, through Knauth, to find out whether Roosevelt and his advisers would welcome legislative consideration of his proposal. If so, Rorty, who did not ask for a definite commitment from the incoming Administration, would turn to Senator Wagner to work out a bill. Rorty apparently felt certain of a positive response on Wagner's part since Isidor Lubin, a Brookings Institution economist who acted as adviser to the senator, was a strong advocate of the plan. Moley, Strauss reported, would see Rorty, if possible toward the first of the year. Moley did not know when Roosevelt would have time to consider the plan and felt Rorty should take the matter up with Wagner immediately rather than wait for a definite reply to his query. This was a partial satisfaction at least of Rorty's request and in a sense cleared the way for the overtures he then made to Wagner. These in turn proved a major source of the senator's sponsorship of the drafting of a start-up plan during April 1933.[18]

The Rorty incident indicated Moley's interest in quick-recovery schemes, but it was the Rand–Oishei re-employment plan which seems genuinely, for a time at least during the interregnum winter, to have captured his, and in some degree his chief's, imagination. The evidence in the Moley Papers argues, tentatively at least, that Moley and Roosevelt seriously weighed whether a re-employment–recovery program should be dramatically unveiled at the outset of the new presidency.

During the last months of 1932, James Rand and John Oishei had worked together in an attempt to persuade Hoover to put their re-employment plan into execution. By January their collaboration had ended as Rand joined with Frank Vanderlip, Vincent Bendix, and a number of other business figures to form the Committee for the Nation. Rand's participation insured that the re-employment scheme would be on the group's agenda, but "reflation" was its first and only immediate objective. Oishei resented the committee, fearing prejudicial reaction if the re-employment plan became associated in the public mind with the committee's plan to "fool with the currency." Abandoning hope of involving Hoover, Oishei turned to the men of the incoming Administration, contacting Moley early in January 1933. Equipped with a "Procedure Chart" illustrating the steps for implementing the plan, with a draft of a radio speech for Roosevelt to use in initiating it and other such paraphernalia, Oishei appears to have had several conversations with Moley during January 1933, the latter declaring in mid-month that the Roosevelt circle was "very interested" in the proposal and was giving it "full attention."

Whether, as Oishei believed, the President-elect came genuinely near to adopting the re-employment plan is unclear; but it seems certain he and his advisers were sorely tempted by the plan's promise of instant recovery. Oishei appears, with the aid of Morris Tremaine, New York State comptroller, to have gained personal access to Roosevelt at least once. During February Will Woodin, designated to take over the Treasury on March 4, discussed the plan with Oishei while Roosevelt and his staff traveled to Florida. "REPORT FAVORABLE PROGRESS WITH WHW. HIS RESEARCH DEPARTMENT ANALYSIS INDICATES SOUNDNESS," Oishei wired Moley on February 16, again urging the plan be readied for immediate implementation. The plan, he told Tremaine on February 23, had been "considered" by Roosevelt, "reported on favorably" by Moley, Berle, and Woodin, and the decision on adoption hung in the balance.[19]

Whether Oishei really was quite so close to success as he believed is doubtful. But his experiences in January and February revealed how ready the incoming Administration was to give serious attention to schemes which promised quick recovery and the return of economic normalcy. The tendency continued unabated during the opening weeks of the new presidency. A few days after the inauguration, James P. Warburg, a New York banker, who, like Strauss, was serving at this point as a Moley aide, drew the latter's attention to Fred Kent's start-up plan and was set the task of evaluating the whole array of such plans, including Oishei's in which Moley still was especially interested. Warburg submitted a preliminary memorandum on March 25, his report on April 4. It is this latter statement to which Moley refers in his memoirs of the New Deal.

The report attempted to categorize and evaluate all the major plans for "restarting industry." The advocates, to many of whom Warburg had spoken, at this point seemed grouped in one of two schools, one believing loans to industry to encourage restarting and re-employment were necessary, the other arguing that guarantees against losses would be sufficient incentive. Warburg advocated calling all these architects into conference to secure agreement on a bill for prompt submission to Congress. All the recovery planners, Warburg was pleased to report, agreed that public works spending or "pure unemployment relief" was inappropriate, a judgment which fitted perfectly with Warburg's conservative position in this regard and which was no doubt an important factor in his enthusiasm for the ideas of the start-up planners. A conversation of late March between Warburg and Moley recorded in the diary kept by Moley's secretary during the winter and spring of 1932/33 reinforces the conclusion that, for Warburg, for Moley, and, no doubt, for Roosevelt too, a strong element in the attractiveness of start-up plans was that they seemed to offer an escape from pressures to spend. Warburg is shown in the diary entry as "tremendously" concerned "as a conservative" over the prospect of a large public works spending program which, he thought, would take the bottom out of the bond market. He was convinced "something more fundamental" would have to be done to "right the balance." Moley seemed to agree with this in principle, though he registered concern over the plight of the unemployed; he apparently believed that public works could not be ruled out altogether, though he noted Roosevelt had criticized their effectiveness in the Forgotten Man speech a year earlier.[20]

Start-up plans came to Roosevelt and Moley from additional sources, most notably, during March, from Meyer Jacobstein, former New York congressman, now a Rochester banker, and Harold Moulton, a trustee of the Brookings Institution and an economist. Their start-up plan required no governmental financial guarantees or outlays, but involved minimum-price setting in key industries with allocation among them of desired increases in employment and production. Roosevelt received this plan first on March 6, and it was drawn to his attention several times during the month.[21]

Against this background Moley and Roosevelt on April 4 discussed the advisability of actually choosing a recovery plan and implementing it. They decided, according to Moley, to defer a decision, believing that "thinking on the subject . . . had not crystallized sufficiently to justify further moves at the time." Then, again according to Moley, the passage in the Senate on April 6 of the Black bill reawakened Roosevelt's interest in such proposals. On April 11 he instructed Moley again to get in touch with the leading recovery-plan authors and to evaluate the relative merits of their plans. From Moley's perspective, as related in his memoirs, of Roosevelt's actions and intentions, it appears that, within a few days of Senate action on the Black bill, the President had virtually decided to commit himself to some amalgam of the several start-up plans Moley and Warburg had previously evaluated. Whether this perspective was adequate can be questioned, however. Roosevelt already had shown he was intrigued by start-up mechanisms which promised reactivation of the economy. But in mid-April he evidently retained reservations about their political and economic workability. His appraisal, given about April 12, of the Jacobstein–Moulton Plan, a brief version of which his uncle Frederic Delano, had penned and given to Louis Howe early in April, reflected a strong note of skepticism. "The President says," Missy LeHand informed Howe on April 13, "to show this [letter] to Mr. Roper with memorandum saying he thinks his uncle is right but perhaps a little ahead of his time." As will be seen, Roosevelt was pushed toward adopting a start-up plan as an Administration measure.[22]

DRAFTING THE N.I.R.A.

Following the lead of Raymond Moley and other New Deal participants, historians have treated Senate passage of the Black bill as a pivotal event. Roosevelt felt the measure was dangerously inflexible, would lead to an actual drop in purchasing power (since it contained no minimum wage provisions), and had to be defeated. Yet simple opposition was out of the question. The measure was too popular, both in Congress and with the voters, especially with organized labor. Opposition had to consist in substitution of a better proposal for stimulating employment and recovery. In the week following April 6, Roosevelt began the search for such a proposal. For five weeks rival proposals jockeyed to influence the recovery plan. The identity of the individuals and groups involved and their strategies, the specific nature of the rival proposals, has remained somewhat obscure. The ultimate result of five weeks of drafting, negotiation, and compromise was the National Industrial Recovery Act which the President sent to Congress on May 17.

In part, the N.I.R.A. seems to accord perfectly with the proclivities Roosevelt showed during the months, down to early April, when the different recovery concepts were competing for his attention and support. In its most important aspect, however, it presents, in the same terms, a genuine puzzle. Given the interest in improved wages and hours which Roosevelt evinced during March and April, the provisions of the Act which mandated labor standards for the codes and which guaranteed the right of collective bargaining are readily understandable. They accord, too, with the Congressional outlook of that spring which made the Black bill so popular. The public works provisions of the Act also seem to reflect the President's outlook of the early Hundred Days. Not only was the appropriation ($3.3 billion for two years) much below the demands of senatorial and other public works advocates, but the arrangements in the Act for the administration of the funds were such as, in effect, to allow the President much discretion over how rapidly they would be disbursed. Roosevelt used this discretion (by separating implementation of the industrial codes and public works provisions, giving the first to Hugh Johnson, the second to the Secretary of Interior, Harold Ickes) to limit drastically the actual expenditure of public works money during 1933.

The third, and most important, aspect of the N.I.R.A. is the one which presents the puzzle. Roosevelt had shown a marked interest in re-employment and start-up plans but almost none in the business plan which revolved principally around antitrust revision and business-controlled price and production stabilization. Yet the Act was almost totally barren of the elements of any of the start-up plans. Rather, it provided for industry-drafted codes of competitive behavior, and suspension of the antitrust laws (in their anti-cartel aspect) relative to these codes. The wage-and-hour standards were almost the only recognizable survival from the start-up plans. The labor provisions, on the grounds that they would increase "purchasing power" and spread work, made it somewhat possible to regard the N.I.R.A. as a recovery measure, as did the antitrust suspension, upon the supposition that unfair and ruthless competition was causing continuing deflation of prices and wages and making revival impossible. This latter argument was one which antitrust revisionists had consistently put forward throughout the depression, and seemingly it had been accepted. Gone were the provisions for the concerted, calculated increases in employment of the Rand–Oishei Plan, for the guarantees against losses suffered by giving greater employment of the Kent Plan, for an orchestrated effort to increase the production of basic industries by appropriate percentages of the Jacobstein–Moulton Plan, or for the bounties to selected industries for augmenting production of the Rorty Plan.

In practice the N.I.R.A. resulted, as the leading student of the NRA has written, in the "triumph of industrial self-government," in a series of codes mainly intended to peg prices, limit production, and increase profits. Labor conditions and employment improved somewhat as the administrators of the Act used their power to approve specific cartelistic practices as a bargaining counter to get improved wage-and-hour standards into the codes. The Act, however, squarely met the goals of the business planners, who had consistently argued that cartelization would lead to recovery. Did the drafters of the N.I.R.A. and the President himself realize this? Was their intention primarily recovery or had they decided to accept the goals of the business planners which were, first and foremost, the shoring up and maintaining of the business structure and, secondarily, recovery? Why were the mechanisms of the re-employment–start-up planners and the wage–hour legislation Perkins was proposing shunted to one side? How the design of the N.I.R.A. was fixed can be discovered only through a more detailed and precise re-creation of the process of clash and compromise between rival approaches than has previously been provided.[23]

Roosevelt's first traceable reactions to passage of the Black bill (which occurred on Thursday, April 6) came on Tuesday, April 11. This was the day on which he told Moley to review recovery plans again; the day on which he told Walker Hines that antitrust revision was out of the question; and, most importantly, the day on which he met with Perkins and the Attorney General and decided to give partial support to the Labor Secretary's substitute proposal to the Black bill. Perkins' substitute provided for a national board to grant limited exemptions to the thirty-hour limit and for industry boards to fix minimum wages, thus following the lines she had laid down during the preceding weeks. A novelty was the provision empowering the Secretary of Labor to limit the hours of operation of any unit of an industry when because of, for example, continuous operation, it was securing a disproportionate share of the market and threatening to displace other units. This provision, if used extensively enough and interpreted broadly, could have served to limit total industry production. There is no evidence, however, that Perkins had this as a concealed purpose. The provision does appear to have had its origin, as Perkins stated, in the insistence of northern textile manufacturers that their states' limitations upon female and child labor would, under a shortening of work shifts, allow southern producers to increase their share of total output to the detriment of employment in the north. Roosevelt discussed all these aspects of the Perkins substitute extensively at his press conference on April 12. Newsmen reported having "learned" that the President approved the measure, but they were not allowed to cite him as the direct source. The same day Perkins met with the House Labor Committee, telling newsmen afterward of her expectation of passage of labor standards legislation during the session and of the way she was seeking to alter the Black bill. During the following two weeks before the April 25 opening of hearings on her substitute, Perkins gradually committed herself fully to the bill, while the position of the President was left ambiguous. Statements given to the press on April 13 by labor leaders, on the 14th by Senate public works advocates, after meetings with the President, represented him as favoring the Perkins approach.[24]

The Perkins substitute, combined with public works spending—the latter of which was in some degree inevitable, so strong was insistence for it within the Cabinet and among leading New Deal supporters in Congress—appears to have been uppermost in Roosevelt's mind as an alternate to the Black bill for ten days or more after the Senate passage. But the President never made the bill an Administration measure and, as business opposition to it mounted during the two weeks before the House Labor Committee hearings opened on April 25, his support seemed to dwindle. In her statement before the Committee on the 25th, Perkins represented the President as favoring wage-and-hour regulation in principle but as not committed to her specific approach.[25]

At the same time he was encouraging Perkins, however, Roosevelt also asked Moley, as we have seen, to look again into the workability of industrial rehabilitation plans. Within two weeks, Roosevelt's indecision had been resolved, as pressure was brought to bear from several sources to persuade him to adopt the start-up approach. These pressures came

from within the Administration, from a senatorial group, and from business groups mobilized behind the Department of Commerce.

Within the Administration, Warburg was the consistent and assiduous
advocate during April of a start-up program. Between April 5 and 14,
he spoke with most of the major figures who had drawn up such programs
and on the latter date persuaded Moley to call them together. On the
following Monday, the 17th, Moley told Warburg to talk with Senator
Wagner, whom, evidently, Warburg was to persuade to take the lead
in forming a definite proposal. The next day Moley and Warburg met
with Wagner and La Follette in the Senate Office Building. Warburg believed, when the conference ended, that he had persuaded the two that a
start-up plan would promote employment better than would public
works, and that they should take the lead in securing a consolidated plan
from the several different proposals and then promote their handiwork.[26]

Wagner was somewhat disingenuous during this conversation, perhaps, for he had already begun to take the lead Warburg was, actually
somewhat tardily, giving to him. Wagner's active interest in recovery
plans dated back to 1931. But it was in the spring of 1933 that he assumed the role of sponsor of them. Moulton and Jacobstein by early
April understood Wagner to be "friendly disposed" toward their plan to
"start the industrial machine moving forward." Wagner evidently regarded their mechanism as a complement to his ambitious public works
program. As he told Arthur Krock of *The New York Times* on April 13,
he was looking for a way to guarantee the effectiveness of construction
spending in reviving the economy. It appears that Wagner in the first
weeks of April was acting entirely independently and trying to prod the
President toward commitment to a recovery plan, just as he was pushing
for far greater public works appropriations than Roosevelt wished to
concede.

This interpretation rests largely on an article Arthur Krock published
in the *Times* on April 14. The article, which caused a mild sensation,
reported that certain members of Roosevelt's circle were drafting a recovery bill which they hoped to persuade him to support. The plan, as
Krock described it, clearly was the Jacobstein–Moulton Plan with elements of the Kent Plan. Other *Times* correspondents on the following
two days reported unnamed officials as denying such a measure was
under way, and conveyed a picture of the Administration as somewhat
confused and embarrassed. It was Wagner himself who inspired the
Krock story, as the newsman later related. On April 19 Krock, with
Wagner probably his source again, published a sequel reporting that the
drafters he had previously described were confident of winning the President's approval since, despite criticism of them within the Administration following the April 14 article, no word had come from the top to
lay their efforts aside. Again Krock described the proposal as a start-up

plan, a compound of Jacobstein–Moulton and Kent, again emphasizing that the "thought behind the plan" was to increase the expansive effect of public works spending.[27]

On April 22 Wagner sent invitations to a number of individuals associated in some way with recovery planning, among them the authors of the best-known plans, including Moulton, Kent, Rorty, and James H. Rand, to gather to draw up a recovery proposal. The meeting of this group on the 25th produced, according to one participant, Malcolm Rorty, agreement on a plan along the lines of the "Kent–Rand–Moulton–Jacobstein plans" but without the guarantees against loss of the Kent Plan. "Premiums for new capital operations, as proposed by myself," Rorty reported, had also been tentatively accepted.[28]

The bill rapidly took on concrete form. Following the meeting of the 25th, a subcommittee headed by Moulton drafted a text which omitted the guarantees or bounties of the Kent and Rorty schemes and reverted simply to the original Jacobstein–Moulton Plan. On the evening of April 28, this subcommittee met with "economists and lawyers associated with the Department of Agriculture." These were, no doubt, Louis Bean and Jerome Frank, with whom Tugwell had been studying recovery plans. Tugwell had written at mid-month in his "New Deal Diary" of his urgent sense of need for rapid mounting of an expansive fiscal policy and of procedures for stimulating production and employment. This group from Agriculture, with Tugwell possibly participating personally, insisted that the Kent and Rorty mechanisms be included in the draft, which was done.[29]

At some point during the last days of April Roosevelt decided to abandon the Perkins substitute and to take up the recovery approach which Moley and Warburg wanted and which Wagner had been pushing since April 13. The Wagner group was called together—"at the suggestion of the President" according to Wagner, at his "insistence" according to Douglas—but it was not until after April 25 that signs appeared that Roosevelt had actually decided to make the shift. April 26 seems the likely date of the decision, for it was on this day that Roosevelt at last moved to have prepared the public works bill which the spenders had been urging upon him since early March. On the 26th Roosevelt informed Ickes he was to head a Cabinet committee to shape a public works bill. But it soon became clear that the Perkins substitute was no longer regarded as the companion to public works. The start-up concept had taken its place. Within a short time, Roosevelt moved publicly toward a tentative commitment to a recovery plan broader than simple wage-and-hour legislation. An April 30 White House press release on Roosevelt's speech before the Chamber of Commerce scheduled for May 4 hinted at this, as did Senator Robinson, the majority leader, in a press statement on May 1 after a conference with the President.

Why did Roosevelt decide to drop plans to modify the Black bill and to follow Wagner's lead instead? One reason—one which Wagner would have resented—was that adoption of a start-up plan offered more hope of keeping public works spending to a minimum. Frances Perkins in her memoirs of the New Deal describes how, at a Cabinet meeting sometime in April during a discussion of public works spending, Lewis Douglas, the Administration's most forceful fiscal conservative, had alluded to a scheme being developed (which, Perkins found shortly afterward, was the Wagner project) which would be far superior to public works spending as a recovery measure. Douglas' memo of April 29 on the Wagner committee's bill, recording the thoughts which, it is reasonable to assume, he was sharing with Roosevelt at just this time, advances the same argument. Roosevelt certainly behaved during the closing days of April as though he was determined to cut public works spending to the bare minimum. On April 29 he met with his Cabinet committee on public works, with Douglas sitting in, and, in a manner Ickes found harsh, parried its proposal for a $5 billion construction program by vigorously belittling the group's evidence that a large supply of worthwhile projects which could be initiated promptly was available. He drew the spending line at $1.5 billion and even committed himself to this minimal figure at a press conference following his meeting with the Cabinet committee. This same meeting discussed ways of "speeding up industry," including unquestionably Wagner's plan and, Ickes told the press, proposals business groups had submitted. These circumstances all point to a link in Roosevelt's thinking, which Douglas was encouraging, between a successfully executed start-up plan and the Administration's ability sharply to limit public works spending.[30]

The other main influence which shifted Roosevelt away from the Perkins substitute was pressure from business and its spokesmen within the Administration, especially John Dickinson, Assistant Secretary of Commerce. The business groups consisted of the same figures who had taken the lead during March and early April in pressing Roosevelt for antitrust revision. Now they had absorbed fully the lesson that their objective had to be cloaked more substantially in the rhetoric of recovery planning to attain success. They converged upon Dickinson and his superior, Daniel Roper, when they realized how fully these two sympathized with the business objectives. The business spokesmen had little or no cohesion by this time, with Harriman, Emery, and Lund, and such leaders as J. Harvey Williams acting largely independently though in parallel fashion.

The immediate reason for the rallying of the business leaders behind Dickinson was to secure defeat of the Black bill. Still the aim was not merely to defeat federal regulation of wages and hours, but to use the prevailing concern with the issue as an opening to secure the long-sought goal of "industrial self-regulation," which now was emphasized as offering the best means of reviving the economy. Both Secretary Roper and Dickinson needed no prompting to interest them in business self-regulation. Dickinson, a Columbia Law School professor before his appointment to the Commerce post, had included trade association work in his practice and had participated in drafting the defense brief in the *Sugar Institute* case, one of the major antitrust cases of the Hoover Administration. One of Dickinson's first moves after becoming Assistant Secretary on April 5 was to ask Frederick Feiker, still the carry-over chief of the Bureau of Foreign and Domestic Commerce, whether the Bureau had investigated "the relation of the Anti-Trust laws to the conduct of business." H. I. Harriman found Roper and Dickinson very willing to discuss sympathetically the Chamber's bills for securing antitrust liberalization. Dickinson agreed to speak on the subject before the upcoming Chamber convention, though he declined to join in open criticism of the antitrust policy. "From the standpoint of public opinion and [an?] attack on the evils of excessive competition . . . an argument in behalf of legitimate cooperation among business men has a better chance of succeeding if it does not take the form of an attack on the anti-trust laws," he told Harriman.[31]

Dickinson needed little prompting to persuade him to champion the immediate business goal of early April: the defeat of the Black bill and the substitution for it of wage-and-hour standards set through industry agreements. The NAM appears to have taken the lead in this undertaking. Roosevelt's rejection of antitrust relief, as James Emery explained to an NAM member, had forced the association to approach the goal "through another angle . . . out of the Black bill." The strategy was to show that "inability to make cooperative agreements with respect to hours of production" had resulted in "cutthroat competition, under-payment of wages and demoralization of industry." Industry regulation of hours of work would, in other words, be substituted for the direct control of prices and production Roosevelt apparently would not concede. While pressing the argument for industry regulation of working hours on Roper, Dickinson, and Perkins, Emery also, in the two weeks following Senate passage of the Black bill, was marshaling all the resources the NAM and the related state manufacturers' associations could muster to block passage of the Black bill in the House. Wavering business groups thinking of working for a compromise which would accept federal work-week standards if the norm were forty rather than thirty hours were whipped back into line. Compromise should be considered only as a last resort, Emery insisted. The Black bill, if enacted, would become the basis for detailed regulation of all aspects of business operations, once the principle was established that goods could be excluded from interstate commerce unless produced under conditions laid down by Congress. Another element in Emery's strategy was to capitalize on the Administration's objection to the provision of the version of the Black bill before the House which excluded foreign goods from American commerce unless they were made under the norms of the bill. The provision conflicted radically with Secretary of State Cordell Hull's trade program and, therefore, in Emery's view, William Connery of Massachusetts, the House sponsor of the Thirty-Hour bill, should be given every encouragement to stand by it. Connery's position, Emery explained to the secretary of the Associated Industries of Massachusetts, brought him "into conflict with the Administration and he therefore needs strong evidence of support . . . particularly from his home district." [32]

The NAM's fundamental objection to the Black bill applied with equal force to the Perkins substitute. Besides, the business goal was not merely industry control of the work week but the control of competition. Opposition to Perkins' measure was, therefore, forcefully expressed well before the House Education and Labor Committee opened hearings on it on April 25. And Dickinson, on April 21, declared war from within the Administration on the Perkins substitute, writing to both Roper and Perkins herself of the disastrous economic and political consequences the measure would bring down upon the Administration, repeating these arguments for Moley on the 26th. He urged consideration instead for giving industry the power to set hours and minimum wages.

When the hearings on the Perkins substitute began on April 25, business spokesmen immediately turned them into a sounding board for opposition to the measure. Industry regulation of wages and hours was urged instead, and, as the hearings went on, business spokesmen were increasingly emboldened to demand cooperative control of production and prices as well. On April 28 the NAM staged a mass meeting of businessmen in Washington which denounced the Black bill in any form and revived the Truce Plan concept of an emergency suspension of antitrust restrictions with industry control of all market decisions under loose federal regulation. "The membership of that meeting broke over the Capitol like a bomb," in Emery's description, while he himself "went through Congress and the departments with aggressive determination." By the next evening, he claimed, "the Cabinet officers were urging the President against the pending proposal." The other major groups which had worked so long for antitrust revision now also re-entered events. Williams and his associates had proposed the antitrust-suspension approach to Dickinson during the previous week as a substitute for the Perkins bill. On May 1 Harriman gave Dickinson a draft bill similar in intent, effect, and mechanics to the NAM's latest proposal, differing mainly in its stress upon permanent relaxation of antitrust standards. The vociferous business opposition to the Perkins bill found support from AFL leaders William Green and Matthew Woll, both of whom, in line with their traditional opposition to minimum wage legislation, now denounced the wage boards the measure provided for. Roosevelt could scarcely have imposed the measure, given the need to enhance confidence and stability, in both the economic and political sense.[33]

The circumstances of late April which persuaded Roosevelt to drop the Perkins substitute and to take up the Wagner group's measure seem clear enough. But another puzzle arises at this point. Why did the N.I.R.A. contain so little of the substance of the start-up approach in the Wagner measure which, as of April 29–31, had become the basis of discussion for a recovery plan? The shift in emphasis toward the business concept of recovery through cartelism was accomplished with startling rapidity. As several writers have pointed out, Dickinson and Wagner were assigned, probably on April 30, the responsibility for finalizing a recovery proposal. The direct participation and remarkable degree of influence which business leaders enjoyed in the work of the Wagner–Dickinson drafting group during the first days of May has not been fully apprehended. Letters of James Emery, the NAM leader, indicate a rapid pace for negotiations on May 1, 2, and 3. Both the Chamber and the NAM were, in this period, circulating recently drafted proposals for allowing businessmen collective control of markets, wages, and hours. Both relied upon extension of the fair competition concept to include mandatory adherence to agreements by industry majorities. The former reluctance to demand coercion of industry minorities was now swept away. The NAM proposal continued the Truce Plan concept of a temporary suspension of the antitrust laws, and this was the main difference now between the Chamber and the other group. The Chamber's May 1 document evidently provided the model which came to dominate the discussions of the next few days, for it outlined in a few hundred words the procedures which formed the core of the N.I.R.A., though it was the NAM suspension-of-antitrust concept which emerged in the Act. The grand aim was to secure, as Emery wrote on May 2, "the rights of self-organization in industry." Evidently the business leaders, no doubt with Dickinson's support, were able to persuade Wagner that elimination of "cutthroat competition" and improvement of wages and hours through industry-wide agreements would, together with public works, be an adequate recovery mechanism.

The Administration, Emery wrote on May 3, was accepting the challenge businessmen had offered to right the economic situation if given the chance. "This is being worked out as an emergency proposal. It will be in the nature of an experiment of self-government within industry if it can be done at all." The positive, directive, mobilizing role of government of the Jacobstein–Moulton approach evidently was talked down.[34]

On May 4 most of the key business leaders who were active in the negotiations with the Wagner–Dickinson committee assembled for a self-congratulatory and self-laudatory session before a large group of conventioneers attending the Chamber of Commerce annual meeting and anxious for a word on the shape of the coming recovery bill. The confidence and assurance displayed were complete. It was clear the speakers felt that the main features of the bill had taken form and that business had triumphed. Recent events had opened, Emery said, "an opportunity which many have long sought to find a chance to determine whether or not industry can organize itself to set up a form of self-government." Somewhat incautiously perhaps, in view of the NAM's long history of moderation in this respect, Emery vented his contempt for "irrational minorities" who now would be controlled. "I personally am rather sick of living under organized minorities in industry or in politics," he said of the non-cooperators of every industry. J. Harvey Williams, Goldthwaite Dorr, and others who spoke all echoed Emery's confident assertion that "self-government was within the business community's grasp." That evening the President, in his talk before the Chamber, seemed perfectly to validate this confidence as he discussed the recovery bill in preparation.[35]

The business spokesmen had learned to stress with plausible arguments and broad promises the public-benefits, recovery-oriented nature of their proposals. James Rand, who was serving on the NAM Steering Committee in continuous session in Washington since late April to influence the recovery legislation, probably revealed the tenor of business argumentation with the Wagner–Dickinson committee when he announced on May 7 that his Committee for the Nation and the NAM, assuming that business was about to secure antitrust liberalization, had adopted a re-employment plan for putting 3,000,000 men back to work within months. It is unclear whether the NAM proposed, at this point, actually to sponsor a particular re-employment plan, but it is certainly true that Rand, Robert Lund, and the Steering Committee had thoroughly discussed the scheme. The most important point here is that the episode confirms that business spokesmen were, during the period of the negotiations, and therefore probably in the negotiations themselves, lavishly promising a dramatic improvement in the unemployment rate if the antitrust barriers were let down. H. I. Harriman's prediction, in late April before the House Labor Committee, of recovery within thirty days of the inauguration of collective control by trade associations is another example in point.[36]

After this swift initial victory of early May, two major problems arose for the business planners before the N.I.R.A. became law and its policies were established. It was discovered that there was a second proposal, prepared by Hugh Johnson, and that the President had appointed a new drafting committee to reconcile the Wagner and Johnson versions. The new committee had on it the "counsel of the railroad unions," as Emery described Donald Richberg, whom Johnson had recruited to help him draft his recovery bill. This was an allusion to one problem: that pro-union provisions might be written into the bill. The other problem was, of course, that the business self-regulation features of the Wagner group's bill might be lost.

Wagner's and Johnson's proposals both went to Roosevelt on May 10. He immediately appointed the new committee, of Wagner, Johnson, Richberg, Dickinson, Douglas, and Perkins. The NAM at once demanded access to the new committee. "Mr. Lund and former Governor Gardiner, of North Carolina, are at the White House discussing the whole subject with the President," Emery wrote on May 11. Lund threatened the NAM's opposition to an unsatisfactory bill. An avalanche of telegrams descended on Washington from NAM members and their sympathizers, including Basil O'Connor, Roosevelt's former law partner, protesting that the new drafting committee lacked appropriate business representation. The President promptly approved formation of a committee of business leaders "to confer with the Drafting Committee." [37]

This business advisory committee consisted of Lund, Emery, Harriman, Lammont DuPont, Charles Hook, and one or two others of lesser fame. Johnson's approach—which was, in Emery's words, "to give the President complete power of organization, authority to set up such machinery as he pleased and permit self-organization or compel organization"—violated the business group's canons. The bill was in a state of flux, Emery wrote on the 12th, and the outcome uncertain. But, he added, "we are steadily resisting every effort to make it of such a nature that it will be a governmental organization and regulation of industry, instead of a self-organization by industry for its own self-control and self-organization." By May 13 the bill was nearly in final form and satisfactory in essentials to both the business advisory committee and the NAM Steering Committee. The former met with the drafting committee for a long session on May 13, objecting to the licensing provision and asking for stiffer import controls; the latter group considered the bill in an all-day session on Sunday, May 14, reacting, it appears, in precisely the same manner. The bill, as one member of the Steering Committee wrote, gave industry the chance to prove itself "capable of self-government." Its long-term effect, he thought, "will be some relaxation of the so-called anti-trust laws after the country gets accustomed to the idea, just as they have become quite inured to business on a large scale in contradistinction to the general wariness of large corporations twenty-five years ago." [38]

The business committees appear to have approved of, or at least acquiesced in, the bill before it was submitted on May 17; but, by the end of May, the NAM Steering Committee was mounting another campaign to secure certain amendments—apparently as a result mainly from a change in the labor provisions of the bill after its submission to Congress. These provisions had caused little difficulty during the drafting stage. The language of Section 7 (a) as originally submitted contained phrasing which the NAM leaders construed as an open shop provision. During the Ways and Means Committee hearings, William Green asked for amendments which strengthened the language barring employers from interfering with the right of workers to organize and forbidding them to require workers to join a company union as a condition of employment. The second of the two amendments which Green requested had an especially important consequence. As James Emery protested later during the Senate hearings on the bill, Green's amendment, which the House had accepted, had the effect of making the union shop permissible. The amendments aroused for the first time the fear among the NAM leaders that the N.I.R.A. might lead to the disruption of company unions. In later years, Emery would insist, as apparently he felt during the hearings, that Wagner's acceptance of Green's amendments was a betrayal of the original agreement on the language of 7 (a). Lund and Emery objected at the White House to the change and renewed their objection to the licensing provision and to the failure to provide drastic import controls. Receiving no satisfaction, they now tried the same tactics which, they believed, had killed the Black bill, calling for a mass meeting of NAM members in Washington for June 3 to build up pressure for their amendments.[39]

Businessmen hardly considered these defects, not even the new labor provision, as warranting the defeat of the whole measure. Many actually favored the licensing provision as a stiff support of the codes and, of all the business association resolutions reaching the Senate Finance Committee, which held hearings on the bill between May 22 and June 1, very few regarded modification of Section 7 (a) as an absolute condition of their support for passage. Spokesmen for the NAM before the Senate Finance Committee were far from suggesting defeat of the measure if their amendments were not accepted, and the Chamber's H. I. Harriman was even more tolerant of the text as the House had passed it.[40]

The text of the N.I.R.A., except for Section 7 (a), conceded to the business concepts on every important point. Self-regulation through codes of fair competition was stressed. The President was, it is true, empowered, if an industry failed to take the initiative, to impose a code, but there was no suggestion that this section could be used to dictate price or production schedules. He was empowered also to impose wage-and-hour standards, but only when an industry failed to provide satisfactory standards in a proposed code.

Despite strong efforts, business leaders failed to persuade the Senate Finance Committee to restore the original wording of the N.I.R.A.'s labor organization provision. This, and what, in the weeks immediately following Roosevelt's signing of the Act on June 16, appeared to be a resistance in the Administration to allowing price- and production-control provisions in the codes, gave businessmen pause. The content of the codes was not specified in the Act, except for the antitrust exemption and the requirement to provide wage-and-hour standards. The text was silent as to whether and to what extent the codes actually would contain price- and production-control provisions. Administration pronouncements during late May and June concerning the program all stressed the wage-and-hour provisions of the proposed codes. Lewis Douglas and Wagner avoided discussion of price and production limitation when they appeared before the House Labor Committee during the hearings on the bill, repeatedly and categorically stating it was intended to eliminate wage cutting and shorten hours and would not lessen, but raise the plane of, competition. "Efficiency, rather than the ability to sweat labor . . . will be the determining factor in business success," Wagner insisted. When Roosevelt signed the bill on June 16, he relied entirely upon the idiom of the start-up concept. Title I, he said, "proposes to put millions of men back in their regular jobs this summer," through work spreading combined with higher wages. He acknowledged the law was "relaxing some of the safeguards of the anti-trust laws," but insisted they still stood "against monopolies that restrain trade and price fixing which allows inordinate profits or unfairly high prices." The NRA *Bulletin* of June 17, "Principles to be Embodied in Codes," omitted even this highly ambiguous reference to price and production provisions, citing and emphasizing those sections of Roosevelt's remarks of the 16th which portrayed the NRA as a vast re-employment campaign in which businessmen were called upon to increase the work force and raise wages without raising prices.[41]

This attitude may have been a reversion, at least a wish to revert, to a start-up program and to avoid fulfilling the agreement of early and mid-May to allow cartelistic provisions in the codes. Later, in *The Blue Eagle,* Johnson would write that for many months before the spring of 1933 he had been calculating how recovery could be restored by spreading work, improving wages, and "repressing" price increases, meanwhile stimulating the producers' goods industries by pouring money into housing and armaments.

Probably this was Johnson's bent and Roosevelt's too, though the former had been so closely associated with Baruch and agreed so thoroughly with the ideas on industrial stabilization which Baruch had purveyed in the earlier stages of the depression that he obviously was in accord with the fundamental business aims.[42]

In any case it is certain that during the weeks following the Presi-

dent's signing of the N.I.R.A. and the promulgation of the code guidelines in mid-June, uncertainty prevailed in most industries whether the
victory won during the drafting of the Act would prove hollow. Though
many industries began the drafting of codes, few had submitted any to
the NRA by early July. In the discussions with the representatives of the
CTI, which was the first group to begin serious code negotiations,
Johnson, as Louis Galambos relates, "talked about eliminating cutthroat competition and destructive practices without fixing prices or restricting production."

Another consideration generated hesitancy also: the fear that a code
might increase labor union strength. Seeking to make good their successes in the drafting of the N.I.R.A. and to secure a ruling which
would nullify any advantages labor might hope to gain from the Act,
the members of the NAM Steering Committee on recovery legislation
and the organization's Board of Directors met on July 10 to draft an
appeal to Johnson. The resulting statement demonstrates quite clearly
that business leaders at this point feared that everything they thought
they had gained might be slipping from their grasp. The NAM petition
asked for "a statement similar to the . . . doctrine laid down by the
National Council of Defense during the World War" when it had decreed,
according to the NAM, that government policy would not interfere with
existing labor representation arrangements—would not, in other words,
interfere with company unions and the open shop tradition. The petition
referred as a matter of equal concern to the fear that the Administration
intended to add to production costs burdens (through increased wages
and shortened hours) without compensation. There was a widespread
"feeling that codes of fair competition adopted should permit correction
of trade abuses, and that they should, in certain cases, permit price ad-
justments." Industry needed assurance, to secure its cooperation with
the program, that these price and competitive relations could "properly
be submitted and receive consideration in the codes as first presented
with the provisions contained therein concerning maximum hours and
minimum wages for common labor."

These demands were presented to Johnson the same day they were
drafted. The NRA head promptly gave explicit assurances on the labor
question. There does not seem to have been a formal reply on the
question of the codes and competition, but businessmen soon learned
that their wishes would be met entirely. Actually the NAM statement of
July 10 was already out of date, for the Cotton Textile code, which
Johnson had submitted to Roosevelt on July 9, had withheld nothing
from the cartelistic objectives of the manufacturers. These objectives had
been moderate, consisting mainly of restrictions upon hours of operation (production control) and upon construction of new productive

capacity. But they had clearly broken through the old wall of prohibitions. The force of law was reversed, compelling the manufacturers now to cooperate rather than compete.[43]

Even though the Cotton Textile code seems to show that Johnson and Roosevelt were prepared, if pushed, to deal with the consequences of accepting the N.I.R.A. as the business leaders had drafted it, there was one further indication that they would, if possible, have avoided conceding any more to cartelism than could be avoided. Only two days after receiving the NAM protest and petition concerning the codes and competition, Johnson announced the beginning of a massive re-employment campaign. All the nation's employers would be asked immediately to participate by signing the Blanket Code, a pledge to reduce the hours of individual workers (thereby spreading work) and increase hourly wages. This President's Reemployment Agreement was, of course, precisely the start-up plan concept which had dominated Roosevelt's planning for recovery until the business leaders had intervened in late April and May to shape the recovery act to their own wishes. The PRA campaign was carried on with remarkable vigor and enormous ballyhoo through the summer of 1933 as employers were urged to sign up and display the Blue Eagle, the emblem Johnson chose as the symbol of cooperation with the NRA. The PRA resulted in little additional employment, it seems, but it did capture the imagination of the people for a time. Demonstrating hope and enthusiasm that recovery could be rapidly achieved by concerted wage raising and work spreading, citizens marched in many major cities during that summer in support of the Administration's plan.

It has usually been assumed that Roosevelt and Johnson launched the PRA campaign because of industrial foot-dragging in code formulation. If the pace of code negotiation were not stepped up, hopes for generating an impulse toward rapid recovery would dim. The PRA, it is thought, was intended to provide the impetus for recovery and also to whip up an atmosphere in which trade associations would be more willing to quicken the process of codification. It is not necessary to reject this explanation entirely to suggest that Roosevelt might have seen the PRA in the first instance as a last chance of avoiding the cartelistic provisions which business would demand in the codes as the price of cooperating in improving wages and hours. What is certain is that as late as July 10 a key group of business leaders, which had been closely in touch with the development of the NRA for weeks, feared that the Administration was looking for a way to renege on the understandings reached in May.[44] It seems clear, also, that, whether or not by the PRA Roosevelt hoped to avoid substantial concessions to the business viewpoint in the industry codes which would be drafted, he was reverting again to the concept which had seemed so attractive to him during the winter and spring of 1932/33: that of somehow jolting the economy back to normal by infusing it with self-generating purchasing power and the psychology of expansion.

Any intention the Administration may have had of moderating cartelism in the codes evaporated. The promise implicit in the Cotton Textile code was fulfilled, and the uncertainties of the NAM spokesmen were cleared up within a brief time. The logjam immediately was broken, and industries presented no fewer than 300 draft codes to Johnson for approval during the first week of August. By mid-month several codes, in addition to the Cotton Textile agreement, had been approved, and the NRA machinery was grinding out additional ones at a quickening pace. In the negotiations with the NRA administrators, business clearly held the upper hand. Concessions from business on labor conditions were bought dearly with more than commensurate government concessions. As a recent historian of the NRA has said, "students of the code-writing process are almost unanimous in noting the weakness of the labor provisions and the triumph of the business point of view." Relatively few codes permitted direct price-fixing, but nearly all prohibited sales below the cost of production. These provisions were used often by code authorities (the policing agencies set up within each codified industry) to limit price competition. More effective, perhaps, were the complicated open price provisions which a very high percentage of the codes contained. These provisions often were precisely of the type which the Supreme Court had found illegal during the 1920s because they lent themselves so readily to price-fixing. The open price system, when it prohibits any sales except at prices announced to all competitors and forbids any lowering of prices until competitors are notified, has the evident purpose of eliminating the occasion and the incentive to cooperate in terms of prices. Limitations upon the weekly permissible hours of plant operation, designed to restrict total industry output, or direct production quotas, appeared in a far smaller percentage of codes, but many of these represented the larger industries such as cotton textiles and lumber. The devices which businessmen sought, and received, approval for were, however, as diverse as American industry itself. Ultimately, over 550 codes would be approved. That a high proportion of them governed relatively minor industries (over half the codified industries employed fewer than 5,000 workers each), which might better have been subsumed under one of the major industry codes, was an additional sign and proof that business viewed NRA mainly as a means to market control.[45]

During the summer of 1933 a boom in production and employment, representing, most economists agree, manufacturers' haste to add to inventories before the NRA program generated higher prices, fostered public belief that the New Deal actually was working. The continuous flow of pronouncements and speeches by Johnson and a horde of NRA spokesmen had the same effect. But, as Hawley has noted, "popular hysteria could not be maintained indefinitely." By September economic indices were again turning down sharply, and a long and soon bitter public debate over the merits of NRA began to develop. From within the NRA, the Consumers Advisory Board and the Research and Planning Division, where orthodox economists such as Leon Henderson were influential, began a policy debate which soon flooded over into Congress where old-line progressives such as William Borah and Gerald Nye took up the argument. The condemnation of the NRA system focused upon two charges: (1) that it was stifling competition, fixing prices and production levels, and actually retarding recovery; and (2) that it was causing structural changes in the direction of monopoly, giving the more powerful firms of certain industries the opportunity to crush smaller rivals. Both charges were overdrawn—even the first one, for in the case of some highly competitive industries, NRA compliance procedures were not intensive enough to make cartel arrangements effective. In competitive industries with strong pre-existing trade organizations, however, and for oligopolistic industries, the codes almost certainly increased cartelistic behavior.[46]

The NRA has been interpreted by Schlesinger as the forerunner of the planned and balanced economy toward which, according to the Galbraithian brand of economic logic, the economic dilemmas of the latter years of the twentieth century are driving Americans. But most commentators have joined in agreeing that it contributed little to recovery in 1933–35, that in some cases it established cartelist patterns which survived the demise of the agency itself, and that it seems to denote a disturbing tendency on the part of businessmen to seize state power and use it to defend their position and improve their wealth in default of their traditionally conceived role of economic innovation and expansion under the imperative of the competitive market. This last point seems especially to deserve stress. In this chapter I have attempted to show how an experiment so much at variance with American ideology and legal tradition came into existence.[47]

NOTES

1. See Hawley, *New Deal and . . . Monopoly*, Chapters 2 and 3, for a description of the code-drafting and the ensuing battle over policy within the NRA.

Ronald Radosh, "The Myth of the New Deal," *New History of Leviathan*, pp. 159–75, argues, from a "New Left" perspective, that the N.I.R.A. and the subsequent policies of the NRA were a purposeful consent to economic policies businessmen wanted. The NRA represented the triumph of "corporate liberalism," and was "meant to evolve into a corporate state." Radosh's analysis is based upon what he deems the implications of the rhetoric of certain Administration participants, not upon detailed study of the drafting and administration of the Act.

2. Schlesinger's account of the background of the NRA in his *Coming of the New Deal* (Boston: Houghton Mifflin, 1959), pp. 87–102, has long been accepted as the fullest and most convincing general treatment. Two more recent accounts, in Hawley, *New Deal and . . . Monopoly*, pp. 19–34, and in Joseph J. Huthmacher, *Senator Robert F. Wagner and the Rise of Urban Liberalism* (New York: Atheneum, 1968), pp. 130–53, accept Schlesinger's basic outline though each contains important elements of originality and, by drawing attention to sources and circumstances previously unnoted or misunderstood, has advanced understanding of the problem. All this is true of another indispensable treatment, in Galambos, *Competition and Cooperation,* Chapters 8 and 9, which emphasizes the role of the men associated with the CTI. The most recent treatment, in Frank Freidel, *Franklin D. Roosevelt: Launching the New Deal* (Boston: Little, Brown, 1973), pp. 408–35, achieves a fresh perspective on the weeks of April 1933 when FDR approached the decision whether to develop a general industrial recovery measure. Freidel stresses certain aspects of those weeks which I, too, believe deserve more emphasis. This is especially true of Secretary of Labor Perkins' substitute to the Black bill. Freidel feels that the railroad reorganization bill influenced Roosevelt's thinking regarding a broader industrial recovery measure, but does not, in my opinion, demonstrate the linkage, though the supposition is a plausible one.

3. The most useful characterizations of the ideas of these three central figures are in Schlesinger, *Coming of the New Deal,* pp. 179–84; Bernard Sternsher, *Rexford Tugwell and the New Deal* (New Brunswick: Rutgers University Press, 1964), pp. 39–50, 109–21; Moley, *After Seven Years* (New York: Harper, 1939), pp. 23–24; and William E. Leuchtenburg, *Franklin D. Roosevelt and the New Deal, 1932–1940* (New York: Harper, 1963), pp. 33–35.

Berle has been credited, especially by Schlesinger, with a stronger tendency toward social control of businessmen than is sustained, I believe, by the record in the Moley Papers of his ideas during the Brain Trust period.

4. Tugwell, *Brains Trust* (New York: Viking, 1968), pp. 34–36, 43–44, 57–60, 97–100, 104–105, 129, 132–35, 158, 168–69, 174–75, 277–78, 303–305, 307, 380, 385, 401–11, 416–18, 462, 471–72, 494, 520–21; *idem, The Democratic Roosevelt* (Garden City: Doubleday, 1957), p. 246. The material in *Navigating the Rapids, 1918–1971: From the Papers of Adolf A. Berle*, edd. Beatrice Bishop Berle and Travis Beal Jacobs (New York: Harcourt Brace Jovanovich, 1973), pp. 61–70, sustains this version of the background of the Commonwealth Club speech. Sternsher, *Tugwell,* p. 47, for the possible discrepancy mentioned in the text.

5. Berle's contribution to the "Memorandum of May 19"—the title given to the file in the Moley Papers, Hoover Institution, Stanford University, containing the items sent to Roosevelt at Warm Springs—is in box 2, Safe file. See also memo for Moley by Berle, November 10, 1932, file 102/1; Berle to FDR, January 12, 1933, file 102/11; Montague to Moley, January 12, 1933, file 113/126; Williams to Moley, November 15, 1932, file 24/33; all in Moley Papers. Berle and Jacobs, *Navigating the Rapids,* pp. 31–59, 77–79.

Berle to Marvin McIntyre, March 30, 1933, Alpha file, Franklin D. Roosevelt Papers, Franklin D. Roosevelt Library. Galambos, *Competition and Cooperation,* p. 190, cites the Dorr papers for information on Berle's contacts during February with the business group. Moley, *First New Deal* (New York: Harcourt, Brace and World, 1966), p. 231.

6. Wilson to Tugwell, July 25 (two letters), October 8, 24, November 28, 1932, Rexford G. Tugwell Papers, Franklin D. Roosevelt Library. Wilson to Moley, October 3, 1932, file 24/1, Moley Papers.

7. Harriman to FDR, January 3, 13, 14, 1933; FDR to Harriman, January 26,

1933, President's Personal File 3572, Roosevelt Papers. "Notes from a New Deal Diary," Tugwell Papers. Harriman, "An Economic Program," February 10, 1933, file 108/21, Moley Papers.

8. "Memorandum for Governor Roosevelt" by Moley, January 10, 1933; memo by FDR, written on about March 4, 1933, Safe file, *ibid.*

9. The similarity of their proposals, in concept and in language, is the only evidence that these parties were actually working together at this time. See Williams to FDR, February 24, 1933, Official File 277; to Marvin McIntyre, March 24, 1933, Official File 105; Warner Hays to Louis Howe, March 16, 1933; Hines to McIntyre, March 23, 1933, Alpha file. For the NAM leaders, see the McIntyre memo, "Visitors Seeing Mr. Howe," March 29, 1933, President's Personal File 8246; all in Roosevelt Papers.

10. Memos for FDR by McIntyre, March 22, 1933, Official File 277 and Official File 259; McIntyre to Robert Lund, April 4, 1933, President's Personal File 8246; to Warner Hays, March 20, 1933, Alpha file; to Williams, March 23, 1933, Official File 105, *ibid.*

11. Raymond Moley to Marvin McIntyre, March 21, 1933; Ellis Searles to McIntyre, March 23, 1933; memo for McIntyre by Adolf Berle, April 10, 1933, all in Official File 175, Roosevelt Papers. Nathan A. Margold to Perkins, April 4, 1933, Coal file, Record Group 174, Records of the Office of the Secretary, Department of Labor, National Archives. (Hereafter cited as RG 174.) Searles to Pat Harrison, January 4, 1933, file 120/24; "Memorandum, Davis-Kelly Bill," n.d., file 34a/5, Moley Papers. *The Secret Diary of Harold L. Ickes: The First Thousand Days, 1933–36* (New York: Simon & Schuster, 1953), pp. 10, 21, 24, 30.

12. Morgan to Marvin McIntyre, March 10, 1933; Moffett to FDR, May 31, 1933, Official File 56–A, Roosevelt Papers. There is much information on the oil conference and subsequent developments in Official File 56, *ibid.*, as there is in the Ickes *Secret Diary*, pp. 6, 9–13, 13–16, 26, 29–30, 31–32, 37, 39–40, 44, 46–47, 49–50.

13. Lawrence to FDR, March 22, 1933, file 94694, RG 40. Emery to C. A. Owens, April 17, 1933; to Charles R. Hook, April 17, 1933. These items are from a collection of Emery's letters from the spring and summer of 1933 in the NAM Papers.

14. Moley, *After Seven Years,* pp. 174, 186; *idem, First New Deal,* pp. 267–71, 273–75; Leuchtenburg, *Roosevelt,* p. 52; Schlesinger, *Coming of the New Deal,* p. 95; Huthmacher, *Wagner,* pp. 138–39, 142–43; Perkins, *The Roosevelt I Knew* (New York: Viking, 1946), pp. 268–70. James P. Warburg, "Reminiscences," Columbia University Oral History Project, pp. 171, 183–84, 207–208, 215–18, for Douglas' attitude. Roosevelt, *Press Conferences of the President,* Microfilms, 12 reels (Hyde Park, N.Y.: Franklin D. Roosevelt Library, 1956), reel 1, April 14, 1933, conference.

15. Perkins to Lehman, December 17, 1932, Herbert H. Lehman Papers, Columbia University. "Memorandum for Miss Perkins: The Case for the Establishment of Minimum Standards of Hours and Wages in New York State" by a Perkins aide, February 15, 1933; FDR to Perkins, n.d.; Perkins to Cross, April 3, 1933; FDR to governors of Pennsylvania, Maryland, Rhode Island, Illinois, etc., April 11, 1933; Perkins to R. S. Payne, April 7, 1933, all in Minimum Wage file, RG 174. "Additional Item for Agenda of President's Conference with Governors on March 6, 1933" by Perkins, Conferences file, *ibid.* Edwin S. Smith to Perkins, March 28, 1933; Thomas J. McMahon to Perkins, March 10, 1933, Textiles file, *ibid.* Perkins to Raymond Moley, February 16, 1933, file 117/22, Moley Papers.

16. "Suggested Statement for Governor Lehman to Make at the Governors

Conference," Conferences file, RG 174. Perkins to Richberg, March 22, 1933, Donald Richberg Papers, Library of Congress. "Recommendations of the Labor Conference Held on March 31, 1933 With the Secretary of Labor," Conferences file, RG 174. Perkins, *Roosevelt I Knew*, pp. 151–52.

17. FDR memo on a legislative program, written on about March 4, 1933, in Safe file, Moley Papers.

18. Memo for FDR by Perkins, July 15, 1932, file 50/17, *ibid*. Rorty to Knauth, November 19, 1932; Knauth to Strauss, November 25, 1932; Strauss to Rorty, December 5, 1932, all in file 19/29, *ibid*.

19. Daniel J. Kenefick to Moley, January 6, 1933; Moley to Kenefick, January 11, 1933, container 13, *ibid*. Oishei to Moley, January 18, 26, February 16, March 7, 1933; to McIntyre; to Tremaine, February 23, 1933, file 116/5, *ibid*.

20. Moley to Oishei, March 24, 1933; Warburg to Moley, March 25, 1933, *ibid*.; "Memorandum for R. M.—Industrial Rehabilitation by Reemployment" by Warburg, April 4, 1933, file 124–60; secretary's diary, March 24, 1933, *ibid*. Warburg, "Reminiscences," pp. 188, 215–18, 243.

A Robert Strauss memo for Moley of February 18 also testifies that interest in quick-recovery schemes ran high during the winter of 1932/33 in the Roosevelt inner circle. Strauss was reviewing proposals on many subjects, including recovery, and noted the popularity of the proposal for issue of scrip money, dated to expire within a limited period. "I must say that I am very sold on it myself as are the other members of the Brain Trust, such as Berle and Tugwell." The memo is in container 14, Moley Papers.

21. Moulton to Raymond Moley, March 6, 1933, Jacobstein to FDR, March 14, 1933; FDR to Moulton, March 21, 1933, file 109/19, *ibid*. The Roosevelt letter states that Lionberger Davis first brought him the proposal. In Jacobstein to Senator Wagner, June 19, 1933, Robert F. Wagner Papers, Georgetown University, there is a different version. "I [Jacobstein] presented the original plan to Dr. Moulton on March 2 and on March 5th a memorandum was carried to President Roosevelt by his uncle, Mr. Delano."

22. Moley, *After Seven Years*, pp. 184–89. *Idem*, *First New Deal*, pp. 283–90. Delano to Howe, April 7, 1933; "Memorandum for L. H.," April 13, 1933, President's Personal File 72, Roosevelt Papers. For a copy of the Delano Plan, "The Industrial Crisis and the Cure," March 31, 1933, see Unemployment file, James Delano Papers, Franklin D. Roosevelt Library.

23. Leverett S. Lyon *et al.*, *The National Recovery Administration* (Washington: The Brookings Institution, 1935), pp. 8–14, provides a detailed outline and commentary upon Title I of the N.I.R.A.; pp. 889–99, the text. See Hawley, *New Deal and . . . Monopoly*, pp. 53–71, for the drafting of the codes; and Moley, *First New Deal*, pp. 276, 292, for the clearest comment on Roosevelt's appointment of Ickes as a means of slowing down even the minimal public works expenditures authorized in Title II of the Act.

24. John Cutler to Perkins, April 8, 1933, Textiles file, RG 174. Perkins to Editor, *Washington Post*, April 20, 1933, Official File 15, Roosevelt Papers. *New York Journal of Commerce*, April 13, 1933, and Washington *Evening Star*, April 14, 15, 1933. Roosevelt, *Press Conferences*, reel 1, April 12, 1933, conference. Freidel, *Launching the New Deal*, pp. 418–21, has an illuminating account of the Perkins substitute, but, I believe, has misunderstood (p. 425) the meaning of Roosevelt's comments upon it at his April 12 press conference.

25. *New York Journal of Commerce*, April 26, 1933. House of Representatives, Committee on Labor, *Thirty-Hour Week: Hearings . . . on S. 158 and H. R. 4557*, 73d Cong., 1st sess., 1933, pp. 1–10.

26. Warburg, "Reminiscences," pp. 371, 378–88, 428, 460–61, 476, 493–94. All

these passages are taken from the Warburg journal, kept in 1933 and reproduced as part of the "Reminiscences," not from his later recollections, which are somewhat unreliable—in any case vague.

27. Huthmacher, *Wagner*, pp. 145–46. Jacobstein to Wagner, April 5, 1933, Wagner Papers. *New York Times*, April 14, 19, 1933. Arthur Krock, "Reminiscences," Columbia University Oral History Project, p. 24.

28. Rorty to Simon Rifkind, March 30, April 4, 1933; to Wagner, April 21, 1933; James P. Warburg to Wagner, April 18, 1933; Wagner to Rorty and others, April 22, 1933, drawers 97 and 101, Wagner Papers. Rorty to Robert Strauss, April 27, 1933, file 119–75, Moley Papers. Huthmacher, *Wagner*, p. 146, gives the full membership of Wagner's group.

29. The full text of the bill produced by Moulton's subcommittee is in the Lewis Douglas Papers, University of Arizona. Attached is a memo of April 29, 1933, outlining the bill and commenting upon it and the circumstances of its drafting.

The "New Deal Diary," Tugwell Papers, in the entry of April 14, 1933, seems to indicate that Tugwell too, in the desperate circumstances of the spring of 1933, was more concerned with having the Administration make a "grand effort toward resumption of industrial activity in normal ways" than with immediate institution of national planning. On April 21 he noted that Bean and Frank were working with him on a review of the "various schemes put forward by Kent, Rorty and others for stimulating private industry." Douglas' memo of April 29 described the result of contact between the Tugwell group and the Moulton subcommittee. What other impact Tugwell made is not clear. His "Diary" entry for May 30, 1933, the only other important passage on the creation of the N.I.R.A, has been relied upon very heavily by Schlesinger and subsequent writers in reconstructing the events of late April and early May. His sequence—dates are not provided—has his group (Bean and Frank) make contact with John Dickinson, presumably in late April; and then this Dickinson/Agricultural Department group meet with the Wagner group to work out a mutually agreeable bill which then had to be reconciled with the bill Hugh Johnson had drafted. Tugwell's recapitulation is no doubt sound, but, after the meeting between Tugwell's group and the Moulton subcommittee on April 29 (which Tugwell omits entirely to mention), his influence seems negligible. The most significant point to emphasize, and this is borne out by both the "Diary" and the Douglas memo, is that Tugwell, like all the other Administration figures involved, was thinking determinedly, in April and May 1933, in terms of restarting the economy.

30. Wagner to James Rand, April 22, 1933, Wagner Papers. Douglas memo, April 29, 1933, Douglas Papers. Ickes, *Secret Diary*, 28, 34. Perkins, *Roosevelt I Knew*, 197–98. *New York Herald Tribune*, April 30, May 1, 2, 1933. *New York Times*, April 29, May 1, 2, 1933. *New York Journal of Commerce*, May 2, 1933.

31. "Memorandum for Mr. Dickinson" by Feiker, April 8, 1933, file 83057; A. B. Barber to W. W. Splawn, April 3, 1933; Roper to Harriman, April 13, 1933; Harriman to Dickinson, April 12, 1933; Dickinson to Harriman, April 15, 1933, file 92001/2; Harriman to Roper, April 8, 1933, file 82248/48, all in RG 40.

32. William F. Long to Emery, April 7, 1933; Emery to H. B. Earheart, April 8, 1933; Orra L. Stone to Emery, April 11, 13, 18, 1933; Emery to Stone, April 12, 17, 22, 1933; C. A. Owens to NAM, April 13, 1933; Emery to Owens, April 17, 1933; to Charles R. Hook, April 17, 1933, NAM Papers. Emery to Roper, April 10, 1933, file 94694, RG 40.

33. *New York Times*, April 20, 1933. Dickinson to Roper, April 21, 1933; to Perkins, April 21, 1933; to Moley, April 26, 1933, file 93124, RG 40. House of Representatives, *Thirty-Hour Week*, pp. 1–10 (Perkins), 26–31 (Jacobstein), 66

(Green). *New York Journal of Commerce,* April 26, 27, 28, 29, 1933. NAM flyers, detailing the April 28 rally and its proposal, file 94694, RG 40. These are mimeographed, dated April 28 and May 2, 1933. Warner Hays to Dickinson, April 17, 1933; Gilbert Montague to Dickinson, April 17, 1933; Dickinson to Hays, April 19, 1933, file 93124; Williams to Dickinson, April 20, 1933; Harriman to Dickinson, May 1, 1933, file 82248/48, *ibid.* Hays to Marvin McIntyre, April 26, 1933, Alpha file; Williams to McIntyre, May 2, 1933, Official File 98, Roosevelt Papers. Emery to Henry D. Sharpe, May 15, 1933, NAM Papers. Walter M. Nones to Roper, May 3, 1933, file 92001/2, RG 40, regarding a conference between Roper and NAM representatives on April 29, 1933.

34. Emery to A. W. Berresford, May 2, 1933; to H. R. Hawthorne, May 2, 1933; to J. M. Manley, May 3, 1933, NAM Papers. On the NAM's "highest respect and regard" for Dickinson during the drafting of the first two weeks of May, H. W. Prentiss to Roper, May 20, 1933, file 94694, RG 40. Several independent sources confirm Emery's portrayal of the easy and quick victory of the first few days of May. George A. Sloan to Donald Comer, May 4, 1933, box 88, Comer Papers, tells of a conversation with Roper on May 3. H. I. Harriman to Henry A. Wallace, file 82248/48, RG 40, comments that the drift of all planners was "in the same general direction, to wit: the development of self-regulation through trade associations, with the government swinging the lariat to make the maverick run with the herd." J. Harvey Williams was in contact with "some of the draftsmen of the Industrial bill" on May 3 and 4 and was fully satisfied; Williams to Marvin McIntyre, May 16, 1933, Alpha file, Roosevelt Papers.

35. Chamber of Commerce, "Minutes—Twenty-First Annual Meeting, May 3, 4, 5, 1933." *The Public Papers and Addresses of Franklin D. Roosevelt* 13 vols. (New York: Random House–Macmillan–Harper, 1938–1950), II 155–58.

36. Rand statement in *New York Herald Tribune* and *New York Times,* May 7, 1933. Benjamin A. Javits had a hand in this proposal: Javits to Raymond Moley, April 10 (obviously misdated—should be May 10), 1933; Moley to Javits, May 20, 1933, file 109/12, Moley Papers. A copy of a statement of the proposal in which Javits stated Rand and Lund had concurred, dated May 10, 1933, was enclosed in John Fahey to Daniel Roper, May 23, 1933, file 94964, RG 40. *New York Journal of Commerce,* April 28, 1933, for the Harriman statement.

37. Emery to E. J. McMillan, May 11, 1933; to Henry D. Sharpe, May 15, 1933, NAM Papers. There are many wires to Daniel Roper on the advisory committee controversy in file 94694, RG 40. O'Connor to Moley, May 11, 1933, file 116/4, Moley Papers.

38. See "The Policy and Action of the National Association of Manufacturers with Respect to the Black and Connery Thirty-Hours Bills and the National Recovery Act," a memo written by Emery in 1948 or 1949 for a planned NAM history, for membership of the NAM advisory committee and some details on its actions. Emery to E. J. McMillan, May 11, 1933; to W. D. Tynes, May 12, 1933, all in NAM Papers. Also, on the committee, "Wagner Bill Links Public Works with Industrial Control," *Iron Age,* 131, No. 20 (May 18, 1933), 795. H. W. Prentiss to Daniel Roper, May 20, 1933, file 94694, RG 40.

There is a genuine problem in the fact that Hugh Johnson appeared on the scene with another recovery proposal at this point. Moley, in *First New Deal,* pp. 283–84, gives the well-known story about accidentally encountering Johnson on April 25 and forthwith turning the recovery planning problem over to him. This is curious because Warburg's journal, as already noted, clearly shows that Moley had gone with Warburg to speak to Wagner about drawing up a recovery proposal on April 18. In *After Seven Years,* p. 188, Moley states he was unaware, when he gave Johnson his mandate, that anyone else in the Roosevelt circle was working on the problem. This appears to be a lapse of memory. It may be that Moley and Douglas (who seems to have been linked with, or at least in touch with, Johnson by the early part of May) decided to try to get control of the drafting back within their immediate purview, away from Wagner and his rather far-flung operation. In any case, the final bill seems to have been completely in accord with the bill the Wagner group produced.

39. Emery, "Policy and Action of the National Association of Manufacturers"; NAM flyer calling for rally of members on June 3, 1933, in Washington, NAM Papers. Schlesinger, *Coming of the New Deal*, p. 99. House of Representatives, Committee on Ways and Means, *National Industrial Recovery: Hearings . . . on H. R. 5664*, 73d Cong., 1st sess., 1933, pp. 116–22. Senate, Committee on Finance, *National Industrial Recovery Act: Hearings on . . . S. 1712 and H. R. 5755*, 73d Cong., 1st sess., 1933, pp. 273–94.

40. Numerous telegrams from business groups on H. R. 5755, dated during late May or early June 1933, are in boxes 52 and 53, Senate 73A–E5, Record Group 46, Records of the Senate, National Archives. Senate, *National Industrial Recovery Act*, pp. 273–94.

41. House, *National Industrial Recovery*, pp. 91–112. *Public Papers . . . of FDR*, II 251–56. *A Handbook of NRA*, ed. Louis Mayers (New York: Federal Codes, Inc., 1934), p. 217.

42. Johnson, *Blue Eagle* (New York: Doubleday, 1935), pp. 164, 196–200.

43. Galambos, *Competition and Cooperation*, pp. 217–24. NAM, Board of Directors, "Minutes," July 10, 1933. *New York Times,* July 11, 1933, for Johnson's reply on the labor issue. Robert Lund to Daniel Roper, July 3, 1933, file 94694, RG 40.

44. Schlesinger, *Coming of the New Deal*, pp. 110–12, 114–16; Hawley, *New Deal and . . . Monopoly*, pp. 53–55, for the PRA campaign.

45. *Ibid.*, pp. 55–56, for an incisive description of the competitive practice elements in the codes. Lyon *et al., National Recovery Administration*, pp. 551–704, for a detailed treatment.

46. Hawley, *New Deal and . . . Monopoly*, pp. 72–90.

47. Schlesinger, *The Politics of Upheaval* (Boston: Houghton Mifflin, 1960), pp. 389–92. Historians have tended to stress positive benefits, for the nation's psychology, for wages and hours, and so on, while accepting the interpretation of most economists that the NRA overall did little to expand production and employment. See especially Leuchtenburg, *Roosevelt*, pp. 67–70.

11

Conclusion

THE NRA RESULTED FROM the interplay of several independent political forces. The labor-purchasing power, public spending, and start-up advocates helped to build up an indispensable context in which novel experiments seemed legitimate and necessary. Lacking this context, the business planners, promising better times through market controls, probably could never have brought off their program. Taking advantage of the momentum these other groups had generated, the business planners were able to subsume their goals and yet write a bill patterned after business concepts. They were in a strong enough position during the early history of the NRA to make their purposes triumph, even though the Administration hoped to make the bill a kind of start-up plan.

The victory of the business planners in 1933 was the culmination of a movement to turn public policy toward favoring cooperative market controls which dated back to the postwar push for antitrust liberalization. The goals of this business movement took a more or less radical direction according to the changing contours of several variables. The postwar wave of revisionism was extremely radical in its goals, outspoken and open in its tactics. It originated in the enthusiasm for cooperative capitalism which businessmen felt as a result of their wartime experience. It was bred, too, of a degree of cocksureness, an overestimate of the nation's gratitude and admiration for the highly touted success of businessmen in mobilizing industry for war. Postwar economic conditions undercut expected public support. The institutional basis for cartelistic market behavior, trade associations, were thrust on the defensive by mid-1919. Harry Daugherty's political needs—more broadly, the Harding Administration's responsiveness to popular moods during the troubled political and economic conditions of the early 'twenties—forced associationism to fight to maintain the traditional cooperative practices which could be reconciled, in principle at least, with traditional concepts of a market-dominated enterprise system. By 1925 economic and political conditions conspired to reopen the question of a wider scope for cooperation which had been so hastily and thoroughly suppressed in 1919. The Coolidge Administration, through the Justice Department and the FTC, encouraged associations to extend their practices to and beyond the limits which prevailing judicial doctrines had laid down, and was purposively preparing a strategy for erosion of those doctrines through appropriately staged litigation.

Hoover's election cut this strategy off, for, despite a well-deserved reputation for championing associationism in business, Hoover had not, as Secretary of Commerce during the 'twenties, tried to push cooperative activities beyond the limits staked out by Supreme Court decisions and beyond the point at which competition and cooperation could be reconciled ideologically. The reasons are rather complex. Hoover accepted the competitive mechanism as the most appropriate ordering device for the industrial system, as the most certain means for obtaining the social fluidity and economic progress which he felt were the basic and all-important accomplishments of American society. But the competitive mechanism was a means, not an end, in Hoover's mind, and he showed at times during the 'twenties a readiness to modify very far toward cartelism his notion of appropriate organization for an industry when, as indicated by the pragmatic test of results, the competitive mode had failed. Two factors—political considerations and the grave difficulties in working out effective regulation for industries excused from the competitive discipline—sharply limited Hoover's willingness to experiment in theory or in practice with the encouragement of more extensive cooperative programs for trade associations than the Department actually did sponsor.

These factors operated in exactly the same way after Hoover became President. Political circumstances forced him to cut off the Coolidge-era strategy for securing a relaxation of antitrust standards from the courts and to prosecute the more notorious examples of quasi-cartelist trade associations. Conviction entered into this decision, too, as it had into his adamant refusal to cooperate with the various proposals for legislative liberalization of antitrust standards. Hoover did accept the rationality of relaxation when experience had shown acceptable economic and social performance otherwise unobtainable. But this was far from accepting a cartelized industrial order the political and economic implications of which Hoover believed horrendous.

It is ironic that, in the last stage of his presidency, Hoover unknowingly did much to create a key element in the context which finally allowed the business revisionists to triumph. He and others in the Administration helped to popularize the start-up concept and gave encouragement to some of the chief authors of specific plans. The revisionists reaped great advantage from the widespread interest in such plans by masquerading their program as one of them. Without this maneuver, success would probably have eluded them, for Roosevelt and his entourage had shown little more inclination simply to concede to the cartelistic viewpoint than had the previous Administration.

The revisionist victory also owed much to the extraordinary context of early 1933. The revisionists were the ablest politicians of the several groups pressing for one form or another of recovery program and were able to channelize these other efforts and make them serve the cause of antitrust liberalization. But there was still another element in the revisionists' success: that the several distinct groups ultimately found the capacity to cooperate or, at least, to work along closely parallel lines. The attempt at consolidation dated back only to the fall of 1932. Before then the different groups—the Chamber, the NAM, the Industrial Group, the Congress of Industries, and others—had pursued independent courses and different, sometimes sharply different, objectives.

The controversy over substantive versus procedural change originated in the later 1920s, at the same time as the revival of interest in revisionism. Active, militant revisionism was based in a specific sector of industry, in the relatively less profitable industries—those which, probably not coincidentally, were also the older and more developed, usually producers' goods, industries. The reason why many business leaders and prevailing sentiment within many such industries favored procedural revision over more radical proposals is quite clear. There was confidence that procedural revision could achieve the desired substantive ends without raising dangerous questions about substituting government regulation for competition. As the Hoover Administration's policies dimmed these hopes for the efficacy of procedural revision and as economic conditions worsened, the swing toward support of substantive revision became ever more pronounced. Eventually the remaining barriers of discretion collapsed and, at the last, the groups still active in the revisionist cause were seeking legalization of full-blown cartelism in which non-cooperators could be suppressed.

The notion that the N.I.R.A. represented a triumph of big over small business is accurate only in a limited and special sense. The major line of division within the business community was between the more and the less profitable industries, with the former not so much opposing revision as braking it, by their indifference and by the hesitancy which stemmed from naturally more acute fears of the government interference which might result from a weakening of the antitrust laws. Industries from the less profitable sector tended to support revision, quite irrespective of the average size of member firms. The oil refining industry, populated by giants, supported revision no more convincedly than did J. Harvey Williams' factory supply and tool industry, most of whose members, while of substantial size, were small by other standards. Within industries whose organizations and leaders were active revisionists there, probably, regardless of the typical size of firms within the industry, always existed a group of firms, of varying size and importance, which shrank from any legal changes which would allow an industry majority to dictate the norms of market behavior. This point of view was rather well submerged throughout the whole period of the revisionist movement but it surfaced occasionally. In 1933, during the drafting of the NRA codes, a specific formalized opportunity to put opposition to majoritarianism on record arose and, as the NRA files show, often was used. These dissenters were usually smaller firms which felt code practices would allow larger competitors some advantage. Often the dissenters were a fringe element or at least an insubstantial element, a small minority, staying alive through price-shading or some other competitive maneuver.[1]

Some interesting aspects of the businessmen's political and social as well as economic norms and goals appear in the rhetoric and tactics of this revisionist movement. Clearly, well before the depression, businessmen in a large segment of industry had decided that acceptable security and profitability required cartelization, regardless of the conflict with the traditional ideals of enterprise and competition. Their preference was to secure the change through indirection, through a kind of conspiracy in which the Justice Department, the FTC, and the federal courts would join, as long as there was hope that such a strategy would succeed. This was a reflection of a fundamental attitude—made even clearer in the rhetoric and some of the maneuvers of the revisionist movement during 1931–1933: that economic power and the determination of economic policy were as much as possible to be reserved to the business community; responsibility and accountability to political agencies to be avoided at all cost.

NOTE

1. This paragraph states the most frequently encountered situation in which an industry minority could be observed during these years in opposition to enforced cartelism. The operative factor in this opposition was that the minority believed it stood to lose somehow if it were compelled to follow market behavior rules designed by the majority. The minority parties in some instances constituted a substantial part of an industry and were on an equal competitive footing with the cooperationists, as Louis Galambos shows in *Competition and Cooperation*, pp. 157–62.

Intra-industry quarrels were often recorded in the NRA "A and B" files which contain correspondence on codes before final approval. In a sample of the "A and B" files for sixteen industries, all of them of substantial importance, several recorded complaints of minority elements, composed of smaller firms, which registered distrust and fear concerning the larger firms of the industry. These seven were the following: Paint and Varnish (105); Lumber and Timber (9); Laundry and Dry Cleaning Machinery (34); Iron and Steel (11); Electrical Manufacturing (4); Ice (43); and Fertilizer (67). The files are in Record Group 9, Records of the National Recovery Administration, National Archives.

BIBLIOGRAPHY

Government Records

Departmental and bureau records in the National Archives, especially those of the Commerce Department and of the Antitrust Division of the Justice Department, formed the core of my analysis of government policies toward trade association activities and toward other economic problems during the Republican era. Each of the Record Groups cited made an important contribution, even if perhaps only on a particular point.

Federal Trade Commission, "Minutes" of the Commission, Federal Trade Commission Building.
RG   9, Records of the National Recovery Administration.
RG   40, General Records of the Department of Commerce. (These include the papers of Robert P. Lamont.)
RG   46, Records of the Senate.
RG   56, General Records of the Department of the Treasury.
RG   60, General Records of the Department of Justice.
RG 122, Records of the Federal Trade Commission, Economic Investigations File (Open Price Associations, Investigations of 1921 and 1925).
RG 151, Records of the Bureau of Foreign and Domestic Commerce. (These include the papers of Frederick M. Feiker.)
RG 174, Records of the Office of the Secretary, Department of Labor.
RG 232, Records of the Federal Oil Conservation Board.
RG 233, Records of the House of Representatives.

Manuscript Collections

The papers of all the Presidents and of a large number of public figures relevant to this study are available, though widely scattered. The most important collections were those of Hoover, for the Republican era, and of Roosevelt and Moley, for the immediate origins of the N.I.R.A. Several other collections played a major role, however, and even those which appear only briefly in the footnotes made significant contributions.

Winthrop W. Aldrich Papers, Baker Library, Harvard University Graduate School of Business
Bernard M. Baruch Papers, Princeton University
John M. Carmody Papers, Franklin D. Roosevelt Library, Hyde Park, New York
Roy Chapin Papers, University of Michigan
Edward T. Clark Papers, Library of Congress
Calvin Coolidge Papers, Library of Congress
Donald Comer Papers, Baker Library, Harvard University Graduate School of Business
James Delano Papers, Franklin D. Roosevelt Library, Hyde Park, New York
Lewis Douglas Papers, University of Arizona

Warren G. Harding Papers, Ohio State Historical Society, Columbus, Ohio

Herbert Hoover Papers, Herbert Hoover Presidential Library, West Branch, Iowa
(abbreviated in the footnotes as CP, HHL for the Commerce Department years, as HHPP for the presidential years)

Arthur Krock, "Reminiscences," Columbia University Oral History Project

Thomas W. Lamont Papers, Baker Library, Harvard University Graduate School of Business

Herbert H. Lehman Papers, Columbia University

Ogden L. Mills Papers, Library of Congress

Raymond Moley Papers, Hoover Institution, Stanford University

National Civic Federation Papers, New York Public Library

National Wool Manufacturers Association Papers, Merrimack Valley Textile Museum, North Andover, Massachusetts

Donald Richberg Papers, Library of Congress

Franklin D. Roosevelt Papers, Franklin D. Roosevelt Library, Hyde Park, New York

Rexford G. Tugwell Papers, Franklin D. Roosevelt Library, Hyde Park, New York

Robert F. Wagner Papers, Georgetown University

David I. Walsh Papers, College of the Holy Cross

Thomas J. Walsh Papers, Library of Congress

James P. Warburg, "Reminiscences," Columbia University Oral History Project
(typed with these recollections is a very helpful journal Warburg kept during the Hundred Days in 1933)

Ray Lyman Wilbur Papers, Hoover Institution, Stanford University

Woodrow Wilson Papers, Library of Congress

Business Organization and Trade Materials, Published and Unpublished

The two largest business organizations each maintained a monthly magazine during the 1920s and '30s: *American Industries* (NAM) and *Nation's Business* (Chamber of Commerce). For most of these years the NAM published a record of its *Annual Convention*. The Chamber's annual meetings are recorded quite fully in typescript volumes in the library of the organization's headquarters building in Washington, D.C. Available for both also are records of board of directors and executive committee meetings. The NAM's are in typescript and are among the historical materials the organization held in its New York headquarters library for many years and recently has deposited in the Eleutherian Mills Library, Greenville, Delaware. The Chamber's are in published form and are available in its library. These collections also contain a considerable number of unpublished records of special meetings, committee reports, and so on. Correspondence in the case of the NAM has not been preserved, except for the very helpful James A. Emery file on the drafting of the N.I.R.A. The Chamber was unwilling to make correspondence files available.

The American Trade Association Executives published a *Proceedings* during the period considered here; it made available, moreover, at its Washington, D.C. office, its helpful but not very full minutes of board of directors meetings. Two trade associations, the National Electrical Manufacturers Association and the Motor and Equipment Manufacturers Association, allowed me to use the records which have been preserved. For both groups this included board of directors minutes; for the NEMA, it included very detailed records of meetings of the association's "Policies Division," the general meeting of all the group's members.

Published sources for the study of business organization activities are very extensive. There are a large number of periodicals addressed to industrialists generally, and nearly every sizeable industry has at least one trade journal devoted to its affairs; many have several. In addition, many trade associations publish records of their annual meetings. I have explored such publications extensively. Originally, I planned to treat the question of what sort of industries tended most to support antitrust revision through a series of profiles of associations. This plan was ultimately abandoned in favor of the statistical approach worked out in Chapters 5 and 7 of this book. In the meantime I acquired a large stock of information about the attitudes of a considerable number of trade associations which contributed greatly to the formation of the ideas presented in those chapters, even though little reference to this background material appears in the citations. Below, a number of the trade journals and association publications, read, in whole or part, for the 1920–1933 period, are listed, serving mainly to illustrate this type of source. Given separately are the several general business periodicals I found especially useful. I came to regard the business newspapers as very helpful for marking out the main outlines and sometimes the details of business reactions to and attempts to change government policies. Especially helpful were the *New York Commercial* (which ceased publication in 1926) and the *New York Journal of Commerce.*

REPRESENTATIVE BUSINESS PERIODICALS OF GENERAL CHARACTER

Advertising and Selling
Annalist
Bradstreet's
Business Week
Commercial and Financial Chronicle
Factory and Industrial Management
Forbes

Industrial Management
Magazine of Business
Magazine of Wall Street
Manufacturers Record
Manufacturing Industries
Printers' Ink
Sales Management

REPRESENTATIVE TRADE JOURNALS AND TRADE ASSOCIATION PUBLICATIONS
(Arranged by Industry)

American Machinist
Automotive Industries

The Canner
Canning Age

Candy Manufacturer
Manufacturing Confectioner
National Confectioner's Association, *Proceedings*

Black Diamond
Coal Age

Electrical Manufacturing
Electrical World

American Fertilizer
Commercial Fertilizer
National Fertilizer Association, *Proceedings*

Foundry

National Association of Ice Cream Manufacturers, *Proceedings*
Ice and Refrigeration

American Iron and Steel Institute, *Proceedings*
Iron Age
Iron Trade Review

Oil, Paint and Drug Reporter

Paper Mill and Wood Pulp News
Paper Trade Journal

Rubber Age
India Rubber World

Textile World

Government Documents

In addition to the Annual Reports of the relevant government departments and agencies, especially those of the Departments of Commerce and Justice, and of the Federal Trade Commission, a number of Congressional hearings and of FTC reports were of major value. A complete bibliography of FTC materials is available in Myron Watkins, *Public Regulation of Competitive Practices* (cited in the next section of this bibliography). I have therefore listed here only Congressional materials, and only the most directly significant of these.

House of Representatives, Committee on Labor. *Six-Hour Day, Five-Day Week: Hearings on . . . H. R. 14105.* 72d Cong., 2d sess., 1933.
——————. *Thirty-Hour Week: Hearings on S. 158 and H. R. 4557.* 73d Cong., 1st sess., 1933.
——, Committee on Ways and Means. *National Industrial Recovery: Hearings . . . on H. R. 5664.* 73d Cong., 1st sess., 1933.
Senate, Committee on Education and Labor. *Thirty-Hour Week: Hearings . . . on S. 5267.* 72d Cong., 2d sess., 1933.
——, Committee on Finance. *Investigation of Economic Problems: Hearings on S. R. 315.* 72d Cong., 2d sess., 1933.
——————. *National Industrial Recovery Act: Hearings on S. 1712 and H. R. 5755.* 73d Cong., 1st sess., 1933.
——, Committee on the Judiciary. *Amendment of Federal Trade Commission Act and Establishment of a Federal Trade Court: Hearings . . . on S. 2626, S. 2627, and S. 2628.* 72d Cong., 1st sess., 1932.
——————. *Concentration in American Industry.* 85th Cong., 1st sess., 1957.
——, Committee on Manufactures. *Establishment of National Economic Council: Hearings . . . on S. 6215.* 72d Cong., 1st sess., 1932.
——, Committee on Mines and Mining. *To Create a Bituminous Coal Commission: Hearings . . . on S. 2935.* 72d Cong., 1st sess., 1932.
——, Select Committee on Unemployment Insurance. *Hearings . . . on S. R. 483.* 72d Cong., 1st sess., 1932.

Secondary Works

The following list is selective, but it includes the most important of two main types of books used for this study. One of these consists of recent scholarly works on politics and economic policy in the 1920s and early 'thirties. The other consists of older materials, dating for the most part from the period itself, which give data on the economic phenomena and discuss the economic problems of the era.

Bain, Joe S. *Industrial Organization*. New York: Wiley, 1959.

Berle, Beatrice Bishop, and Jacobs, Travis Beal, edd. *Navigating the Rapids, 1918–1971: From the Papers of Adolf A. Berle*. New York: Harcourt Brace Jovanovich, 1973.

Blair, John M. *Economic Concentration: Structure, Behavior and Public Policy*. New York: Harcourt, Brace, 1972.

Blaisdell, Thomas C. *The Federal Trade Commission*. New York: Columbia University Press, 1932.

Burns, Arthur R. *The Decline of Competition*. New York: Columbia University Press, 1936.

Clark, J. D. *The Federal Trust Policy*. Baltimore: Lord Baltimore Press, 1931.

Cuff, Robert. *The War Industries Board: Business–Government Relations During World War I*. Baltimore: The Johns Hopkins University Press, 1973.

Davis, G. Cullom. "The Transformation of the Federal Trade Commission, 1914–1929." *Mississippi Valley Historical Review*, 49, No. 2 (September 1962), 437–55.

Edwards, Corwin D. *Maintaining Competition*. New York: McGraw-Hill, 1941.

Epstein, Ralph C. *Industrial Profits in the United States*. New York: National Bureau of Economic Research, 1934.

The Federal Antitrust Laws: With Summaries of Cases Instituted by the United States. New York: Commerce Clearing House, 1949.

Foth, Joseph H. *Trade Associations: Their Services to Industry*. New York: Ronald Press, 1930.

Freidel, Frank. *Franklin D. Roosevelt: Launching the New Deal*. Boston: Little Brown, 1973.

Galambos, Louis C. *Competition and Cooperation: The Emergence of a National Trade Association*. Baltimore: The Johns Hopkins University Press, 1966.

Green, Marguerite. *The National Civic Federation and the American Labor Movement, 1900–1925*. Washington, D.C.: Catholic University of America Press, 1956.

Hawley, Ellis W. *The New Deal and the Problem of Monopoly*. Princeton: Princeton University Press, 1966.

———. "Secretary Hoover and the Bituminous Coal Problem, 1921–1928."*Business History Review*, 42, No. 3 (Autumn 1968), 247–70.

———. "Herbert Hoover, the Commerce Secretariat, and the Vision of an 'Associative State,' 1921–1928." *Journal of American History*, 61, No. 1 (June 1974), 116–40.

Himmelberg, Robert F. "The War Industries Board and the Antitrust Question in November, 1918." *Journal of American History*, 52, No. 1 (June 1965), 59–74.

———. "Business, Antitrust Policy and the Industrial Board of the Department of Commerce, 1919." *Business History Review*, 42, No. 1 (Spring 1968), 1–23.

Hoover, Herbert C. *American Individualism*. Garden City: Doubleday, 1922.
————. *Memoirs*. 3 vols. New York: Macmillan, 1952.
Huthmacher, Joseph J. *Senator Robert F. Wagner and the Rise of Urban Liberalism*. New York: Atheneum, 1968.
Huthmacher, Joseph J., and Sussmann, Warren, edd. *Herbert Hoover and the Crisis of American Capitalism* (with essays by Ellis Hawley, Robert Himmelberg, Gerald Nash, and Murray Rothbard). Cambridge: Schenckman, 1974.
Johnson, Hugh. *The Blue Eagle*. New York: Doubleday, 1935.
Jones, Franklin D. *Trade Association Activities and the Law*. New York: McGraw-Hill, 1922.
Kaysen, Karl, and Turner, Donald F. *Antitrust Policy: An Economic and Legal Analysis*. Cambridge: Harvard University Press, 1959.
Kolko, Gabriel. *The Triumph of Conservatism*. New York: Free Press, 1963.
Leuchtenburg, William E. *Franklin D. Roosevelt and the New Deal, 1932–1940*. New York: Harper, 1963.
Lyon, Leverett S., et al. *The National Recovery Administration*. Washington: The Brookings Institution, 1935.
McCoy, Donald. *Calvin Coolidge: The Quiet President*. New York: Macmillan, 1967.
Means, Gardiner C. *The Structure of the American Economy: A Report Prepared by the Industrial Section of the National Resources Committee*. Washington, D.C.: Government Printing Office, 1939.
Miller, John Perry. *Unfair Competition*. Cambridge: Harvard University Press, 1941.
Moley, Raymond. *After Seven Years*. New York: Harper, 1939.
————. *The First New Deal*. New York: Harcourt, Brace, 1966.
Murray, Robert K. *The Harding Era: Warren G. Harding and His Administration*. Minneapolis: The University of Minnesota Press, 1969.
Myers, William S., ed. *The State Papers and Other Public Writings of Herbert Hoover*. New York: Doubleday, 1934.
Myers, William S., and Newton, Walter H. *The Hoover Administration*. New York: Scribner, 1936.
Nash, Gerald. *United States Oil Policy, 1890–1964*. Pittsburgh: University of Pittsburgh Press, 1968.
National Industrial Conference Board. *Trade Associations: Their Economic Significance and Legal Status*. New York: NICB, 1925.
Naylor, Emmett Hay. *Trade Associations: Their Organization and Management*. New York: Ronald Press, 1921.
Nelson, M. N. *Open Price Associations*. Urbana: The University of Illinois Press, 1923.
Noggle, Burl. *Teapot Dome: Oil and Politics in the 1920's*. New York: Norton, 1962.
Nutter, G. Warren. *The Extent of Enterprise Monopoly in the United States, 1899–1939*. Chicago: The University of Chicago Press, 1951.
Paull, Irving S. *Trade Association Activities*. Bureau of Foreign and Domestic Commerce. Washington, D.C.: Government Printing Office, 1927.
Pearce, C. A. *Trade Association Survey*. Temporary National Economic Committee Monograph No. 18. Washington, D.C.: Government Printing Office, 1941.
Perkins, Frances. *The Roosevelt I Knew*. New York: Viking, 1946.
The Public Papers and Addresses of Franklin D. Roosevelt. 13 vols. New York: Random House–Macmillan–Harper, 1938–1950.
Radosh, Ronald, and Rothbard, Murray, edd. *A New History of Leviathan: Essays*

on the Rise of the American Corporate State. New York: Dutton Paperbacks, 1972.

Romasco, Albert U. *The Poverty of Abundance: Hoover, the Nation, the Depression.* New York: Oxford University Press, 1965.

Roosevelt, Franklin D. *Press Conferences of the President.* Microfilms, 12 reels. Hyde Park, N.Y.: Franklin D. Roosevelt Library, 1956.

Scharfman, I. L. "The Trade Association Movement." *American Economic Review Supplement,* 16, No. 1 (March 1926), 203–18.

The Secret Diary of Harold L. Ickes: The First Thousand Days, 1933–36. New York: Simon & Schuster, 1953.

Schlesinger, Arthur M., Jr. *The Coming of the New Deal.* Boston: Houghton Mifflin, 1959.

———. *The Politics of Upheaval.* Boston: Houghton Mifflin, 1960.

Sternsher, Bernard. *Rexford Tugwell and the New Deal.* New Brunswick: Rutgers University Press, 1964.

Stocking, George W. *Workable Competition and Antitrust Policy.* Nashville: Vanderbilt University Press, 1961.

Swain, Donald C. *Federal Conservation Policy, 1921–1933.* Berkeley: University of California Press, 1963.

Thorp, Willard L., and Crowder, Walter F. *The Structure of Industry.* Temporary National Economic Committee Monograph No. 27. Washington, D.C.: Government Printing Office, 1941.

Tosdal, H. R. "Open Price Associations." *American Economic Review,* 7, No. 2 (June 1917), 331–52.

Tugwell, Rexford G. *The Democratic Roosevelt.* Garden City: Doubleday, 1957.

———. *The Brains Trust.* New York: Viking, 1968.

Warren, H. G. *Herbert Hoover and the Great Depression.* New York: Norton, 1959.

Watkins, Myron W. *Public Regulation of Competitive Practices in Business Enterprise.* New York: NICB, 1940.

Whitney, Simon N. *Trade Associations and Industrial Control: A Critique of the NRA.* New York: Central, 1934.

Wiebe, Robert H. *Businessmen and Reform: A Study of the Progressive Movement.* Cambridge: Harvard University Press, 1963.

Wilbur, Ray Lyman, and Hyde, Arthur M. *The Hoover Policies.* New York: Scribner, 1937.

Index